About Pfeiffer

Pfeiffer serves the professional development and hands-on resource needs of training and human resource practitioners and gives them products to do their jobs better. We deliver proven ideas and solutions from experts in HR development and HR management, and we offer effective and customizable tools to improve workplace performance. From novice to seasoned professional, Pfeiffer is the source you can trust to make yourself and your organization more successful.

Essential Knowledge Pfeiffer produces insightful, practical, and comprehensive materials on topics that matter the most to training and HR professionals. Our Essential Knowledge resources translate the expertise of seasoned professionals into practical, how-to guidance on critical workplace issues and problems. These resources are supported by case studies, worksheets, and job aids and are frequently supplemented with CD-ROMs, websites, and other means of making the content easier to read, understand, and use.

Essential Tools Pfeiffer's Essential Tools resources save time and expense by offering proven, ready-to-use materials—including exercises, activities, games, instruments, and assessments—for use during a training or team-learning event. These resources are frequently offered in looseleaf or CD-ROM format to facilitate copying and customization of the material.

Pfeiffer also recognizes the remarkable power of new technologies in expanding the reach and effectiveness of training. While e-hype has often created whizbang solutions in search of a problem, we are dedicated to bringing convenience and enhancements to proven training solutions. All our e-tools comply with rigorous functionality standards. The most appropriate technology wrapped around essential content yields the perfect solution for today's on-the-go trainers and human resource professionals.

www.pfeiffer.com

Essential resources for training and HR professionals

"This book makes an invaluable contribution to the fields of organization development, change management, and strategic planning, as well as to the individuals who lead and consult in organizations including executives and senior managers and internal and external consultants who assist organizations in their efforts to survive and thrive in the current fast-paced, highly competitive, global, complex, and ever-changing marketplace."
—Jeanne Cherbeneau, president, Cherbeneau & Associates

"The message in this book is not only why enterprise-wide change (EWC) is critical to organizations that want to survive and be successful, but also how to implement this change. The examples of what not to do versus how to do it right were very helpful. The comprehensive details and examples given about other companies make the book's message and information even clearer. It's one thing to write about a topic, but to actually get your point across is another. The authors put together a beginning-to-end process on EWC in one book that is easy to read and implement."
—Lori L. While, senior vice president, Valley Credit Union

"This book provides valuable context and content to enable the reader to understand and apply the Systems Thinking concepts. It provides the tools that are needed to actually start and sustain an enterprise change effort in a planned and systematic method. This book also presents an excellent introduction to the framework for the complex process of enterprise-wide change. It's a great road map!"
—Mary Jefferies, director, human resource services, Alberta Environment

"This is not some esoteric 'fad of the decade' book, it addresses, in a very pragmatic way, the various elements that need to be considered when developing a change management process in a Systems Thinking context."
—Dennis A. Looney, vice president of operations,
    Apex-Carex Healthcare Products

"Haines' book gives practitioners and project managers a comprehensive map with principles and guides to navigate the change process."
—Aaron S. L. Pun, former chairperson, Hong Kong Society
    for Training and Development

"*Enterprise-Wide Change* is filled with examples and real-life applications, as well as checklists and tools."

> —Denise Bryson, vice president, client services,
> New Client Marketing Institute

"The great value of this book is the way it manages to weave together the various elements of the strategic process in a simple and practical model."

> —Miguel Guilarte, professor, Fielding Graduate Institute, and
> founder and CEO, Transforma Management Consulting

"*Enterprise-Wide Change* is easy and quick to read. It pulls together lots of diverse ideas into one source. This book offers steps in the model that are very specific, as well as many case examples and clearly marked tools, questions, and charts."

> —John Clarke, director of training, development, and quality,
> Cameco Corporation

Practicing Organization Development

**The Change Agent Series
for Groups and Organizations**

MISSION STATEMENT

The books in this series are intended to be cutting-edge, state-of-the-art, innovative approaches to organization change and development. They are written for and by practitioners interested in new approaches to facilitating effective organization change. They are geared to providing both theory and advice on practical applications.

SERIES EDITORS

**William J. Rothwell
Roland Sullivan
Kristine Quade**

EDITORIAL BOARD

**David Bradford
W. Warner Burke
Edith Whitfield Seashore
Robert Tannenbaum
Christopher G. Worley
Shaolin Zhang**

Other Practicing Organization Development Titles

Organization Development at Work: Conversations on the Values, Applications, and Future of OD
Margaret Wheatley, Robert Tannenbaum, Paula Yardley Griffin, and Kristine Quade

Finding Your Way in the Consulting Jungle: A Guidebook for Organization Development Practitioners
Arthur M. Freedman and Richard E. Zackrison

Facilitating Organization Change: Lessons from Complexity Science
Edwin E. Olson and Glenda H. Eoyang

Appreciative Inquiry: Change at the Speed of Imagination
Jane Magruder Watkins and Bernard J. Mohr

Beyond Change Management: Advanced Strategies for Today's Transformational Leaders
Dean Anderson and Linda Ackerman Anderson

The Change Leader's Roadmap: How to Navigate Your Organization's Transformation
Linda Ackerman Anderson and Dean Anderson

Guiding Change Journeys: A Synergistic Approach to Organization Transformation
Rebecca Chan Allen

Balancing Individual and Organizational Values: Walking the Tightrope to Success
Ken Hultman with Bill Gellermann

The Conscious Consultant: Mastering Change from the Inside Out
Kristine Quade and Renée M. Brown

Organization Development and Consulting: Perspectives and Foundations
Fred Massarik and Marissa Pei-Carpenter

Relationships That Enable Enterprise Change: Leveraging the Client-Consultant Connection
Ron A. Carucci, William A. Pasmore, and the Colleagues of Mercer Delta

Rewiring Organizations for the Networked Economy: Organizing, Managing, and Leading in the Information Age
Stan Herman, Editor

The Innovation Equation: Building Creativity and Risk Taking in Your Organization
Jacqueline Byrd and Paul Lockwood Brown

Enterprise-Wide Change

Superior Results
Through Systems Thinking

Stephen G. Haines, Gail Aller-Stead, and James McKinlay

Pfeiffer
A Wiley Imprint
www.pfeiffer.com

Practicing
Organization
Development

Copyright © 2005 by John Wiley & Sons, Inc.

Published by Pfeiffer
An Imprint of Wiley
989 Market Street, San Francisco, CA 94103-1741   www.pfeiffer.com

Library of Congress Cataloging-in-Publication Data

Haines, Stephen G.
  Enterprise-wide change : superior results through systems thinking / Stephen G. Haines.
     p. cm. — (Practicing organization development)
  Includes bibliographical references and index.
  ISBN 0-7879-7146-4 (alk. paper)
  1. Organizational change. 2. System theory. I. Title. II. Practicing organization development series.
  HD58.8.H345 2005
  658.4'06—dc22

                                                                                2004008461

Acquiring Editor: Matthew Davis   Manufacturing Supervisor: Bill Matherly
Director of Development: Kathleen Dolan Davies   Editorial Assistant: Laura Reizman
Production Editor: Nina Kreiden   Illustrations: Lotus Art
Editor: Rebecca Taff

Printed in the United States of America
Printing   10 9 8 7 6 5 4 3 2 1

Contents

Part B
Practical Application to Enterprise-Wide Change   97

List of Figures, Tables, and Worksheets

Preface

THE ADDISON-WESLEY SERIES on Organization Development is legendary in the Organizational Development field and the basis for the change field. Its impact on the field of OD, and on the authors in particular, was and still is profound.

This new Jossey-Bass Series is the 21st-Century version of the original theory and practice series. The three editors of the earlier books were Edgar Schein, Warren Bennis, and the late Richard Beckhard—true pioneers, founders, and "godfathers" of the field.

Richard Beckhard's contribution to that series, *Organization Development: Strategies and Models* (1969), contains the first well-known definition of Organization Development (and by implication, the entire change consulting field). It has been a central touchstone for us for more than thirty years, and is more relevant today than ever before as the definition for Enterprise-Wide Change.

Beckhard (1969, p. 9) defined Organization Development as an effort (1) planned, (2) organization-wide, and (3) managed from the top to (4) increase organization effectiveness and health through (5) planned interventions in the organization's processes, using behavioral-science knowledge.

This definition is consistent with the creation of this book. In many ways, this book traces its roots and line of sight directly back to Richard Beckhard, the pioneers of the change field, and beyond.

In 1954, Ludwig von Bertalanffy, an Austrian biologist, co-founded the Society for General Systems Research in collaboration with four interdisciplinary Nobel Prize winners. They were the first to begin a search for the *unity of science* among living systems on earth. Our earth, after all, is just one big living system.

A wealth of research exists about the Society's fifty-year search for this universality of life—the "General Systems Theory" (GST) of living systems on earth. For those interested in their research and findings, we recommend their annual yearbooks. This is much of the source of our interpretation and translations. For further information, see www.isss.org, the successor to the Society for General Systems Research.

Von Bertalanffy was a renaissance man who influenced many of the great scientists and theorists of the 20th Century, including Peter Drucker, Margaret Mead, economist and Nobel Prize winner Kenneth Boulding, and Buckminster Fuller. Jay Forrester, MIT professor, was another who focused on the mathematics of Systems Dynamics, an application of Systems Thinking. By the 1970s, the study and pursuit of General Systems Theory and Systems Thinking had formally taken root in twenty-three nations.

Perhaps not surprisingly, however, true Systems Thinking is relatively unknown in North America today. The Science of Living Systems is better known in Europe and Asia. Thanks in part to the Internet, the awareness and knowledge of Systems Thinking is growing. This book is created to provide a strong foundation in Systems Thinking as it applies to Enterprise-Wide Change.

General Systems Theory has never fully penetrated mainstream business consciousness. Instead, it bubbled underground, out of sight. But within the past decade, the elegant simplicity of the natural and living world has begun to be discovered by the business world.

Within Systems Thinking, these natural scientific laws are organized into four elegantly simple concepts:

1. There are seven levels of living (open) systems;

2. There is a normal way all living systems undergo change (the natural cycles of life and change);

3. The ABCDE systems model represents how living systems naturally function; and

4. There are twelve laws of natural (living) systems on earth.

Systems Thinking is a comprehensive yet simple and integrated science. It is a way to analyze and build synergy for Enterprise-Wide Change through

- Developing a high-level view to better scan the environment and marketplace

- Thinking backwards from the vision, marketplace positioning, and core values on how to achieve them

- Building key outcome success measures to clarify desired results

- Developing core strategies to deal with business and human issues to move an entire organization toward its ideal state in approximately three years

- Executing Enterprise-Wide Change processes across the organization, level by level, unit by unit

- Building and sustaining business excellence and positioning over the long term

The change field is not only about satisfying people. It is also about assisting enterprises in improving productivity, serving the customer, meeting financial goals, and addressing societal and stakeholder satisfaction. Effective change consultants must deal successfully with strategy, marketplace positioning, customer value, business excellence, employee satisfaction, and complex, organization-wide execution of cultural changes.

Many change consultants are highly skilled in working at the team, task force, and interpersonal levels of change. This book is intended to increase their skills in operating at the senior management and enterprise-wide levels.

In our increasingly complex and interconnected world, the Systems Thinking Approach is a way to find success facilitating elegant simplicity on the far side of this complexity. Enterprise leaders and change consultants must acknowledge and deal with organizational complexity, head-on.

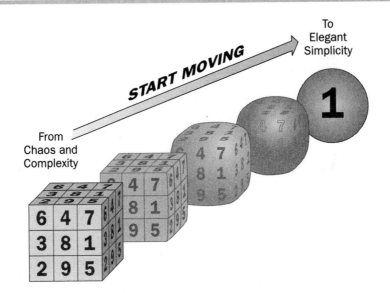

Acknowledgments

WE WOULD LIKE TO THANK five different groups of people without whom this book would not exist.

First, we want to thank the many CEOs, senior managers, and clients who have taught us much more about Enterprise-Wide Change than we ever taught them. The proof is in the fire of execution, and we have been privileged to help them make a positive difference with their shareholders, customers, and employees, and with society as well.

Second, we would like to thank our professional colleagues in and out of the Centre for Strategic Management with whom we have shared, collaborated, debated, and learned about Systems Thinking and Enterprise-Wide Change. As our change consultant practices have honed the concepts and techniques in this book, we have learned and grown from our successes and failures.

Third, we would like to thank the many people who reviewed this book in its second and *final* form. They have helped shape this book into a manuscript for the marketplace. Our sincerest appreciation goes to Jeanne Cherbaneau, Dennis Looney,

Erin Campbell-Howell, Mary Jefferies, John Clarke, Aaron Pun, Frank McLean, Yves LeBienvenu, Dennis Blair, Miguel Guilarte, Denise Bryson, and Lori White.

Fourth, we want to deeply thank our spouses and families for their support, encouragement, and tolerance for the amount of time we had to devote to this book's creation. Thank you, Colleen, Martin, and Jayne, our support team leader.

Last, and most important, we want to offer our deep gratitude, thanks, and admiration to the three series editors, who have sponsored and cajoled us, read our manuscript, and offered innumerable and invaluable suggestions to immensely improve this book: Kristine Quade, William Rothwell, and Roland Sullivan.

Enterprise-Wide Change

Introduction

Change is the only law, and those who look only to the past or present
are certain to miss the future.

John F. Kennedy

TRYING TO CREATE AND SUSTAIN fundamental change throughout
an entire enterprise is an audacious undertaking.

Purpose of this Book

This pragmatic, hands-on book provides a comprehensive overview and practical
details of the science, research, and practice of a Systems Thinking Approach to
Enterprise-Wide Change to achieve superior human and business results.

This book will benefit progressive CEOs, executives, managers, and change consultants of all types, including internal and external organization development
(OD) professionals. It is written for planning, finance, quality, and HR executives
and professionals, as well.

In the 21st Century, we all need to move outside the boundaries of Industrial Age thinking to keep up with the ever-increasing pace and scope of worldwide change. Thinking differently—adopting a Systems Thinking Approach—leads to acting differently, which in turn leads to success in system-wide change.

This book provides the reader with four outcomes:

1. Build Frameworks for Facilitating Complex Enterprise-Wide Change

Systems Thinking provides CEOs, executives, and change consultants with frameworks for facilitating complex, Enterprise-Wide Change. These frameworks provide knowledge and specific techniques to make sense of the complexity of (1) the organization's marketplace environment, (2) the organization itself, and (3) the Enterprise-Wide Change process.

2. Conduct Holistic Organizational Diagnosis and Design

Systems Thinking is holistic and synergistic, and provides comprehensive views of the organization and its components in relationship to each other and the system as a whole. Its focus on outcomes, rather than just individual problems, creates far better odds that a large-scale change will succeed.

3. Provide Superior Decision-Making Abilities

Systems Thinking enhances the strategic thinking skills and decision-making abilities of CEOs, executives, and change consultants. It is a superior way to deal with the complex tradeoffs inherent among employee satisfaction, operational excellence, economic return, customer value, and societal contribution.

4. Achieve and Sustain a Unique Marketplace Position

Systems Thinking enhances senior management's ability to identify, achieve, and sustain the organization's unique differentiation and successful positioning in its marketplace. Russ Ackoff, Peter Senge, and others have written volumes about the effectiveness and application of Systems Thinking to management decision making.

Organization of the Book

I think, therefore, I am.

René Descartes

Part A: Introduction to Systems Thinking and Superior Results

The first part of the book consists of three chapters and serves as an introduction to its unique elements. The first element is the Science of Systems Thinking, *the natural way the world works.* The book's second unique element is its focus on changing the enterprise as a total entity—Enterprise-Wide Change. This book presents an integrated, holistic, and systems change process that requires a unique methodology.

Chapter One provides the definitions and fundamentals of Enterprise-Wide Change and shows how it differs from other kinds of change.

Chapter Two describes the different ages of life on earth and what is happening now that is causing us to deal with the massive complexities we experience. A new science, a unity of science, and our next age of life on earth is introduced: the Systems Age.

Chapter Three sets the context of the science of Systems Thinking, the foundation for this book. It details the four Core Systems Concepts of Living Systems that guide our lives: the Seven Levels of Living Systems, the Rollercoaster of Change, the ABCs of Systems Thinking, and the twelve natural characteristics of life on earth.

Part B: Practical Application to Enterprise-Wide Change

The second part of this book consists of six chapters that present a sequence of practical yet holistic steps to successfully complete the Enterprise-Wide Change journey. It moves from a preparatory Smart Start to Clarity of Purpose, to Simplicity of Execution, to Wave After Wave of Enterprise-Wide Change. Last, we cover the multi-year nature of this unique change.

Chapter Four helps ensure that we engineer success up-front by providing a Smart Start to this journey. Chapter Five is about strategic thinking and a need for clarity of purpose. It is about working on the enterprise, a helicopter view. It includes the four missing elements to strategic direction that must be clear at the beginning of any Enterprise-Wide Change: environmental scanning, marketplace positioning, core values, and success measures.

Chapter Six is about a newly researched Enterprise-Wide Change Assessment tool built on the Malcolm Baldrige National Quality Award Criteria for Performance

Excellence. This Enterprise-Wide Assessment successfully eliminates the "big three" failure issues organizations potentially fall prey to when attempting EWC.

Chapter Seven is about working *in* the enterprise—the complex, confusing, and conflicting details and views of its inner workings that can prevent effective change. It provides the keys to Simplicity of Execution as strategies and actions are cascaded down to ensure clarity of purpose, clarity of accountability, and reinforcement of rewards to engage the entire enterprise in the journey.

Chapter Eight addresses the complex and chaotic six stages of the actual change process everyone naturally goes through. What we term the "Cascade of Change" flows down and across the organization over and over again, wave after wave, and unit after unit. In this chapter we detail how all change and OD interventions described by other authors can be seen as subsets and parts of Enterprise-Wide Change.

Chapter Nine includes how to sustain superior results year after year by developing the required organizational capacity. We explain the need for continual reviews, booster shots, and annual updates to keep the change journey moving forward, year after year.

Part C: How to Begin Enterprise-Wide Change

At this point, you will have been introduced to the concepts of Systems Thinking applied to Enterprise-Wide Change. Now we give some practical ways to begin creating and sustaining business excellence.

Chapter Ten provides some bite-sized options on how to tailor Enterprise-Wide Change to your specific needs and situation. Not every enterprise needs to use every idea in this book, especially smaller firms or those without a need for a full transformation. All enterprises, however, must deal with change in some way in today's dynamic environment. Chapter Ten shows us how to begin.

Special Features

This book is designed to help progressive executives, change consultants, and organizational development (OD) professionals learn Systems Thinking to achieve superior results. It is best appreciated as a whole with the chapters building one on the other.

We have used several special icons and content features:

- We begin each chapter with PURPOSES, in keeping with the #1 Systems Question: What are our desired outcomes?

- In Part B, CONTEXT appears after each chapter PURPOSE to help you keep the big picture clearly in mind (the helicopter view).

- A comprehensive CASE STUDY about East Coast Federal Credit Union appears in Chapters Four through Nine near the end of the chapter.

- RECAPS sum up key ideas at the end of each chapter in Parts A and B. We also include some worksheets to assist with the practical application of that chapter's concepts and activities.

- THINK DIFFERENTLY sections reinforce key points through application of actual examples and stories of systems thinking successes and analytic thinking failures. (For obvious reasons the names of the clients and colleagues involved in these stories remain confidential.)

- QUESTIONS TO PONDER are probes to further your learning.

- Websites that may be of interest are listed at the end of this book, along with a bibliography of key books in Systems Thinking and Enterprise-Wide Change.

Part A

Introduction to Systems Thinking and Superior Results

THE FIRST PART OF THIS BOOK is an introduction to its two unique aspects: (1) the Science of Systems Thinking, the natural way the world works and its roots in biology and the behavioral sciences beginning in Vienna, Austria, over fifty years ago and (2) its focus on changing the enterprise as a total entity, what we call Enterprise-Wide Change. Much has been written about strategic planning for an entire enterprise—as well as about specific organization development and change interventions within organizations. However, there is little written about working on an entire enterprise in a way that deals with the economic, people, and customer elements in a totally integrated, holistic, and systemic fashion.

> Problems that are created by our current level of thinking can't be solved by that same level of thinking.
>
> *Albert Einstein*

A Helicopter View: Now let's get in a helicopter for a better view of Enterprise-Wide Change.

①

The Fundamentals of Enterprise-Wide Change

Change your thoughts and change your world.

Norman Vincent Peale

Chapter Purposes

- To understand how Enterprise-Wide Change (EWC) is fundamentally different from other forms of organizational change

- To learn three main reasons why an estimated 75 percent of major change efforts fail

- To gain a high-level overview of the Enterprise-Wide Change sequence

Obsolescence . . . as a result of the current paradigm shift, the standard way of doing business is rapidly becoming obsolete and irrelevant.

Welcome to the Future

Enterprise-Wide Change is becoming an increasingly large part of the landscape in today's dynamic 21st-Century environment. What do we mean by this?

Enterprise

An Enterprise (business, company, establishment, firm, organization, corporation, and so forth) is

- A business organization
- A systemic and industrious activity
- An undertaking—especially one of great scope, complication, or risk

Synonyms include *business, company, establishment, firm, organization,* and *corporation.* Enterprises are systemic, complex, industrious entities and include all public, private, and not-for-profit organizations. They are not just for-profit undertakings.

Change

Change is a word with which we are all familiar, meaning *to alter something.*

Enterprise-Wide Change

Enterprise-Wide Change (EWC) has a major impact on the entire organization and is usually strategic, large-scale, chaotic, complex, and/or radical in nature.

Examples of Enterprise-Wide Change initiatives and activities include

- Installing an Enterprise Resource Planning system (ERP)
- Creating a new high-performance culture
- Focusing on business and operational excellence
- Conducting mergers, acquisitions, joint ventures, and alliances
- Installing major new technologies
- Executing strategic and business plans
- Becoming more customer-focused
- Becoming a global company
- Improving customer service
- Desiring major growth and expansion
- Downsizing, outsourcing, and major cutbacks
- Restructuring and redesigning the organization
- Improving Six Sigma and quality
- Changing supply-chain management
- Developing and deploying major new products
- Transforming an entire enterprise
- Significantly increasing creativity and innovation
- Creating new businesses

Enterprise-Wide Change includes many of the organization-wide changes in which OD consultants (also called "change consultants" throughout this book) are typically involved, such as team building, visioning, leadership and executive succession planning, talent development, HR planning, process improvement, and change execution.

Enterprise-Wide Change concepts also apply to community and societal changes such as fundamental changes in

- Health care
- Education
- Child care
- Crime
- Security

The Systems Thinking Approach

A system is a set of components that work together for the overall benefit of the whole.

Systems Thinking is

- A way of seeing the whole as primary, the parts as secondary
- A higher-level way to view, filter, and mentally frame what we see in the world
- A worldview that considers the whole entity or enterprise, along with its fit and relationships to and with the environment
- A tool for finding patterns and relationships among subsystems and learning to reinforce or change these patterns to achieve specific outcomes
- A shift from seeing elements, functions, and events to seeing processes, structures, relationships, and outcomes

The phrase "Systems Thinking" became a popular buzzword in organizational change theory after the 1990 publication of Peter Senge's best-selling *The Fifth Discipline*. While Senge's *fifth discipline* is, in fact, Systems Thinking, many people misuse the term today. They use it to refer broadly to *anything* that links together and fits with something else—a list of related topics, for instance, that are somehow important to training and development or some other specific goal. That would be, at best, an integrated list, not a complete Systems Thinking view.

Systems Thinking is a science—the Science of Living Systems on Earth.

Achieving Superior Results

The approach to this level of change needs to be different. This book is about *thinking differently* regarding EWC. To be successful in such a complex set of tasks is management's ultimate challenge.

Superior results include

- Employee satisfaction
- Customer satisfaction
- Economic benefits for shareholders, and for owners
- Contribution to society

 THINK DIFFERENTLY

We often think about *what* we think, but we seldom think about *how* we think.

The Uniqueness of Enterprise-Wide Change

Unlike traditional change efforts, Enterprise-Wide Change (EWC) is a complex, systemic, laborious undertaking. It is not to be taken lightly.

A doctor would be guilty of malpractice if she or he operated on a patient without appropriate knowledge, skills, and a deep understanding of anatomy, genetics, and the patient's current health and medical history. In the same way, leaders and change consultants cannot responsibly impose change initiatives on their own "patients" (the organization as a whole, fellow managers, employees, customers, suppliers, owners, the community) without a full understanding of EWC's unique elements and demands.

Six distinct characteristics of EWC separate it from less comprehensive change initiatives (see Figure 1.1):

1. Major structural and fundamental impact—EWC has a major structural and fundamental impact on the entire organization or business unit in which change is to occur. Energetic leadership is required at multiple levels to succeed.

2. Strategic in scope—The change to be effected is strategic. It links to the business's unique positioning in a dynamic and highly competitive marketplace (including the public sector marketplace).

3. Complex, chaotic, and/or radical—The change is complex and chaotic in nature, or may constitute a radical departure from the current state—even to the point that desired outcomes and approaches to achieve them may be unclear.

4. Large-scale and transformational—The scale of desired change is large and will result in a significantly different enterprise. It will be transformed.

5. Longer timeframe—The desired change will require years of focused attention with multiple phases and stages.

6. Cultural change—The rules of the game change: the norms, guideposts, policies, values, and guides to behavior.

Authors' Note: We hesitate even to use the word "transformation," as it has become an overused catch phrase for all kinds of change. Often it is about giving a new name to old stuff and selling change interventions on the basis of their sex appeal or the latest fad. Evolutionary or point-to-point change efforts are inadequate in the face of systemic Enterprise-Wide Change.

Figure 1.1. Types of Change Management

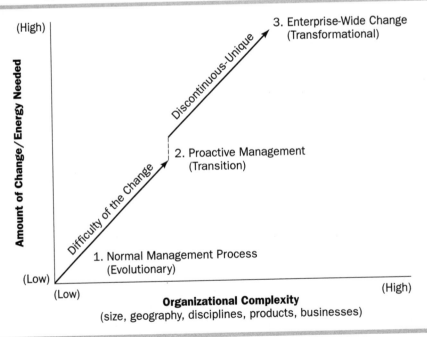

Any large-scale Enterprise-Wide Change will entail at least some of the following characteristics:

- Multiple transitions
- Incomplete transitions
- Uncertain future state(s)
- Multiple changes over long periods of time
- Changing priorities
- Conflicting demands
- Changing players
- Resistance to change
- Loss of focus
- Inadequate resources
- False starts
- Derailments
- Delayed payoffs
- Ambiguity/awkwardness

When *starting over from zero,* these characteristics are normal and to be expected. Persistence and perseverance are essential.

 THINK DIFFERENTLY

Boeing is trying to "think differently" to reinvent itself to become a defense contractor, not just an airplane manufacturer. They are undergoing EWC to reposition themselves into an additional business and marketplace through acquisitions in the defense industry.

Its headquarters is now in Chicago, not Seattle, and it has acquired numerous other defense contractors, including much of Rockwell International. However, in looking beyond their aircraft roots, many analysts feel Boeing is losing significant ground to the European Airbus competitor.

A dual focus on Enterprise-Wide Change and their current business is required for their future success. This is a very public Enterprise-Wide Change process we can all observe.

Questions to Ponder

- Do you agree with these definitions of Enterprise-Wide Change? The Systems Thinking approach to superior results? Why or why not?

- Can you think of other examples of Enterprise-Wide Change?

- Do you agree with the six unique characteristics of Enterprise-Wide Change? Why or why not?

21st Century: Revolutionary Worldwide Change and Its Implications

In the complex and dynamic 21st Century, CEOs, executives, change consultants, and organization development professionals need new modes of thinking to effectively manage organizations. The approaches to thinking and management that worked in the 20th Century and during the Industrial Revolution are no longer relevant in today's fast-paced Information Age.

Systems Thinking tells us that enterprises are not simply the sum of their components or parts. Instead, they are the end result of all of their processes, systems, and people—a complex web of interdependencies and interrelationships.

As many leaders have discovered, changing just one part of an organization without considering the rest of the system often results in unpredictable, unintended, and undesirable consequences elsewhere in the system.

Thinking differently can lead to acting differently and achieving better results.

Since the fall of the Berlin Wall in November 1989, a flood of change has enveloped the world. The Iron Curtain collapsed, along with most communist regimes worldwide. The European Union and Euro currency came into being. Eastern Bloc countries joined NATO and the EU, while a *global village*, working around the clock with interlocking economies, sought freer trade through WTO, GATT, NAFTA, and MERCOSUR. The ascendancy of networked computing brought the Internet, extranets, and intranets into even the smallest businesses across North America, Europe, Asia, and the rest of the world. Satellites and wireless global communications united even the remotest areas of the globe. Genetics research came of age; the human genome was mapped in its entirety; and the biotech revolution is underway.

The 21st Century has fostered a radically changed business climate. A global recession rages. Now worldwide competition grows more intense. Corporate corruption and greed are uncovered almost daily. Industries blur into one another as substitutions and new product lifecycles shorten. Employees feel helpless and over-whelmed with new demands, complexities, and intensity in the workplace. Companies see a shift in the power balance as consumer demands take center stage. Simultaneous pressure for commodity pricing and erosion of marketplace positioning take their toll. Cultures must shift as flexibility, speed, and responsiveness mean survival, even as demands rise for economies of scale and lower costs.

One thing is certain: Business as usual won't cut it anymore—not in government, not in the private sector, not in the not-for-profit world, and certainly not in the military.

> The history of mankind is strewn with habits, creeds, and dogmas that were essential to one age and disastrous to another.
>
> *James Reston*, New York Times columnist

▶ THINK DIFFERENTLY

21st Century U.S. warfare such as Operation Iraqi Freedom (which they thought ended in April 2003) has found the *silver bullet* for military success: *coherent joint warfare.* Yet systemic nation-building did not follow.

This is defined as the highest level of joint force integration (Army–Navy–Air Force–Marines–Coast Guard–FBI–CIA), progressing from specialized joint operations to synergistic joint operations where joint forces will be thoroughly integrated to fully exploit the synergism of land, sea, and air combat capabilities—a systems view.

> *David Vergun (2003). "Coast Guard Brings Order to Varied Fleet of 1,500 Boats."* Sea Power, *August 2003, p. 35.*

Authors' Note: Cause and effect can be greatly separated in time and space, as the above is a direct result of the Goldwater–Nichols Defense Reorganization Act of 1986. It mandated joint operations and unified combatant commands such as the central command led by Army General Tommy Franks in 2003. The aftermath of April 2003 is a monumental tragedy owing to lack of both a Smart Start and Clarity of Purpose and no integrated simplicity of execution. Unfortunately, the same systems view of nation-building in Iraq was absent. It required a worldwide intervention system to have a chance to succeed.

The good news is that society and enterprises have moved beyond looking for the one right, simplistic silver-bullet answer to their chronic and diverse issues and problems. They are starting to apply multiple solutions to patterns of events and issues. However, we believe that they may not fully understand the context, or systems within systems, in which all these complex issues exist.

It is tempting and comforting to look to top executives who have transformed their companies in these dynamic times. The best advice we know of is the widely quoted view from GE's former CEO:

> If you are still doing things now the same way you did them five years
> ago, you are doing something wrong.
>
> *Jack Welch*

This book provides a roadmap for Enterprise-Wide Change using an *integrated Total System Thinking Approach* that identifies, considers, and leverages the impact of isolated organizational change. Senior management's ability to identify, achieve, and sustain a unique position in the marketplaces is improved significantly when their decisions are based on a more holistic, humanistic, and systems orientation.

The Secret of Constant Growth

Living, growing systems change. This means that no matter what journey an organization is undertaking, every organization is constantly required to change or die. All enterprises must simultaneously service the current business and create the future business. It is the not-so-secret of constant growth (Figure 1.2).

Figure 1.2. The Secret of Constant Growth

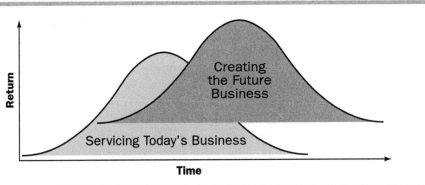

Source: Andrew Papageorge, www.goinnovate.com

The secret of constant growth means that executives and managers have two full-time jobs:

1. Serving today's business in a stressful, dynamic, consumer-oriented world where more demanding customers are driving products and services toward commodity pricing

2. Creating future business amidst the pressure of the daily business for current results

The secret of constant growth is simple:

- Work IN the business and you feed yourself today
- Work ON the business and you feed yourself next year

Fritjof Capra, Ph.D., a world-renowned physicist and systems theorist who co-wrote the film *Mindwalk*, explores the fundamentals of Systems Thinking:

One of the foremost signs of present-day society is the presence of massively complex systems that increasingly permeate almost every aspect of our lives. The amazement we feel in contemplating the wonders of industrial and informational technologies is tinged by a sense of uneasiness, if not outright discomfort.

Though these complex systems continue to be hailed for their increasing sophistication, there is a growing recognition that they have brought with them a business and organizational environment that is almost unrecognizable from the perspective of traditional management theory and practice. (Capra, 2004)

The global society at large and the nations, companies, and cultures of which it is composed are approaching a transformation, moving through the Information Age to the Systems Age. Many people, however, are not yet fully aware of the impending transformation. It will be a distinct competitive advantage to learn early how Systems Thinking can be used to guide enterprises to superior results.

75 Percent of All Major Changes Do Not Succeed

The vast majority of major organizational change efforts fail to achieve their intended and desired outcomes.

We know of no single comprehensive study that quantifies the exact percentage of failed change initiatives. This is not surprising, as it would be quite unusual to have CEOs admit to this. However, consultants, executives, and business professors alike seem to agree that the most likely outcome of a significant change initiative is failure to achieve its desired intent and superior results. This should not be too surprising when we realize that both the technical and social complexity of our lives and organizations is so great that it makes successful change very difficult.

Anecdotal evidence, decades of experience in the change field, smaller research studies, and numerous conversations with other prominent consultants and writers suggest our staggering belief that approximately *75 percent of all major change initiatives fail to fully meet their initial objectives.* This is despite a multi-billion-dollar consulting industry dedicated to Enterprise-Wide Change.

In post-mortem analyses, one dominant characteristic we at the Centre for Strategic Management have found in failed initiatives is that they are fragmented efforts. They rely on outmoded analytic methods and tactics. And they almost universally attempt to address a systemic problem in a piecemeal one-best-way, silver-bullet fashion.

What follows is a short list of myopic approaches to systemic problems—and the typical consequence of unintended results that leads to the 75 percent failure rate.

Job Cuts and Downsizing

In the past twenty years, more than sixty million jobs have been eliminated from American organizations, according to the American Management Association (www.amanet.org). The economic effects of technology, computers, robotics, and so forth have been enormous. Today, there is no such thing in business as a career or lifetime job. Outsourcing and offshoring will continue.

Many companies that were leaders in the Industrial Revolution have fallen on difficult times and decimated their human organizations in an attempt to maintain profitability. The massive downsizing of corporate America, however, has not achieved its desired effect. The American Management Association's survey of member companies conducted each year since 1990 has repeatedly found that downsizing fails to produce higher results. Fewer than half the companies that cut jobs reported an immediate increase in operating profits, while less than one-third reported an increase in productivity.

Fragmented Reengineering Fads

A number of popular management/business books advocate incomplete and fragmented tactics that make change sound simple and easy. Business process reengineering, to take just one example, was popularized in Michael Hammer and James
Champy's 1993 book *Reengineering the Corporation: A Manifesto for Business Revolution.*

For most enterprises that attempted reengineering, the effort did not work out as
intended. CFOs (rather than someone with a more natural customer and sales
focus) often led reengineering projects; consequently, reengineering too often simply became a massive cost-reduction program that destroyed capabilities, core competencies, and customer value.

Hammer, in his second book, *Beyond Reengineering: How the Processed-Centered
Organization Is Changing Our Work and Lives* (1996), acknowledged that many efforts
failed because the reengineering industry neglected to factor in the human element—a critical flaw.

Lack of Customer Orientation

Despite common sense and the abundance of research on its value, far too few companies achieve a customer orientation. Organizations are often driven instead by
(1) regulatory decisions, (2) operational efficiencies, (3) anything to make a profit,
or (4) product orientation.

The Gallup organization, located in Washington, D.C., has found that, while
many organization leaders talk a good game about the customer being king, more
than 70 percent of all managers feel performance is driven more by internal operating measures than by any kind of external, customer-focused ones.

Silver-Bullet Change Consulting: Fads

Management consultants and authors who tout their method as the sole path and
silver bullet to corporate salvation often compound existing problems. The one-best-
way approach promulgated by leading management authors and gurus has
resulted in fad after fad. Every year, each new fad goes through the same inevitable
lifecycle:

- Introduction of new ideas
- Early adoption of new ideas
- High acceptance and widespread dissemination of new ideas

- Misuse of or lip service to the ideas
- Criticism and decline of the approach
- Search for the next Holy Grail

However, no *one-best-way* can solve all ills—not even this book. Our goal in writing this book is to improve the *probability* of successful Enterprise-Wide Change.

Resistance to Change

Gallup polls have shown that more than two-thirds of business leaders resist change. Understandably, like most of us, they have a vested interest in protecting the status quo, do not like to lose control, and may not feel comfortable about what to do about the needed changes.

The stock market, of course, drives publicly held companies to be quarterly and short-term oriented. As a result, company executives are often rewarded for maintaining a consistent small increase in earnings, as seen, for example, in the Freddie Mac scandal in 2003.

Gallup polls also show that 74 percent of all employees in the United States are *disengaged* from their work—and worse yet, 19 percent are *actively disengaged* from (and may even sabotage) their company. This news is devastating for those searching for superior business results.

Strategic Planning Fragmentation

The highly respected strategist and professor Henry Mintzberg, in his book *Strategy Safari* (1998), examined ten different strategic planning processes and found none to be effective.

Our Centre's own research (since 1990) comparing fourteen different *strategic planning* models found the same ineffectiveness and fragmentation. Fewer than 25 percent of all planning models studied had any form of pre-planning or efforts to ensure the effort was organized and tailored to each unique situation up-front.

More than half of the models did not even link the strategic plan to the annual plan and budget. None of them dealt with helping to organize implementation Game Plans.

It is no wonder many plans are never implemented and fall prey to the SPOTS syndrome (Strategic Plan on Top Shelf . . . gathering dust) as noted in *The Systems Thinking Approach to Strategic Planning and Management* (2000). Data we have collected lead us to estimate that only about 25 percent of all strategic plans are ever successfully executed.

Inadequate Change Frameworks

In our research on thirteen popular organizational change models, we found

- Only four focused on the customer
- Few had a focus on outputs and goals, as opposed to process alone
- Many did not focus on the need for cross-functional teams as vehicles for integrated change
- Less than one-third included strategic thinking or planning as a guide for the change effort
- Fewer than half dealt with organizational culture as a key variable
- Many did not look at the values and beliefs of the organization

In general, these change models were technical, operational, or mechanistic in nature. They usually did not deal with the issue of people's hearts and minds being in tune with the desired changes. Only one of the thirteen included adequate feedback mechanisms, and only one out of thirteen used a system and processes to manage change strategically. The results can be found in *Reinventing Strategic Planning for the 21st Century* (2002).

The "Big Three" Enterprise-Wide Failure Issues

Based on our research, there are three normal, natural, and predictable issues that contribute to 75 percent of all major changes failing to achieve their desired intent. Outlined below, the first one produces a guarantee of failure up-front, and the last two are symptoms of partial success because of an either-or mindset.

1. A Piecemeal Approach to a Systems Problem

- This involves a variety of multiple mindsets, holistic frameworks, and consultants employing different models, concepts, and silver bullets instead of applying a single mindset based on an organization as a living system.

2. A Primary Focus on the Economic Alignment of Delivery

- This approach focuses on productivity, processes, and bottom-line economics without attending to the cultural attunement issues. Both elements are needed.

3. A Primary Focus on the Cultural Attunement of People

- This approach focuses on egalitarian, participative people processes without incorporating the economic alignment issues. Combining both elements is critical to success.

Instead of telling you more about these three ways to fail, in this book we recommend an alternative approach to Enterprise-Wide Change that combines solutions to the "big three" causes of failure with one holistic mindset that focuses on integrating both economic *alignment of delivery* and the *cultural attunement* with people. The results are

Full Success—A Totally Integrated Systems Solution

- An Enterprise-Wide, Systems Thinking Approach to business excellence that combines economic alignment, cultural attunement, and a single holistic mental map to assess and guide the change that achieves superior results (profits–growth–customer–culture–sustainability)

In sum, the reality is that there are so many reasons change fails that it is not surprising that only about 25 percent of change efforts are fully successful. This is particularly true for large-scale Enterprise-Wide Changes.

The Search for the Silver Bullet

Attempts to change organizations with the latest silver bullet ignore two powerful principles of organization:

1. Organizations are perfectly designed for the results they get.

2. Success comes from individuals who take accountability for their actions.

Alignment and Attunement Concepts Expanded

Most EWC journeys tend to be under-funded and under-resourced, especially in terms of people, when one considers the complexity and magnitude of the planned change. Change consultants sometimes don't help matters with their terminology. The talk today is about the *alignment of people* in the enterprise in support of the desired changes. Alignment is an industrial and mechanical term. It is appropriate when discussing assembly lines, robots, and technical systems. *Alignment of delivery* is an appropriate term. *Alignment of people* is not.

The authors would like to belatedly thank Roger Harrison, a pioneer in the OD field, for this distinction learned more than thirty years ago in a long-forgotten session. This distinction may seem a small change, but the leverage it makes possible is enormous.

People are *living systems.* We don't function like robots. People have feelings, emotions, a brain, and a spirit, *in addition to* hands and feet that perform physical work tasks. When change consultants use the term *alignment* to refer to people, they are inadvertently downplaying the human requirements for successful Enterprise-Wide Change.

Attunement is a musical term that means *to bring into harmony*—to ensure that each instrument in an orchestra or band is tuned exactly the same way as all the others. The proper term for what executives need to do with people in an enterprise is attunement. Collaboration is required to bring our hearts and minds into harmony with each other and with the higher-level system goals.

You can force alignment, but you cannot force attunement.

Note: For those interested in reading more on the tension between alignment and attunement, we highly recommend Michael Beer and Nitin Nohria's *Breaking the Code of Change* (2002). In 1998, a Breaking the Code of Change conference was held at the Harvard Business School. Professors and executives were asked to compare, contrast, and debate two theories of change: Theory E (creation of economic value) and Theory O (development of an enterprise's human capability and culture to implement strategy). Their conclusions support the views in this book.

⟩ THINK DIFFERENTLY

A large West Coast financial services enterprise underwent a massive turn-around and EWC process. The process was a rousing success because the new CEO and executive VP cared deeply about both the economic alignment and cultural attunement issues. The executive VP was the internal executive in charge of the program management office and the external consultant was the president of University Associates (an external consulting firm).

Even though more than fifty managers and executives were individually terminated for poor performance, morale and profits went up dramatically in the first full year after the new CEO was hired. And . . . no lawsuits for wrongful termination were filed.

Questions to Ponder

- What revolutionary changes do you see going on in the world today?
- Do you agree that Enterprise-Wide Change is fundamentally different from traditional change? Why or why not?
- Do you agree with our "big three" reasons why Enterprise-Wide Change fails? Why or why not?

Final Thought—Great Results and Great Frustrations

We want to be clear that there are many cases of CEOs, executives, and change consultants who are very successful at achieving superior results for their organizations—both in terms of the *economic alignment of delivery* and the *cultural attunement with people*. We will give some examples of them throughout this book.

However, we also know that there is ONE GREAT FRUSTRATION regarding change in enterprises and businesses by executives, employees, and change consultants alike. It is a great frustration that we all don't seem to see the same picture. Each of us personally thinks that our picture is THE CORRECT PICTURE. This leads to frustration with each other and the lack of superior results for customers, stockholders, employees, and the community. This lack of both yin and yang strategies is one of the overarching themes of this book (Figure 1.3).

Figure 1.3. The Yin and Yang of Strategies

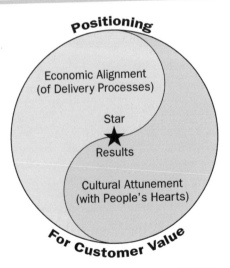

Preview: The Enterprise-Wide Change Journey

There are three goals of Enterprise-Wide Change. This book covers the three goals and an entire process to achieve them in depth.

Three Goals in Enterprise-Wide Change

Prework: Use a Smart Start with a Systems Thinking foundation

Goal #1: Develop an overall enterprise-wide clarity of purpose, with a game plan for dramatic change.

Goal #2: Ensure simplicity of execution, with enterprise-wide systemic change.

Goal #3: Build and sustain business excellence and superior results, year after year.

This book approaches each goal in depth, giving you both a theoretical foundation and practical tools you can use to guide EWC efforts. Obviously, it would be unusual for an enterprise to use all of the points of this book—even our clients rarely do. But this book gives you a template from which to choose and tailor your Enterprise-Wide Change effort.

Prework: Build a Smart Start

The prework concept in Chapter Four is the most commonly skipped, missed, or ignored part of any EWC. There are real, non-negotiable preconditions for successful systemic change that must be in place before an Enterprise-Wide Change process can hope to succeed. Smart Start helps enterprises to engineer success upfront before the formal beginning of the journey.

We recommend that senior management first undergo a two-day retreat. The goals of this *Smart Start* are

- To educate the executives on Enterprise-Wide Change
- To assess issues critical to the Enterprise-Wide Change
- To tailor the EWC process to your needs and unique situation
- To organize the EWC effort to fit your size, budget, and focus

Prework: Lay The Systems Thinking Foundation

Competence and a foundation in the core technologies of Systems Thinking are critical for executives and change consultants who undertake EWC. In Smart Start, enterprise leaders learn the assumptions, mental models, and methods that will help them to understand their organization's challenges and strengths from a full Systems Thinking perspective.

Terms like "mental map," "model," "paradigm," "framework," "concept," "worldview," and "Weltanschauung" (German for *view of the world*) are similar words for a collective mindset, a way in which humans understand (or misunderstand) the world in which we live.

Specific change interventions typically use a narrow analytical mental map. While the interventions have value, even the best of these is only partially successful. No one can begin to maximize the overall potential business excellence and superior results without a systemic mental map of some kind.

Our belief is that Systems Thinking is one excellent mental map to understand an organization. We also believe there is much to be gained by carefully choosing elements of other change models and methodologies. Just remember to integrate them within some kind of holistic approach. There are other kinds of large-scale change approaches in this Pfeiffer Practicing OD Series that the reader is invited to review as well.

THINK DIFFERENTLY

The U.S. Coast Guard is now part of the new Department of Homeland Security. In the post–9/11 world of terrorism we now live in, the Coast Guard has taken on added importance.

They are now seeing increased funding for their mission. Historically, their fleet of over 1,500 boats was of dozens of different types. They ranged from 19 to 52 feet long, of many different manufacturers, with all kinds of different engines, and many different type hulls. Local commanders had carte blanche authority to purchase almost any type of boat needed (even with special modifications), 188 different stations, sixty aids-to-navigation stations, and dozens of Marine Safety Offices, on their own—an example of analytic thinking run amuck. The complexity of this hodgepodge approach caused many problems from readiness to safety, sea handling, proficiency, maintenance, parts, training, and transferring personnel.

Now, with a more Systems Thinking view, they have a plan to transition to four standardized classes of shore-based response boats. One manufacturer is building all new 117-foot Fast-Motor Lifeboats and 47-foot highly maneuverable Fast-Motor Lifeboats. In addition, all 25-foot Small Response Boats are being built by another manufacturer and all 41-foot Medium Response Boats will have a contract awarded in 2004.

The boat fleet will now be standardized—not quite as systemically as Southwest Airlines, with only one 737-type aircraft, but a huge systems improvement for the Coast Guard.

Goal #1: Achieve clarity of purpose

Gaining true clarity of purpose requires conducting, identifying, and clarifying four parts of the Game Plan, if they are not already in place:

1. Conducting an environmental scanning process of relevant external factors
2. Developing enterprise-wide positioning (desired outcomes) that articulates the overall direction/vision of the enterprise
3. Clarifying core values, which are the guiding principles for decision making throughout the change effort
4. Setting measurable goals for the process—year by year if necessary

 THINK DIFFERENTLY

A large, thirty-year-old, employee-owned engineering business had been doing well by the standards of a plan that had been developed five years before. The entrepreneur-founder CEO had fired the president and COO within the past year. Running the business had been left to the executive team (with rotating leadership) during the vacuum.

As is typical of organizations at this stage, the executive team often received conflicting messages from the CEO regarding strategy and change. The executive team knew it couldn't afford to wait for the new president to be hired before a new EWC plan was developed. They embarked on a journey to refine the organization's vision, values, and positioning and completed a comprehensive future external environmental scan.

It took months for a new president to arrive, but in the meantime, the organization had its EWC plan in place and a solid base for the new president to build on. It also enabled the executive team and new president to work effectively with the entrepreneur-founder-CEO.

Goal #2: Ensure simplicity of execution

During EWC efforts, you obviously cannot know everything in advance. The Game Plan has to be a living, breathing process that is continuously re-created as it unfolds. Goal #2 is where execution of change formally begins in all its gory, chaotic, and complex details.

Without a systems orientation, this is, unfortunately, often the place where change consultants and executives start—thus ensuring piecemeal failure up-front by failing to adequately lay the groundwork that emerges from the prework (Smart Start) and Goal #1.

Goal #2 requires regular meetings of an Enterprise-Wide Change Leadership Team. It is supported by a Program Management Office with detailed tracking and regular reporting about issues, results, and measures of success.

Goal #3: Sustaining business excellence

Key actions at the end of each year include recycling back through the prework and all three goals again (wave after wave of change):

- Reviewing and assessing the business alignment and people attunement results from the last year

- Assessing how well you are "walking the talk" on your core values

- Developing further action plans to correct for a values breakdown—areas of weakness or failure

- Assessing the results of the first year of the EWC Game Plan itself

- Refining the Enterprise-Wide Change Game Plan for the next twelve months, adjusting core strategies and their key initiatives as necessary

Chapter One Recap

1. Richard Beckhard's original definition of Organization Development in *Organization Development: Strategies and Models* (1969) is still as relevant today to Enterprise-Wide Change. Organization Development is an effort that is planned, organization-wide, and managed from the top to increase organization effectiveness and health through planned interventions in the organization's processes using behavioral-science knowledge.

2. Enterprise-Wide Change is fundamentally different from other traditional changes. It has a major structural impact, is strategic in nature, is complex,

chaotic, or radical, is on a large scale, is system-wide, and occurs over a longer timeframe.

3. An estimated 75 percent of major change efforts fail.

4. The "big three" Enterprise-Wide Change failure causes are (1) an analytic, piecemeal approach to systems problems (multiple conflicting frameworks and mindsets); (2) focusing mainly on the economic alignment of delivery; and (3) focusing mainly on cultural attunement and involvement with people.

5. Three goals in Enterprise-Wide Change are to (1) develop an overall enterprise-wide clarity of purpose, (2) ensure simplicity of execution with enterprise-wide systemic change, and (3) build and sustain business excellence and superior results, year after year.

Seeking a Unity of Science for Living Systems

Great spirits have always encountered violent opposition from mediocre minds.

Albert Einstein

Chapter Purposes

- To explain the differences between Analytic Thinking and Systems Thinking
- To provide an overview on the science, research, and history of thinking about living systems on earth

In one way or another, we are forced to deal with complexities, with *wholes* or *systems* in all fields of knowledge. This implies a basic reorientation in scientific thinking.

Ludwig von Bertalanffy, from General Systems Theory: Foundations, Development, and Applications

It should be borne in mind that there is nothing more difficult to arrange, more doubtful of success, and more dangerous to carry through than initiating changes in a state's constitution.

The innovator makes enemies of all those who prospered under the older order, and only lukewarm support is forthcoming from those who would prosper under the new.

Their support is lukewarm partly from fear of their adversaries, who have the existing laws on their side, and partly because men are generally incredulous, never really trusting new things unless they have tested them by experience.

In consequence, whenever those who oppose the changes can do so, they attack vigorously, and the defense made by the others is only lukewarm.

So both the innovator and his friends are endangered together.

Machiavelli

Complexity Versus Simplicity: Our Different Views of the World

Look at the two boxes in Figure 2.1:

Figure 2.1. Simplicity Versus Complexity

Simplicity

Complexity

What a difference between the simplicity of a sunset versus the complexity of our communities! The world is complex—and becoming even more so with technological inventions and innovations. We have a complex, interconnected world economy and global Internet communications that actually obscure the realities of how life functions naturally on earth as we asphalt over much of it.

To make this point, we recommend using a Rubik's Cube analogy (Figure 2.2) throughout your change effort.

Figure 2.2. Rubik's Cube

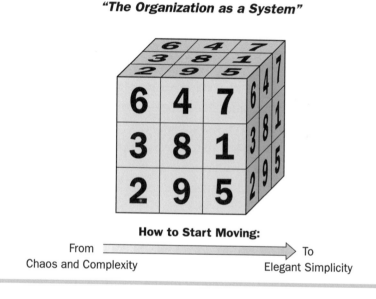

"The Organization as a System"

How to Start Moving:

From   To
Chaos and Complexity   Elegant Simplicity

The Rubik's Cube is a deceptively simple puzzle that offers a nearly perfect illustration of the nature of complex problems and the necessity to abandon analytic thinking when dealing with complexity.

Hungarian designer Erno Rubik invented the six-sided, six-colored cube in 1974. Rubik did not intend to create a puzzle per se; he was more fascinated with solving the problem of creating the inner workings of the cube which would allow each axis of a 3-by-3 cube to rotate freely.

Once he had solved the engineering problem of how to create the cube's mechanism (itself a breakthrough in Systems Thinking), Rubik next began to understand the enormous complexity inherent in the deceptively simple cube. Rubik himself has described the moment when he recognized that his invention presented a problem that transcended analytical solutions when he applied color to each of the six sides and began twisting:

> It was wonderful to see how, after only a few turns, the colors became mixed, apparently in random fashion. It was tremendously satisfying to watch this color parade. Like after a nice walk when you have seen many lovely sights you decide to go home.
>
> After a while I decided it was time to go home. Let us put the cubes back in order. And it was at that moment that I came face to face with the Big Challenge: What is the way home? (Erno Rubik from M. Bellis, 1997)

It took Rubik a month to find the way home on the cube, the first time around. Mathematicians have calculated that there are nearly forty-three quintillion independent configurations in the cube. If one were to approach solving the cube randomly, by simply twisting and trying one combination after another, it would take many lifetimes to find, let alone try, all the possible permutations.

A Rubik's Cube today comes with instructions that explicitly state that the solution cannot be found by approaching just one color or one side in isolation. It is, in fact, impossible to solve the puzzle in its entirety by attempting to *fix* just one *problem* at a time.

By 1983, the puzzle Rubik had invented had entered popular consciousness, baffling engineers, scientists, and ordinary citizens alike. There were scrambled cubes in lockers, on tabletops, hooked to key rings, and even on bedside tables. Books about how to solve the cube burned up the charts.

Today, you can even play with *virtual* versions of the cube via the Internet (check out www.rubikscube.com). There are dozens and dozens of highly theoretical explanations posted in cyberspace about models required to solve it.

It is possible to solve a mixed-up Rubik's cube without supercomputers. Small groups of cube enthusiasts, in fact, have come up with several systems to do so, and today there are *speed-cubing* competitions where practiced gamers restore a jumbled cube to its initial state in a matter of seconds. In 1983, it was widely reported that a seven-year-old Norwegian boy was able to successfully complete the puzzle time and time again. Yet he *could not explain how he achieved this feat in words.* He simply did not have the language necessary to do so.

The thinking required to generate reliable solutions to the puzzle of the cube had to transcend analytic, one-piece-at-a-time thinking, explanations, and language.

Complexity in organizations and enterprises is of a similar nature. One twist or even a series of changes intended to *solve* one aspect of an organization's problems may give the illusion of a solution—until you look at the rest of the system and realize that the myopic focus on one side has left others to become even more jumbled, as a predictable yet unintended consequence.

Enterprise-Wide Change, like Rubik's Cube, requires a continuing holistic systems thought process and view of the world (all six sides of the Rubik's cube) to solve. Our view of the world today must also change.

Western civilization has evolved through a series of ages—periods of time in history or human progress marked by the prominence of a particular approach to reality (Figure 2.3):

- The Hunting and Gathering Age of nomadic life (eons)
- The Agricultural Age of farming and ranching (thousands of years)
- The Industrial Age of machines, assembly lines, and mass production (250 years)
- The current Information Age of computers, telecommunications, and the Internet (ongoing; roughly fifty years)

The first noticeable trend in this progression is that the length of each approach to the world (and the worldview that underlies the approach) has become shorter and shorter. If the trend continues, a shift to the next age is rapidly approaching.

The Information Age often overwhelms people. We believe part of this response to complexity and chaos is the result of attempting to solve problems with mindsets and tools that have been losing efficacy since the Industrial Age. The next *age* could be a leap or shift to a conscious *Systems Age*.

⟫ THINK DIFFERENTLY

Despite our enormous knowledge, technology, and sophistication in the Western world, why is it we have chronic issues that our mindsets and problem-solving approaches cannot solve? Chronic issues such as homelessness, crime, drugs, health coverage, education, and poverty are resistant to our current attempts to solve them. How we think about them has a lot to do with it.

Figure 2.3. The Changing View of Our World

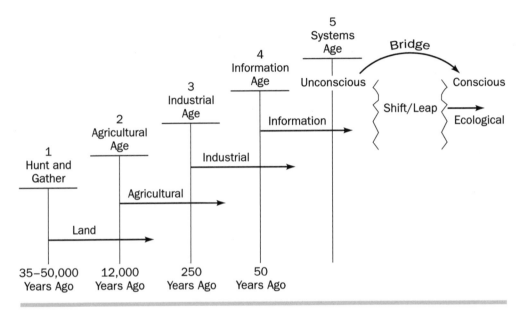

Shifting View of the World
(4.5 Billion Years Old)
Through Changing Thought Patterns

Ever since early NASA astronauts saw a faraway Earth floating in space, we've become increasingly aware that humanity and the Earth are part of a vast, interdependent universe—a system in which we play but one small part. Photos of the Earth taken from space allow us a view of the planet itself as a single organism—a worldview that is relatively new in science and philosophy.

Very few organizational leaders or change consultants can be astronauts in space with a broader view of planet Earth. We can, however, still get a different perspective—*a helicopter view* that offers a wider, more comprehensive perspective. Gaining this view requires curiosity and imagination. It requires looking farther out, beyond today. It requires entertaining *what-ifs.*

The Helicopter View of Life

A *helicopter view* of the organization from 5,000 feet above the ground provides a higher and broader perspective. It requires letting go of details about the enterprise's parts, its departments, and the details of its day-to-day operations. It encompasses focusing on the environment and all its components—customers, competition, and government.

To succeed in the business environment of the 21st Century, leaders need to gain the same higher-level perspective on the enterprises they guide. And in the larger scheme of things, if humanity is to continue to thrive as a species, we also need to make this new perspective a way of life. One of the worst things we could do at this point in history is to *avoid* thinking about our world in different ways.

Some additional historic paradigm shifts are

- Mass production to mass customization
- Mainframes to PCs to wireless
- Full-time employees to flexible work hours and cottage industries to outsourcing
- British Hong Kong to Communist China to the world's manufacturing center
- Wax cylinders to vinyl records to CDs to MP3 downloads
- Betamax to VHS to DVD
- Electronic tubes to transistors to chips to nanotubes
- Ballooning to biplanes to propeller planes to jets to space shuttles

On the other hand, a few examples of paradigm shifts that were missed at the time are embodied in the following statements, which at the time may have seemed obviously *correct* but in retrospect belie the flaws in the assumptions behind them.

- "Everything that can be invented has been invented." Charles H. Duell, director of U.S. Patent Office, 1899
- "There is no likelihood that man can ever tap the power of the atom." Robert Millikan, Nobel Prize winner, Physics, 1923

- "I think there is a world market for about five computers." Thomas Watson, CEO, IBM, 1943

Whatever you call them, mental models are based on our prevailing beliefs and assumptions—generally unexamined. Thinking differently about the world requires identifying and scrutinizing the assumptions that underlie the mental model through which we approach problem solving.

We are in the middle of a global paradigm shift, away from the assumptions of the fragmented, mechanistic Machine/Industrial Age and toward a larger, clearer, holistic view of *all* the changes and shifts that are occurring. This paradigm shift will allow us to understand and change entire systems, rather than analyzing and attacking one crisis at a time—one after another.

We must begin to see the forest, not just the trees. When we look at our world in this broader way, it becomes easier to see that what we've been doing no longer works. We've used up our energies—and our resources—putting out brush fires in increasingly more circular and destructive patterns.

Old mind maps, tools, techniques, and solutions left over from previous paradigms are past their best-before dates. We still are not seeing, however, a shift to something else that *does* work, a more holistic frame of reference. As futurist H. B. Gelatt puts it in *Creative Decision Making: Using Positive Uncertainty* (1991), "These conditions of turbulence make old paradigms dysfunctional, but paradigm paralysis sets in . . . [that] leads to personal blind spots, because a way of seeing (a paradigm) is also a way of not seeing. Paradigm paralysis is when we become incapable of seeing that things are no longer the way they used to be."

THINK DIFFERENTLY

During an extensive EWC process with a large government department, the director of HR reported that he and the director of finance had been trying to solve a problem for days, with no success. They decided to shift their paradigm and approach. They agreed to use a facilitator and the higher-level Systems Thinking Approach they had learned through the corporate EWC process. Within one hour, they had the solution.

By focusing on the desired outcome first, rather than on the problem itself, as they had been doing, they found they were not "locked on the problem." This experience helped them to understand the power of this new way of thinking, and they went to work to make it a core competency in the organization.

Questions to Ponder

- What is your opinion of the *shifting views of the world*? What are their implications?

- Does the *helicopter view of life* make sense to you? Why or why not?

- Can you think of other historical paradigm shifts in this world?

Analytic Thinking: A Mindset Left Over from the Industrial Age

All the problems of the world could be settled easily if people were only willing to think. The trouble is that people often resort to all sorts of devices in order not to think, because thinking is such hard work.

Thomas J. Watson

Since the Machine Age and Industrial Revolution, mechanization and machines have colored how we look at the world. Assembly lines, mass production, and countless machines brought with them the idea that the universe itself is a machine, not an organic, living system. Mechanistic or analytic thinking has spawned prevalent (and damaging) assumptions about the nature of people and the world itself.

Analytic Thinking Assumptions: Micro Smart and Macro Dumb

- *Reductionism:* If you take anything apart or reduce it to its lowest common denominator, you will ultimately reach indivisible elements. For instance, we repair car motors by taking them apart to work on their smallest parts.

- *Analysis:* If you take the entity/issue/problem apart, breaking it up into its components, you can solve it. Then you aggregate all the solutions and reassemble things. Analysis tends to explain things through parts, rather than a view of the whole. Even today, analysis is probably the most common technique used in organizations. Managers *cut their problems down to size,* reduce them to a set of solvable components, and then reassemble them into one solution. Many managers continue to see analyzing as synonymous with thinking.

- *Mechanization:* In this set of assumptions, virtually every phenomenon begins and ends with a single relationship: cause and effect. Environment is irrelevant. Indeed, the basis of modern scientific methods is the isolation of variables in highly controlled laboratories—an artificially closed systems view of the world.

While reductionism, analysis, and mechanism may appear to resolve problems initially, they almost always fail to provide long-term, longer-lasting solutions. Analytic thinking is such a common way of thinking that it is unconscious. Because its central, mechanistic, linear approach is to diagnose and treat only one issue at a time, other issues must wait their turn, causing further problems and unintended consequences. It's an inherent deficiency of this thinking mode.

Analytic thinking usually assumes one cause for one effect and asks, "Is it *either, or?*" Paired with reductionism, analytic thinking makes us "micro-smart and macro-dumb"—good at thinking through individual elements, like solving one side of Rubik's Cube, but prone to missing the larger, more important picture. Too often, we find ourselves with five unintended jumbled "other" sides as a result of analytic approaches to change.

Analytic Thinking Is Becoming Obsolete

The reason analytic thinking is less effective in business today than it was in earlier ages is that the global economy is increasingly complex, interconnected, and interrelated. Analytic thinking doesn't usually consider all environmental factors as it looks for one-and-only-one best way. The environment, other systems, relationships between and among systems, and multiple and circular causalities surrounding the enterprise have great impact on daily functioning. Yet analytic thinking often looks inward instead of considering these relationships, multiple solutions, interdependencies, and environment.

 THINK DIFFERENTLY

What do you see when you look at relationships between the war on terrorism, high oil prices, environmental concerns, tough economic times, the dot.com bubble bursting, retirement, and savings losses?

Well, the Japanese automakers are onto something new. They led the way in 2004 with hybrid gas-electric cars that get 50+ miles per gallon with regular gasoline. Yet they have not sacrificed convenience, style, space, and power. The cars are reasonably priced, too.

On the other hand, General Motors had no hybrid technology as a shorter-term building-block program. Instead they opted for a *one-best-way* longer-term hydrogen fuel cell program (with a ten-year possible marketing payoff). According to *Business Week* (October 27, 2003), "Detroit is missing the boat, as it is really dangerous to assume there will be only one technology in future cars."

Analytic Thinking Has Run Amuck

Here are examples from the United States that result from an analytic approach:

- *IRS rules and regulations:* More than 4,000 pages of regulations governing the taxation system cost American citizens an estimated $400 billion each year simply to comply with them.

- *Educational code in California:* More than 6,800 pages and eleven volumes end up restricting schools and school districts from attempting innovative approaches to teaching.

- *Car models:* General Motors has eighty-four car and truck models, according to a recent newspaper ad. People are continually confused as to what is different about each of the models, since many have the same *platform base* or foundation.

- *Specialized government districts:* Thousands of disconnected regulatory districts govern minute bits and pieces of public infrastructure, services, and property. Water districts, assessment districts, school districts, and so forth treat each fragment of public administration in isolation, almost always failing to consider the whole of public service and infrastructure in their decisions and policies.

- *Federal intelligence agencies:* An alphabet soup of sixteen federal agencies concerned with intelligence (NSA, CIA, FBI, CIA, and so on), none of which were effective in preventing the September 11, 2001, tragedy. Will the complex Homeland Security Department fix this?

- *Company SKUs:* Companies often have thousands and thousands of SKUs (stock keeping units), even though many sell poorly (80/20 rule).

- *Pricing cabbage:* The U.S. Department of Agriculture directive on pricing cabbage—something that would seem on its surface to be a simple matter—is reportedly 15,629 words long.

- *Health care:* Thousands of small, specialized entities and programs are often based on categorical grants created for singular yet important problems and solutions.

- *Congressional subcommittees:* Too many to enumerate. Every time a new issue comes along, Congress seems to establish a new fragmented yet overlapping subcommittee.

Analytic, piecemeal, and reductionist thinking resists considering multiple issues and their relationships at the same time or taking a larger view of entire systems.

When we approach a complex system and attempt to recognize multiple and delayed causes for every effect, we can become overwhelmed quickly and retreat back into the perceived "safety" of considering individual pieces of a problem in isolation. Unfortunately, as with a Rubik's Cube with just one side solved, the end result is often the unintended consequences on the other sides of the organization.

> We live and work in an analytic prison. Working hard within this prison
> produces nothing. We cannot remodel the prison; we must get rid of it.
> To do this, a transformation is required. Cooperation between people,
> companies, government, countries. There will be joy in working. Every-
> one will win.
>
> *Dr. W. Edwards Deming,*
> *April 21, 1992, presentation,* The New Economics

Eleven Signs of Analytic Thinking

You know you are in the presence of *analytic thinking* when

1. Discussions lack clear purposes or outcomes.

2. People are asking (or endlessly debating) artificial "either/or" questions.

3. Discussions center on finding the "one best way" to do something . . . without ever asking those closest to the problem for *their* solutions.

4. Discussions are focused on direct "cause-and-effect" without awareness of circular causality or environmental factors.

5. Simplistic solutions and "Quick Fixes" are suggested before any search for multiple root causes.

6. Issues and projects are separated into *silos* rather than considered in the context of the larger enterprise (and its other parts).

7. Discussions are activity-oriented, without clarity of purpose.

8. One of the first steps is an assessment of the current situation instead of a future-oriented environmental scan and statement of desired outcomes.

9. Decisions are being made without first exploring their possible unintended consequences on the rest of the organization.

10. Feedback and openness are sacrificed in the name of politeness and protecting fragile egos.

11. Discussions, terminology, and proposed solutions threaten to collapse under their own weight and complexity.

Questions to Ponder

- Do you believe that analytic thinking is becoming obsolete? Why or why not?

- Can you think of other areas where analytic thinking has run amuck?

- Can you think of other signs of analytic thinking?

Systems Thinking Contrasted with Analytic Thinking

From an early age, we're taught to break apart problems in order to make complex tasks and subjects easier to deal with. But this creates a bigger problem . . . we lose the ability to see the consequences of our actions, and we lose a sense of connection to a larger whole.

Peter Senge

Make no mistake; breaking away from analytic and sequential thinking won't be easy. It's been an integral part of our society for a long time. In fact, we rarely differentiate analytic, linear thinking from other types of thinking; we tend to see them as one.

In *Ackoff's Fables: Irreverent Reflections on Business and Bureaucracy* (1991), Russ Ackoff reminds us: "We [have been] attempting to deal with problems generated by a new [systems] age with techniques and tools that we inherit from an old [mechanistic] one."

Systems thinking is about thinking in a new way—thinking synergistically, wherein 1 + 1 = 3 (Table 2.1).

Table 2.1. Synthesis Versus Analysis

Synthesis	The combinations of parts or elements so as to make a whole.	Analysis	Separation of a whole into its component parts; an examination of a complex entity, its elements, and their relationships.
Synergism	Interaction of parts such that the total effect is greater than the sum of the individual parts (2 + 2 = 5).	Reductionism	Narrowing down; the attempt to explain all biological processes by the same explanations that chemists and physicists use to interpret inanimate matter. It reduces complex data or phenomena to simple terms—for example, oversimplification.

General Systems Theory: The Unity of Science

In the 1950s, a biologist from Vienna, Ludwig von Bertalanffy, proposed the idea of a general theory and Science of Living Systems. What von Bertalanffy and his colleagues understood is that *living systems are the natural order of life on earth.*

The theory they proposed would embrace all living levels of science, from the study of a single living cell to the study of the planet as a whole. These pioneers of Systems Thinking sought to unlock the secrets of living systems and to generalize and classify their findings. They wanted to create a recognizable standard of scientific principles that could then be artfully applied to virtually any discipline, be it geology, physics, sociology, or business.

This Science of Living Systems helps people see patterns in the world and identify specific leverage points that can be used to produce lasting, beneficial changes within systems. This science and discipline they called General Systems Theory (GST) focuses on finding the unity of science for all living systems on Earth. It is a scientific, heavily researched, and holistic way to think about living systems. It is the foundation for this book. Its roots include

- Biological research on living systems, begun in the 1950s
- The Society for General Systems Research (SGSR), established in 1954 by four prestigious Nobel Prize–winning interdisciplinary scientists and thinkers:

    Ludwig von Bertalanffy, biologist and renaissance thinker

    Anatol Rapoport, applied mathematician and philosopher

    Ralph Gerard, physiologist

    Kenneth Boulding, economist

The successor to the Society is now called The International Society for the Systems Science (ISSS) and continues this research today (www.isss.org). Even in the 1960s the Society had twenty-three chapters around the world, publishing in the Society's Annual Yearbooks. Today, the teachings and writings of such "Renaissance" professors of management as Russ Ackoff from the University of Pennsylvania, Jay Forrester from the Massachusetts Institute of Technology (MIT), and Gene Ericson from George Washington University are continued.

In "A Classification of Systems" in the *1972 Yearbook* of the Society for General Systems Research/Academy of Management Research, Geoffrey Vickers put it in layman's terms:

The words *General Systems Theory* imply that some things can usefully be said about systems in general, despite the immense diversity of their specific forms. One of these things should be a scheme of classification.

Every science begins by classifying its subject matter, if only descriptively, and learns a lot about it in the process. Systems especially need this attention, because an adequate classification cuts across familiar boundaries and at the same time draws valid and important distinctions which have previously been sensed but not defined.

In short, the task of General Systems Theory is to find the most general conceptual framework in which a scientific theory or a technological problem can be placed without losing the essential features of the theory or the problem.

General Systems Theory states that parts play roles in light of the purpose for which the whole exists. No part can be affected without affecting all other parts. In other words, when studying any system, be it organizational, organic, or scientific in nature, the place to start is with the whole system in its environment (helicopter view); all parts of the whole—and their relationships to one another—are secondary.

◗ THINK DIFFERENTLY

In a number of EWC cases, colleagues have had the privilege of long discussions with CEOs about their careers, goals, personal lives, and life visions. This is especially true with CEO-owners of companies and their families.

Instead of starting with an Enterprise-Wide Change process, they have to first look at their whole lives in their environment and become clear about their own strategic life plan. Once they look at their own lives, they understand how they would personally be impacted by the transformational changes they want for their organizations.

In one highly visible retail case, a colleague facilitated the family through their strategic life plan. They then decided to proceed with an EWC process. They worked for two years to build their firm's capacity for high growth. Once it was clear they were positioned and moving in that direction, they sold the firm to a large, extremely well-known retail firm, each family member walking away as a multi-millionaire.

For more information on developing a life plan, see Haines (2000).

The Systems Around Us: The Basic Unit of Life

Clarity and *simplicity* are what's left over after everything else fails. Everywhere we look, we can see living, breathing examples of systems in our lives, in organizations, on our Earth, and floating in the vast universe. In a Systems Thinking view of the world, human beings are simultaneously the creators of systems, systems ourselves, and parts of larger systems. Some different kinds of systems include

- *Mechanical/electrical systems:* Cars, clocks, assembly lines
- *Electronic/telecommunications systems:* Personal computers, networks, the Internet, digital cable systems, satellite and cellular communication systems
- *Biological systems:* Birds, fish, animals, insects, plants

- *Human systems:* Individuals, social groups, teams, tribes, families, organizations, communities, nations

- *Ecological systems:* Deserts, oceans, forests, eco-regions, the Earth as a planet

There are also countless combinations of the five types of systems outlined above. All enterprises are combinations of these.

Don't lose sight of the fundamental point that human life on Earth is a living societal system overall, with supporting and manmade mechanical, electrical, and electronic systems. This global, human, social system exists within the context of the ecological and biological systems that naturally make up the Earth.

At the highest level, humans share a planet with all other forms of life, protected by a fragile layer of ozone, which preserves the conditions necessary for life as we know it. At this and every other level of life, we exist as part of many *inter*dependent systems.

When one key element of a system in our lives changes, it simultaneously affects many other elements in our lives. Life itself is made up of complex and interdependent systems. Think of how many aspects of your life changed when you graduated from school, moved away from home, married, had children, changed jobs or companies, or retired.

Natural and Universal Laws: The Basis of Systems Thinking

One of the fundamental assumptions behind General Systems Theory is that the Earth and the systems that comprise it (including human systems like teams and organizations) are governed by natural and universal laws. If we can correctly identify and understand these, we have a better chance of successfully interacting with, and transforming, the systems of which we are a part.

Some of the natural and universal laws of life on Earth are

- Four seasons (ask farmers and schoolchildren)
- The life cycle (ask parents, doctors, and nurses)
- The food chain on land and in the water (ask marine biologists, fishers, and hunters)
- The sun and the moon (day and night)
- 365 (plus a few hours. . .) days in a year

We believe: If life on Earth is governed by the natural laws of living systems, then a successful participant should learn the rules.

Simplicity on the Far Side of Complexity

I wouldn't give a fig for the simplicity this side of complexity, but I'd give my life for the simplicity on the far side of complexity.

Justice Oliver Wendell Holmes

Any idiot can simplify by ignoring the complications, but it takes a real genius to simplify by including the complications.

John E. Johnson, TEC (The Executive Committee) Chair

In Systems Thinking, we seek the elegant simplicity that underlies complexity. The difference between simplicity and simplistic thinking, however, cannot be overstated. The critical differences are outlined in Table 2.2.

Table 2.2. Simplistic Thinking Versus Elegant Simplicity

Simplistic Thinking	Reflects a mechanistic view
	Ignores complexity
	Advocates one best way
	Sees direct environment-free cause-effect
	Tends toward isolated, singular change efforts
	Advocates independent solutions (such as training or better communications alone)
	Settles rapidly on quick fixes that ultimately fail
	Creates more problems than there were at the outset
Elegant Simplicity	Provides a better view of complex solutions
	Uses a framework to see complexity and its web of inter-relationships and make sense of it
	Takes a holistic and complete view, such as a view of Earth from space
	Sees the whole as primary and the parts as secondary—but understands all and uses this understanding for analysis, design, and practical execution
	Is sophisticated, disciplined, and critical
	Looks for ways to capture the complexity of the situation

Most of Science Is Now Converging on Systems Thinking

Many fields of thought and scientific disciplines today are recognizing and dealing with the interrelationship of processes and patterns—*the art of Systems Thinking in its broadest sense.* We have identified forty-five of them. (For further information visit www.SystemsThinkingPress.com.)

Each of these scientific fields begins by identifying common system characteristics and principles, even though the details and applications are still being discovered and articulated. These systems apply to every living system at every level—individual, couple, team, family, organization, community, society, and the planet. What we see changing on one system level will also affect another system level, which in turn affects yet another level, and so on.

Questions to Ponder

- What mental models in your own life need changing?

- Is the distinction between simplistic thinking and elegant simplicity clear? Can you think of two examples?

- Can you think of or have you observed any other sciences converging on Systems Thinking?

Chapter Two Recap

Nothing is so painful to the human mind as a great and sudden change.

Mary Shelley, Frankenstein

1. We have proceeded through four ages on Earth—hunting, agricultural, industrial, and now information.

2. Complex systems require a different way of approaching problems.

3. We are beginning to move toward the next age, the Systems Age.

4. Systems Thinking is a natural way to think—a new orientation to life.

5. Science, paradigms, mindsets, worldviews, models, frameworks, and concepts are all about our approach and thought patterns in viewing our world.

6. Chronic problems continue to exist, both in society and in organizations. Why can't we resolve them? Why are they so resistant to solutions? Answer: Lack of a systems view.

7. We are often *micro smart and macro dumb* in dealing with our problems, resulting in Quick Fixes that often fail, especially over the long-term.

8. General Systems Theory has sought a *unity of science* for living systems on Earth that continues today.

9. There is a vast difference between simplistic thinking and thinking that strives for elegant simplicity.

10. It is important for executives and change consultants to internalize all the key principles and questions of Systems Thinking to achieve superior results in Enterprise-Wide Change.

11. Systems Thinking is the Science of Living Systems on Earth.

12. If life on Earth is governed by the natural laws of living systems, then a successful participant should learn the rules.

What's the Difference?

What are you thinking?

or

How are you thinking?

Foundations of the Systems Thinking Approach

Chapter Purposes

- To understand the four core concepts of Systems Thinking

- To understand the twelve scientific and natural characteristics of living and open systems

- To understand some guiding principles that underlie a Systems Approach to Enterprise-Wide Change

How we think is how we act, is how we are, and determines the results we get.

Changing people's habits and way of thinking is like writing your instructions in the snow during a snowstorm. Every twenty minutes you must rewrite your instructions. Only with constant repetition will you create change.

Donald L. Dewar

What Do These Numbers Represent? 26—12—10—3—2—4

Despite enormous complexity in the natural world and human societies, a different perspective allows us to see the simplicity underlying it all. From a natural perspective, the numbers above have the power to break down complexity into far simpler foundations. Consider some of the foundations of modern life in the Western world.

26—The English language is arguably the most complicated on Earth, with at least 650,000 common words and phrases. Yet at its foundation, just 26 letters—the Roman/Latin alphabet—form the entirety of the language.

12—From classical to jazz to folk songs to rap, every musical composition in the West is created from just twelve musical notes—an octave of seven "whole" or "natural" notes (the white keys on a piano), and five sharps and flats (the black keys).

10—The Western base-ten mathematical system has only ten building blocks (the digits zero through nine).

3—The foundations of color are three basic colors of visible light (red, yellow, and blue). Combinations of those three colors, when they hit the eye, result in the literally millions of colors we observe in the natural world.

2—The entire Information Age and computer revolution was built on just two digits—zero and one.

4—DNA has four building blocks—two strands in a double helix, each strand containing two pairs of information. Four is also the number of core concepts in Systems Thinking.

Just as natural phenomena can be understood in terms of these numbers, human enterprises can be understood through fundamental and natural concepts and characteristics. In this chapter we outline each of the four core concepts of Systems Thinking briefly. Each will be explored more fully in the second half of this book.

Simplicity is the essence of beauty.

The Underlying Simplicity of the Systems Thinking Foundation

A half-century of rigorous research on the Science of Systems Thinking has been translated, interpreted, and updated by the authors. Four related main concepts emerged in the research, which can be used to clarify and simplify how to view complex enterprises. These are

1. Seven Levels of Living Systems
2. Natural and Predictable Cycles of Change
3. The Simplicity of Systems Thinking Is *Backwards Thinking*
4. Twelve Characteristics of Living Systems

Systems Concept #1: Seven Levels of Living Systems

Kenneth Boulding first outlined the seven natural levels of living systems in *The Meaning of the 20th Century* (1964). These seven levels represent the hierarchy and network of living systems.

1. *Cells:* The basic unit of life
2. *Organs:* The organic systems within our bodies
3. *Organisms:* Insects, bacteria, animals, fish, birds, and humans
4. *Groups:* Families, teams, departments, units, etc.
5. *Organizations:* Firms, companies, private, public, and not-for-profit organizations
6. *Community and/or Society:* Microclimates, ecosystems, neighborhoods, communities, cities, states, provinces, nations, regions within countries
7. *Supranational Systems:* Eco-regions, continents, Earth

Systems Within Systems

While these seven levels may initially appear to be discrete and separate from each other, Systems Thinking tells us that each system level is nested within other systems, exists in relationship with every other system, and affects every other system. Every system level exists in a nested, hierarchical relationship with every other system (systems within systems). The Russian stacking dolls are a great analogy. Each one is unique and distinct, yet includes all the same characteristics of each other doll—just the size is different (see Figure 3.1).

Figure 3.1. Matryoshka or Russian Stacking Dolls

In this book we focus on Enterprise-Wide Change of the living and open system level 5, organizations. In doing so, we must at a minimum focus on four of Boulding's seven levels:

Level 3: Organisms (employees)

Level 4: Groups (teams or functional departments)

Level 5: Organizations (total organization)

Level 6: Society

Each systems level, of course, also interrelates and reacts to other living systems at higher and lower levels, in addition to other systems at its own level.

Within systems, there are numerous *collaborations, collisions, and relationships* among, within, and between individuals (one-to-one), teams and departments (department-department or cross-functional teams), and the organization (organization-environment/organization-organization).

The bridges between levels created by these relationships and interactions comprise additional levels, as follows:

Level 3A: One-to-one relationships

Level 4A: Relationships between departments

Level 5A: Relationships between the organization and its environment (Levels 6 and 7)

Thus, this book considers seven natural, hierarchical levels of organizational reality that must be recognized and addressed in large-scale, complex change efforts, shown in Figure 3.2.

Figure 3.2. The Seven Natural Rings of Reality

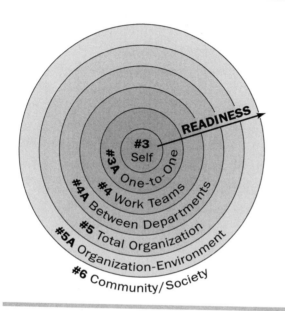

Environment Includes:
- Other people/groups
- Other organizations
- Customers/competitors
- Society/community
- Regions/earth

Increased Readiness:
- Complexity/chaos
- Readiness/willingness
- Skills/competencies growth

Note: Rings 3-4-5-6 are four of the "Seven Levels of Living Systems"

Rings 3A-4A-5A are "Collisions of Systems" with other systems

The farther out one travels through the rings of reality, the more complex the system is and the more collaborations, collisions, and relationships occur. This is due to the fact that when you work at any of the six levels, all the levels inside it are automatically included and impacted by the change initiatives. Intervening at the level of an enterprise requires proportionally much greater skill, willingness, and readiness to deal with this complexity. Just like a Rubik's Cube, organizations have over one trillion *moves,* many of them wrong.

One final critical concept to note is this: As Einstein pointed out, the solution to a systems problem is often found at the next higher level of system (or interaction of systems).

◗ THINK DIFFERENTLY

A senior management team-building effort was truncated early on as the organization hadn't fully made the transition to the new outside CEO. One internal long-serving executive was still the person people looked to for direction.

Until the organization dealt with this situation (who was the CEO anyway?), the team building would not succeed. The CEO was confronted with this and was told that the team building would fail. Instead he had the matter resolved with his board of directors. Then the team building was successful.

Systems Concept #2: Natural and Predictable Cycles of Change

The natural world does not operate in a linear, sequential fashion. The way of natural life and open systems is to move gradually and incrementally through cycles of change—day and night, up and down, awake and asleep—slowly growing, changing, and evolving, as seen in Table 3.1.

Table 3.1. Examples of Natural Cycles of Change

Earth	Civilizations	Enterprises
Ocean tides	Inca, Aztec, Mayan empires	Start-up
Volcanoes	Chinese dynasties	High growth
Whale and bird migration	Roman Empire	Maturity
Lunar cycle	British Empire	Decline
Day and night	Persian Empire	Renewal

Change is constant. Humans, as living systems, keep on changing. It is a natural part of life and death. The key is to *find simplicity on the far side of complexity*.

For example, it is sometimes easier to write a long letter than a short one. You usually have to write the long one first and then pull the essence into a short form—just as we have distilled these concepts into an elegantly simple book. This is what the science of Systems Thinking is all about.

There are many uses of this concept during changes of all types, as we shall see. The basic sequence of change looks like Figure 3.3.

Figure 3.3. The Rollercoaster of Change

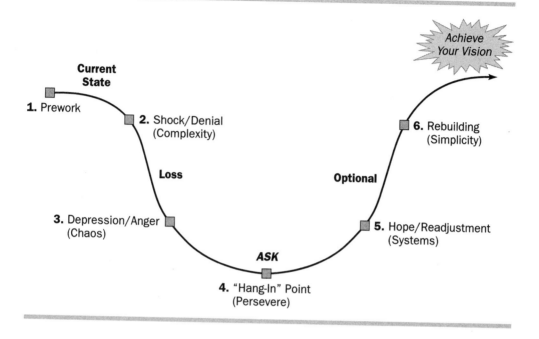

In Enterprise-Wide Change, this concept becomes important because it describes a natural and predictable set of stages through which a system must pass if it is to successfully implement a change initiative.

The phenomenon is written about in many fields and disciplines, including mental health and family therapy. Elisabeth Kübler-Ross (1969) wrote a best-selling book on it and William Bridges (1991) talks about the *Neutral Zone* in his book.

Years ago, we coined the phrase *Rollercoaster of Change* to describe this natural law, because a rollercoaster is a simple metaphor for understanding the dynamics of successful change. Cycles of *stability—change—instability—new stability—and change all over again* are normal and natural, the product of several characteristics of living systems, like dynamic equilibrium and entropy.

⮑ THINK DIFFERENTLY

This entire book is about shifting our thinking from the dominant Western analytic thought process to one of a systems view of the world. In a real sense, many readers may undergo this rollercoaster as part of reading and internalizing this book.

First and foremost, enterprise leaders must manage and lead *themselves* through the Rollercoaster of Change. Then, and only then, can they lead others through the Rollercoaster. Everyone goes through these stages at different rates, depths, and times.

The question is not *if* employees will go through the Rollercoaster, but *when, how deeply, for how long*. And will they successfully reach the other side? This last question is a big issue. Executives are trained in the skill of *telling* others what to do. In the Rollercoaster of Change (Stage 2) telling is only the *skill* of inducing shock and denial, and then depression and anger, in your employees.

It is a given each of us will go through the losses associated with Stages 1 and 2 (Prework and Shock/Denial) of the Rollercoaster. Going through Stages 5 and 6 (Hope and Rebuilding) is optional and often depends on someone leading the change process effectively. Let's explore each of the six stages of the Rollercoaster of Change.

Stage 1: Prework (Smart Start)

During this phase, using a Systems Thinking Approach (and a Smart Start, as we will later see), the enterprise and leadership prepare to undertake EWC.

Stage 2: Shock/Denial (Complexity)

Due to a system's tendency toward equilibrium, all it takes to induce Stages 2 and 3 (shock, denial, anger, and depression) throughout the organization is an announcement of a major change initiative.

The change process, once begun, is often irreversible. *Once you start the change, you cannot go back and erase what you started.* Attempting to reverse changes already begun just kicks off another Rollercoaster of Change, only this time from the spot at which you tried to reverse the process. Since this is usually at Stage 3 (*depression*), it generally means that the new Rollercoaster will take employees deeper down into depression. Rarely will it get you out of the hole you are digging for yourself or your employees.

Stage 3: Depression/Anger (Chaos)

This is a time of high uncertainty and anxiety. In EWC, managers need to spend a great deal of time assisting their employees through this change and addressing WIIFM (What's in It for Me?) questions.

Depression is normal and to be expected, as is resistance to change. The worst thing an executive can do is to tell people they *should not feel that way.* The more you tell people this, the more they will resist (action-reaction). We must listen to their fears, emotions, and concerns; venting is a natural, normal, and healthy part of the process. Leaders must encourage this to occur and have the coaching skills to handle it when it does.

What helps people through Stage 3 is a *sequence* of actions:

1. Listening

2. Asking questions

3. Empathizing, and *only then*

4. Explaining the vision and its significance

> People don't care how much you know until they know how much you care.
>
> *Steven Covey*

Stage 4: Hang-In Point (Persevere)

This is where most change efforts fail. The pain of change is greatest at this point. Willingness to persevere and "tough it out" is crucial. Failure to hang in and persevere is the key reason for failure of EWC, because leadership cannot motivate and lead people through the pain of disequilibria. Instead, leaders may attempt to *quit* the change, as they realize conditions are now worse than they were before the attempt at change. In the Rollercoaster of Change, *things always get worse before they get better.* It is natural, normal, and highly predictable!

Stage 5: Hope/Readjustment (Systems)

The only way through Stage 5 and up the (optional) right side of the Rollercoaster is through strong, unwavering leadership. Leaders must help clarify each person's new role in the system and explain new expectations and requirements, while at the same time building each person's maximum involvement and understanding of WIIFM.

Stage 6: Rebuilding (Simplicity)

Only when the difficult first five stages are completed can leaders create a critical mass with high performance in support of desired changes. The importance of not only *buy-in,* but also *stay-in* throughout the Rollercoaster of Change process is critical.

Executives and change consultants must first understand and manage this process for themselves, and only then help others. Every employee *will* go through the rollercoaster—at different rates, depths, and times depending on their unique individual makeup and perceptions about how they are impacted by the changes.

 THINK DIFFERENTLY

A colleague was involved in a government-wide EWC downsizing initiative. The workforce reduction target totaled 2,000 positions, which was 17 percent of the workforce.

After eliminating vacant positions and providing an attractive voluntary early retirement package, which generated a high uptake, about 350 positions had to be eliminated to meet the goal. The change team handling the EWC decided that a support mechanism was warranted for those who were hit with an involuntary job loss. Career counseling support was provided to ensure that all of the 350 individuals were able to obtain new jobs of equal or better caliber within one year of their job loss.

At the end of the year, all but one person had secured new employment that met the criteria. This individual had been offered four jobs, but had rejected each one. She was so deeply entrenched in Step 3—depression and anger—that she could not bring herself to see any hope or possibility that was offered to help her move to Steps 5 and 6 of the Rollercoaster. She had taken up permanent residence in the valley of despair.

In dealing with the Rollercoaster of Change, there are *major questions* to ask yourself and others.

Questions to Ponder

- Not if, but *when* will we go through shock?
- How deep is the trough? How long will it take?
- Will we get up the right side and rebuild? At what level will we rebuild?
- How many different work-related rollercoasters will we experience at once?

- Are there other changes occurring simultaneously in our lives?

- How do we deal with normal resistance? Will we hang in and persevere?

Systems Concept #3: The Simplicity of Systems Thinking Is *Backwards Thinking*

What Does a System Look Like?

How does a system—any system—operate? Can you draw a system at its most basic level?

Draw a system here:

All systems (especially living systems) take inputs from the environment and transform them into different and better outputs back into the environment. Effective systems provide outputs, which then cycle back around (feedback) to the system again as new inputs to enhance system effectiveness.

> The great successful men [women] of the world have used their imaginations. . . .They think ahead and create their mental picture, and then go to work materializing that picture in all its details, filling in here, adding a little there, altering this a bit and that a bit, but steadily building—steadily building.
>
> *Robert Collier*

Where to start?

Backwards Thinking

Begin with the end in mind.

Steven Covey

Backwards Thinking is the core of where to start in Systems Thinking. Steven Covey's famous quote makes this point very clearly. A real difference between Systems Thinking and analytic thinking is the *beginning* place.

Systems Thinking is about design.

Design is the organizing principle in Systems Thinking. It is about how to design the organization based on its ideal desired future vision (vision, purpose, positioning, and values). Analytic thinking is different. It does not begin with the end in mind.

Analytical thinking is about sense-and-response. The organizing principle in analytical thinking is our normal action-reaction mode or the sense-and-response way of living and behaving.

It is quite simple to draw a system. It might look like the one in Figure 3.4.

Figure 3.4. The Simplicity of Systems Thinking—The ABCs

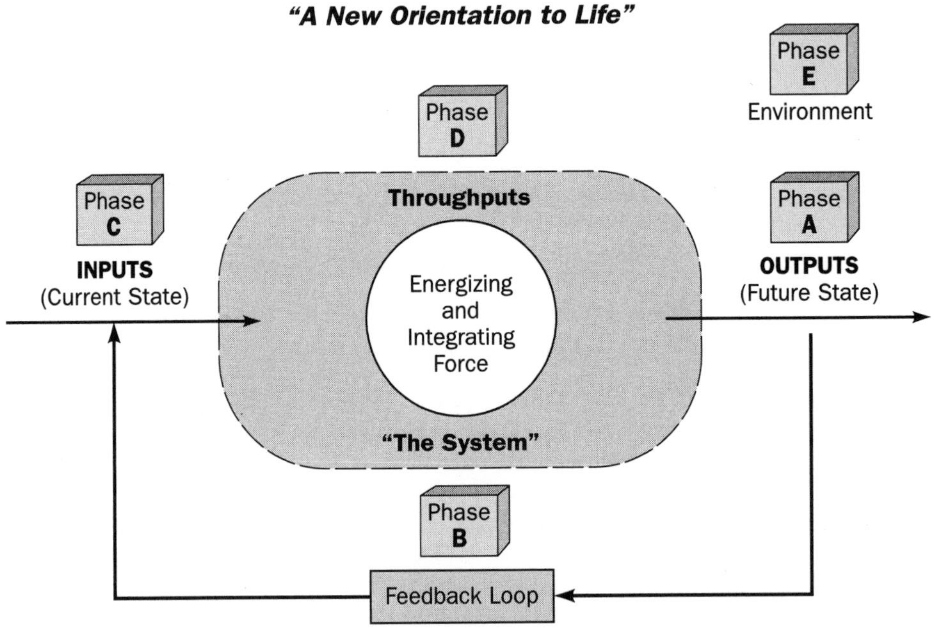

Systems Thinking allows complex problems to be approached through elegant simplicity by allowing leaders to *first* focus on outcomes, and *then* to think and work backwards to identify numerous potential pathways to reach the desired outcomes. In turn, exploring many alternatives makes it easier to find solutions that best fit and optimize all of the parts and relationships within the system toward achieving these outcomes.

By thinking in terms of outputs, the feedback loop, inputs, and then throughputs last as Phases A-B-C-D (and the environment, the all-pervasive E), executives and change consultants can use Systems Thinking to diagnose and make change more effectively by thinking *right to left,* rather than the analytic tradition of reading and proceeding *left to right.*

Right to left thinking yields a "gap" between the outputs and inputs of the system, leading to creative, innovative, and more comprehensive solutions that drive you to your desired outcomes.

Left to right traditional thinking solves today's problems, but has no "gap" to close to achieve a future vision.

The ABCs of Enterprise-Wide Change

The Systems Thinking diagram in Figure 3.4 provides an elegantly simple way to reduce complexity by focusing attention on

- The system as a whole
- Its outputs/outcomes
- Feedback within the environment
- Its inputs
- Its throughputs

From the diagram, we can see that five strategic questions underlie the Systems Thinking approach to Enterprise-Wide Change. We refer to these questions as the *ABCs* of Enterprise-Wide Change.

The questions begin with the future environment and the *end* in mind and work backwards from there to trace possible paths to those desired outcomes:

- *Phase A: Where do we want to be?* The first systems question must answer the desired outcomes of the target system, within its context, environment, and the other levels of systems that surround it.

- *Phase B: How will we know when we get there?* Phase B identifies what signs and mechanisms in the feedback loop can indicate that the desired outcomes have been achieved. How will we measure our results? This phase often reveals that additional work is required on the first question. Goals may be too broadly defined and may need redefinition.

- *Phase C: Where are we now?* This question defines the gap between the present state and the desired future.

- *Phase D: How do we get there?* Phase D uses Systems Thinking to define and implement strategies and tactics that will integrate all of the processes, activities, relationships, and changes needed to close the gap and create the desired outcomes identified through Phase A.

- *Phase E: What other factors could change in the future environment that we need to consider?* The last (but really ongoing) question is one of the most important (and often missed) components of change. Failure to adapt to a changing environment is one of the greatest reasons for the decline and death of organizations.

From an ongoing change perspective, this A-B-C-D-E Simplicity of Systems Thinking framework is circular, as it occurs over and over again as cycles and cycles of change. Thus, the application of Systems Thinking for this book is as seen in Figure 3.5.

Figure 3.5. The ABCs of Enterprise-Wide Change

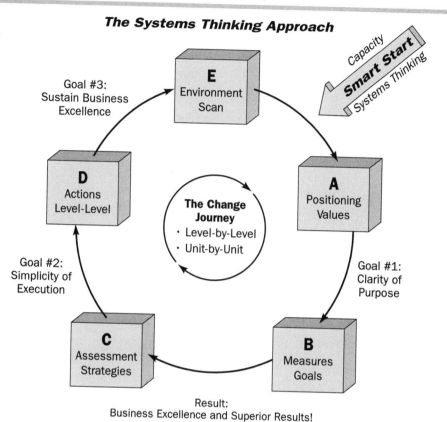

Systems are circular. So is Enterprise-Wide Change. After Phase E, we come back around to Phase A.

Analytic and sequential problem solving, by contrast, is vastly different. It often includes only two of the five phases of change (Phases C and D):

- Analytic problem solving starts with today's current state, issues, and problems.

- Analytic problem solving breaks issues and/or problems down into their smallest components (Phase C).

- It solves each component separately (Phase D).

- Analytic problem solving generally has no future-oriented, far-reaching vision or goal (Phase A); it simply aims for absence (or solving) of the identified problems.

Questions to Ponder

- Is this ABC model how you tend to think and act in every aspect of your life today, both at work and at home?

- Is it clear how the *ABCs* of EWC are an application of the Simplicity of Systems Thinking?

- What does *Backwards Thinking* mean to you? Can you explain it in a concise manner in your own words?

Systems Concept #4:
Twelve Characteristics of Living Systems

At the most fundamental systems level, von Bertalanffy and the others who started the Science of Systems Thinking researched and listed just twelve characteristics that form the standard and predictable systems behaviors that are always present in living systems. (They have been adapted here, with our own comments, from Vickers, 1972.) These are the yearly research results from the Society of General Systems Research mentioned earlier.

The first six of these characteristics apply to the living system as a whole, while the last six describe the inner workings of a living system. Keep in mind that it is the *relationship* and *fit* of all these parts and *characteristics* into one *whole system* that is key, not just each characteristic standing alone.

The Whole System:
Living Systems Characteristics #1–#6

Characteristic #1: Holism (Living Systems Are Whole Entities with Unique Characteristics)

Holism is the principle that says the whole is not just the sum of the parts and, conversely, that a system can be explained only as a totality. Holism is the opposite of elementism, which views the whole as the sum of individual parts.

The difference between the two ways of thinking becomes apparent when it is applied to the question, *what is the value of a human body?* Elementism would break the hypothetical body down into its chemical components like oxygen, nitrogen, carbon, and so on. On that basis, the present "net worth" of a human body is approximately $4.50 (www.coolquiz.com/trivia/explain/docs/worth.asp, September 10, 2003).

In contrast, with the system intact, the value of the components of one human body (including such components as fluids, tissues, and organs) is estimated at nearly $45 million (www.soundmedicine.iu.edu/archive/2003/quiz/humanWorth.html; September 10, 2003).

And of course, no value whatsoever can be placed on the whole living human. *It is literally priceless.* Such is the principle of holism, and the basic definition of a system: A holistic unit has overall purpose and a transformational synergy that transcends its component parts.

 THINK DIFFERENTLY

One CEO in the service sector believed strongly that a corporate strategic plan is just a roll-up of lower-level plans.

This is an excellent example of analytical thinking that resulted in poorly coordinated implementation, turf battles, and silos. The board eventually replaced him as their services became bureaucratic, uncoordinated, and confusing.

Characteristic #2: Living Systems Are Open Systems

Living systems can be considered in two ways in relation to their environment: (1) relatively closed or (2) relatively open. Open systems exchange information, energy, or material with their environments. Biological and social systems are inherently open systems; mechanical systems may be open or closed.

A closed system is one that is isolated from its outside environment. Experimental, sterile chemistry labs and clean rooms in computer chip manufacturing are examples of relatively closed systems. There are, however, few fully closed systems in the world. Only a vacuum is a totally closed system—and does not occur naturally in our world.

All living systems are either relatively more open or more closed to their environment. Figure 3.6 shows the continuum.

Figure 3.6. Open Versus Closed Systems

Closed	Relatively Closed	Relatively Open	Open

Living systems, by definition, are open systems. They are interactive with their environment and actively adapt to fit into that environment to a greater or lesser extent.

 THINK DIFFERENTLY

Excellent organizations are immediately identifiable by their intense desire to be open to feedback and by their constant search for information from the environment that will help them thrive and lead. Bill Gates at Microsoft has a biannual environmental scanning week-long offsite with key futuristic experts to ensure he stays ahead of today's dynamic and competitive environment.

Characteristic #3: Living Systems Have Defined Boundaries

All systems have boundaries that separate them from their environments. Relatively closed systems have rigid, impenetrable boundaries, whereas relatively open systems have more permeable boundaries between themselves and a broader suprasystem. Open systems can more easily integrate and collaborate with their environments. Boundaries are easily defined for biological systems, but are difficult to delineate in organizations and ecological or social systems such as communities.

 THINK DIFFERENTLY

Access to worldwide instantaneous communications resulted in General Electric becoming more open to best practices across organizational boundaries. General Electric continues to call this concept *boundarylessness*, ever since the days of Jack Welch as CEO.

In organizations, the boundaries are relatively open, making them somewhat vague in terms of knowing and fully understanding their limits. Welch wanted no limits to their search for better ideas and practices.

Closed boundaries tend to lead to fragmentation, internecine battles over turf, separation, and parochialism. The ideal is integration, collaboration, and harmony with the environment.

THINK DIFFERENTLY

One of our colleagues facilitated a clarification of a government enterprise's mission and warned them to be careful to think differently about boundary distinctions. They were unclear where their boundaries and responsibilities ended, and where the boundaries of individual citizen responsibilities began. They eventually realized that "big government" got started this way, ultimately making citizens more dependent on government. They decided their existing large boundaries were robbing citizens of vitality, spirit, and self-initiative.

Characteristic #4: Living Systems Transform Inputs into Outputs

Open systems are transformational in nature. That is, living and open systems receive inputs from the environment, transform these inputs in some way via throughput and processes, and then send outputs back into the environment. This produces feedback and begins the loop of new inputs one more time.

At the most basic level, for example, the system we call the "animal kingdom" takes inputs (food and water) and transforms them into energy to sustain life. The animals' throughputs and outputs in turn pollinate plants, affect populations of other animals, fertilize soil, serve as food for other species, and, after death, return vital nutrients to the earth itself. This web of inputs, throughputs, and outputs constantly changes one kind of matter or energy into another.

THINK DIFFERENTLY

On a more positive note, society's move to recycle waste has led to using the waste as input into many new businesses and new industries we see every day—plastic, paper, cans, tires, batteries, computers, and in Europe even cars.

Characteristic #5: Living Systems Require Feedback to Continue Living

Information about outputs of the system in turn feeds back as inputs into the system, leading to changes in the transformation process and achieving more effective future outputs. Evolution is an expression of this characteristic in action.

The value of feedback in improving effectiveness and maintaining a desired steady state cannot be overstated. Feedback is key to stimulating learning and change. There is no "bad" feedback. Bad news, in fact, can help guide leaders to find root-underlying causes of problems in the enterprise.

> ### ◗ THINK DIFFERENTLY
>
> A retail chain had, as a desired outcome, to become a "learning organization." When the consultant they hired removed the rhetoric surrounding the term "learning organization," the retail chain saw the need to gather as much positive and negative feedback as possible in order to become a learning organization. They then acted on it to create new learnings. As they improved their feedback processes, they began to increase learning and growth at all systems levels—individuals, teams, and organizations.

Enterprises often receive little feedback on performance in relation to customers. They do, however, receive financial feedback on a regular basis, a reflection of the value and primacy of financial measures. Better and more regular customer and employee feedback makes for better data-based decision making, which we will discuss further in Chapter Four.

Characteristic #6: Living Systems Pursue Multiple Outcomes

Action toward *multiple* outcomes or goals is a characteristic of all living systems. Social systems, for example, seek multiple goals if for no reason other than that they are comprised of individuals and subgroups with different objectives. One need only look at any government body to verify this characteristic of systems.

In terms of Enterprise-Wide Change, this characteristic demands that members agree on a detailed and common vision and marketplace positioning to focus and coordinate their actions toward a cohesive set of goals. At the same time, WIIFM is a natural question each individual continually asks. Organizations must delineate benefits to each employee to individually motivate employees to work toward common goals.

The clash between individual and organizational goals can cause conflict and lost productivity for all concerned, a lose-lose situation. Add this to dehumanization, unnecessary hierarchy, bureaucracy, and mechanization of work, and the result is often an alienated workforce.

THINK DIFFERENTLY

In facilitating an extensive EWC in a school district, union-management relationships were a huge roadblock. Artificial either/or thinking had led to conflict, instead of everyone embracing multiple outcomes and cooperating and
dialoging to find common goals. After two years of being the neutral third party
in bargaining negotiations, the consultants were able to move the parties to
embrace a common higher vision of "all students learning." Everyone could
support that vision.

Combining characteristics 1 through 6 of System Concept #4 results in a Systems Model (Figure 3.7) that describes the natural functioning of a system within
its environment.

Figure 3.7. The Simplicity of Systems Thinking—The ABCs

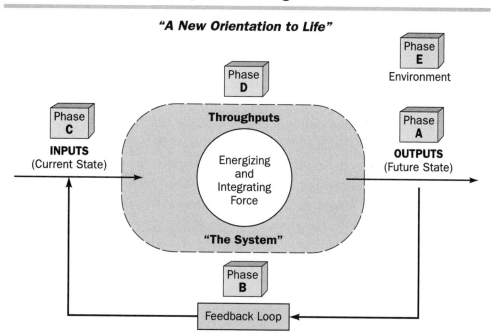

In summary these characteristics—repeated here for clarity and emphasis—are

#1. Holism—the system itself

#2. Open System—to the environment

#3. System Boundaries—that receive inputs and provide outputs into the environment

#4. Inputs → Throughputs → Outputs

#5. Feedback Loop—to recycle learnings and status of results

#6. Multiple Outcomes—living systems have multiple goals

The Inner Workings of Systems: Living Systems Characteristics #7–#12

The second set of six characteristics of living and open systems concerns the inner workings of systems.

Characteristic #7: Living Systems Display Equifinality

Equifinality recognizes there are many ways to the same ends. In mechanistic systems, there is a direct cause-and-effect relationship between initial conditions and the final state. Action begins at a prescribed point, passes through one set of steps, and arrives at one predictable outcome.

Social systems operate differently from mechanistic, mechanical, and electronic systems. Equifinality is the principle that the same results can be achieved with different initial conditions and through different means and pathways.

Equifinality offers a basis for flexibility, agility, and empowerment, because it suggests many roads can lead to the same destination. Social organizations can accomplish their objectives with diverse inputs and with varying internal processes, and there is usually not just one "best" way to solve most problems.

In EWC, the mindset that there is no one best way to solve systemic problems is the primary reason why defining commonly agreed-on, multiple goals is crucial. The question "What?" must be answered before turning to "How?"

▶ THINK DIFFERENTLY

As part of a California-based financial service company's EWC journey, the CEO and executives saw a need to empower their entire workforce to be known as the best in customer service (their desired marketplace positioning). They are now in the middle of a three-year journey starting with senior management and slowly cascading its way throughout the organization. They now appreciate the diversity of input and leadership to solve problems more effectively. They have learned to stop fighting and insisting on the one and only best way.

Things are much more complex today, and decisions are being made closer to the customer. This financial service company is increasing their profits, customer service, and employee satisfaction—all at the same time.

Characteristic #8: Living Systems Are Subject to Entropy

Entropy is the natural tendency for all living systems to run down over time. Entropy is a natural characteristic of all open (living) systems. They slowly break down, deteriorate, lose organization, and eventually die.

The good news is that entropy can be arrested in open systems. Entropy may even be transformed into *negative* entropy—a process through which social and organizational systems can become more organized and enhance their ability to transform themselves through new inputs, energy, and resources from the environment. In the enterprise, this input process occurs through education and learning to transform organizations and sustain superior results.

Entropy is what leads to a system's obsolescence, rigidity, decline, and death. Addressing and reversing entropy is one of the primary processes of Enterprise-Wide Change.

 THINK DIFFERENTLY

A robotics firm embarked on an EWC journey. Its leadership built an excellent Game Plan for Change. They felt it was so clear and compelling that their employees would implement it once it was communicated and understood. Management declined to enlist outside assistance with implementation, however, and went it alone, using the existing structure.

The change effort failed due to a lack of follow-up, reinforcement, and new energy. Management wanted everything up and running on autopilot—the antithesis of what actually makes change happen successfully. The executives were initially concerned about employee *buy-in*, but employee *stay-in* was far more important and difficult to achieve.

Characteristic #9: Living Systems Are Hierarchical

All relationships among discrete systems are hierarchical. Any given system is composed of subsystems (lower-order systems) and is, itself, part of a suprasystem (higher-order system). In the natural world, for example, the predatory food chain is an inescapable hierarchy found both on land and in water. Simpler organisms (plankton, seaweed, grasses, shrubbery) are consumed as inputs by more complex organisms (fish, deer, cattle), which in turn become inputs for even more complex organisms (sharks, whales, bears, wolves, humans).

The secret to successful Enterprise-Wide Change is to simplify and flatten the hierarchy as much as possible and *go with the flow* of life in a self-organizing, natural way, without the imposition of rigid, bureaucratic, complex, and artificial structures.

One of the challenges of Enterprise-Wide Change is to reduce the naturally negative effects of hierarchy. Rigidity and bloated bureaucracies based on command-and-control assumptions amplify the negative effects of hierarchy and assume that lower-level systems can be fully controlled. But they cannot—not for long, and not predictably. The existence of hierarchy and its inherent conflicts requires *participation and involvement*—a key construct in Enterprise-Wide Change.

Characteristic #10: Living Systems Have Interrelated Parts

Systems working optimally have their elements coordinated to maximize the power of the whole. If we maximize the *elements* of a system, by contrast, we usually inadvertently damage the whole. Consider the practice of "doping" in sports. An athlete who attempts to artificially maximize just one element—muscles—through steroid use ends up doing serious long-term damage to the larger system (his or her body).

 THINK DIFFERENTLY

A colleague was called into a large automotive firm that was failing to execute its EWC Game Plan. "Silos" were ruling the day, and interdepartmental conflict was the norm.

The consultant worked with executive leadership to demonstrate the necessity of involving all the competing departments to plan and achieve higher-level business goals. When some individual departments attempted to continue to try to maximize their influence in the organization, the CEO finally replaced two department heads who had been detrimental to other departments—and to the firm as a whole.

Balancing the demands of each department was difficult, but it became the key responsibility of executives as common goals and yearly EWC action priorities were developed. If the organization itself was to succeed, it needed to become a system in which departments worked together to maximize the whole, not the parts.

Characteristic #11: Living Systems Tend Toward Dynamic Equilibrium

Living systems have a dynamic quality even as they resist change. The concept of dynamic equilibrium within a steady state is closely related to entropy.

Closed systems eventually attain an equilibrium state with maximum entropy (death or disorganization). In contrast, open systems may attain a state in which a continuous inflow of materials, energy, information, and feedback produce a dynamic yet steady state. This is a natural state of balance and stability, which is why established societies, cultures, and enterprises are resistant to change. *They are like rubber bands that stretch out, bounce back, and are difficult to break.*

Humans (as systems and parts of larger systems) tend to resist change and cling to their routine—the dynamic equilibrium—of the present state. Resistance to change often leads to short-term myopic WIIFM views and actions as well as passive resistance. In EWC, culture change requires breaking through the state of equilibrium and modifying behaviors of *all* employees and many aspects of an organization's internal workings.

 THINK DIFFERENTLY

Another retail firm decided to focus on employee empowerment. Leadership knew they needed to change the organizational culture. They decided to address their cultural problem by providing training on empowerment. Unfortunately, the culture that surrounded the training defeated the intent of the training and failed to spur lasting change. A dynamic tension existed during training, but eventually old habits, ruts, policies, and procedures reasserted themselves and defeated the good training intentions.

Characteristic #12: Living Systems Produce Internal Elaboration

Internal elaboration leads naturally to greater complexity. Open systems such as enterprises tend to move in the direction of greater differentiation, complexity, and higher levels of potential effectiveness. The theory of evolution is an example of the characteristic of internal elaboration, demonstrating that life on earth changes and adapts itself to environmental inputs through selective survival and propagation of individuals within the system of a species.

In enterprises, internal elaboration can also lead to organizational complexity and bureaucracy in its worst form. Government rules and regulations are a natural expression of the negative outcomes of internal elaboration (remember the 15,629 words in the cabbage pricing guidelines in Chapter Two).

Because open systems naturally tend to an increase in complexity, EWC demands vigilance against unnecessary proliferation of bureaucracy and the natural ossification that results from it. *Simplicity wins the game every time.*

 THINK DIFFERENTLY

Every few years Marriott Corporation performs a "zero-based budgeting process" in which leadership questions each policy, procedure, practice, and expenditure. The aim is to "prune" the organization's complexity and ensure that needless bureaucracy does not take root and grow stronger in the organization.

These last six characteristics, which form the inner workings of any living system, can also be used as the basis for a further elaboration of the ABCDE systems model already presented.

To summarize:

#7. Equifinality

#8. Entropy

#9. Hierarchy

#10. Relationships

#11. Dynamic Equilibrium

#12. Internal Elaboration

These final six characteristics can be simply depicted as shown in Figure 3.8.

Figure 3.8. The Inner Workings of a System

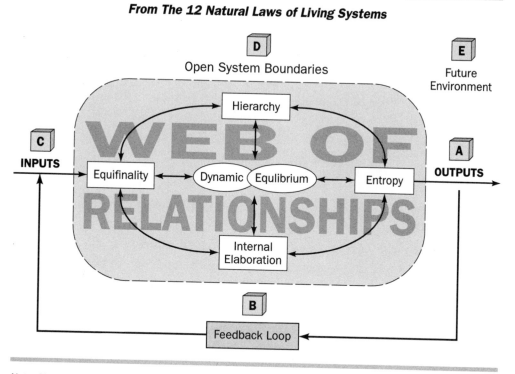

From The 12 Natural Laws of Living Systems

Note: Characteristic #10 (interrelated parts) is represented in this diagram as the *web of relationships*, as it is all-pervasive inside a system.

Questions to Ponder

- Do the first six characteristics make sense to you as a holistic view of a system in relationship with its environment? Why or why not?

- Are there any *inner workings* of a system other than characteristics 7 through 12 that you can think of?

- Which of these twelve characteristics of living systems are clear to you and which are not? Why is that?

Some Guiding Principles of Systems Thinking

Success or failure in the Systems Thinking approach to Enterprise-Wide Change depends on the adoption of a coherent set of *guiding principles* to help predict what might need to be changed. These guiding principles also clarify how change can be leveraged in EWC. The list of guiding principles, like the entire Science of Living Systems, is ever-growing and expanding.

As von Bertalanffy (1998, p. 18) said, "In one way or another, we are forced to deal with complexities, with *wholes* or *systems* in all fields of knowledge."

As you begin to assimilate and master Systems Thinking applied to Enterprise-Wide Change, you can use these guiding principles to keep you on track. Each principle is reinforced with *key systems questions* that can also help you with Enterprise-Wide Change.

In addition, two preconditions must be met before Systems Thinking principles can be successfully applied to a given situation:

- *The entity to be changed must be clearly understood* (Seven Rings of Reality). Successful change requires identifying which of the Seven Natural Rings of Reality is the subject of a planned change. Leaders must be clear about the entity they are targeting. Is it an individual, a team, a family, a business unit, a community, or an organization? What are its boundaries? Is it relatively open or closed in its environmental interactions? The question that must be answered based on this precondition is, "What entity, system, or collisions of systems are we dealing with?" For example, "Are we trying to change an entire enterprise or two enterprises related through an alliance or partnership?"

- *All systems are linked to other systems—some larger, some smaller—in a hierarchy* (systems within systems). No living system is independent of any other. We are all, as human beings, linked to a greater or lesser extent to all others on this planet in a hierarchy of systems. Organizational linkages are subject to the same hierarchy characteristics. Within our identified system and Seven Rings of Reality, what level(s) of the system are impacted by our change? For example, are we trying to change the CEO, the senior management team, or one division, function, or department of the firm? EWC is unique in that we are trying to change the whole organization or entity, including all the people, processes, and parts, in some way as well.

Once the two preconditions have been met, change leaders can then approach an Enterprise-Wide Change systematically, based on the following guiding principles and their related systems question.

Principle #1: Systems Are Multiple-Goal-Seeking Organisms

Develop clarity and agreement on this principle before beginning any actions. Keep in mind that there are usually multiple outcomes, not either/or questions that come from reductionist thinking. Other words for outcomes include *vision, ends, goals, objectives, mission,* and *purpose* (the *what*).

This principle relates to Systems Question #1: *What are the desired outcomes?* Without agreement on ends, our actions will never have a chance of succeeding. Once the *what* is clear, there are many ways to achieve the same end (the *how*) through empowerment.

For example: When groups get stuck, it is often because they have lost sight of their purpose or outcomes. If you want a *showstopper* in a meeting, just use Systems Question #1: *What are your desired outcomes?* Refocus the meeting to be more productive. This needs to become an inherent part of any change consultant and leader's day-to-day thought process. This question needs to become as much a part of your toolkit as your cellular telephone, your computer, your car, your paper, and your pen.

Principle #2: Feedback Is the Breakfast of Champions; Be Flexible and Adaptive (The Feedback Loop)

In today's complex and fast-changing world, the ability to come up with initial solutions is not nearly as important as the ability to generate reliable and constant feedback and to adapt in order to achieve our desired outcomes. The ability to be flexible and adaptive (for example, to learn, grow, change, and adapt to changes in the environment) is crucial. Economies of speed are replacing economies of scale as a key competitive edge. Feedback is the key need in today's learning organizations. It will help them learn, grow, and adapt at all levels of the organizational system (individuals, teams, and the organization as a whole).

This principle relates to Systems Question #2: *How will we know we've achieved our goals?*

For example: What measures or metrics of success does your EWC have? Are they tracked and reported on a regular basis? Feedback is the breakfast of champions. Be flexible and adaptive.

Initial solutions are not nearly as important as the ability to generate reliable and constant feedback and adapt to achieve our desired outcomes.

THINK DIFFERENTLY

A colleague was engaged in conducting a corporate-wide organizational review as part of an EWC for a large federal government department in one of its regional office operations. She applied a technique called a *values audit*, where staff were asked to comment on the capacity of the staff to "walk the talk" as highlighted through their core values.

About 20 percent of the staff responded to the assessment. Despite some extremely powerful data captured in the summary report, the senior executive responsible for this project paid no attention to the results. He wouldn't even consider the data. His response created a significant division within the staff ranks, because so many of the staff felt that senior management had little or no interest in hearing what was really going on within the organization. The change initiative suffered a major setback as a result of this myopic response by the project leader.

Principle #3: Work and Align the Entity to Be Changed from the Outside In, Not the Inside Out

Remember to employ Backwards Thinking. To gain clarity from the beginning, start with the future environment, the wants and needs of the customer, and your desired future outcomes. Then work backwards from the environment into the organization to determine how to meet those current and future customer needs. At the same time, keep meeting the multiple outcomes of other key stakeholders.

Align all employees, suppliers, the entire organization, and business processes across departments to achieve these outcomes. This is the conceptual basis for business process reengineering. Unfortunately, it is often fragmented into departmental elements or internal cost-cutting activities. Customer impact is too often ignored.

This aligns with Systems Question #3: *What will be changing in the environment in the future that will impact us?*

For example: Has your change process included a *future* environmental scan—both external to your enterprise as well as inside the enterprise but outside the process—and taken this into consideration?

> ## ⫸ THINK DIFFERENTLY
>
> A large consumer goods organization reconfigured its global manufacturing strategy, basing the decision to relocate the manufacturing of one product primarily on reduced labor costs in the new region. Once the plant was established, the organization discovered it was not achieving the savings originally anticipated and needed an EWC process. The electrical power source was unreliable and unpredictable, the area was subject to hurricanes in November, and shipping by sea was restricted for two months of the year. The local population (employment pool) was engaged in an independence movement against the local government. Production was severely affected, and the product had to be airlifted to meet delivery commitments (instead of shipping by sea).
>
> After being introduced to the skill of future environmental scanning as a way to start an EWC, the client stated that if they had completed a more comprehensive future external environmental scan, they would not have relocated their manufacturing facility as they did (work outside first and then work in the organization).

Principle #4: The Whole Is More Important Than the Parts

The relationships and processes are key (holism and subsystems). The synthesis of how the parts fit and link together in an integrated process in support of the whole outcome is the most important assessment.

An analysis of each part's effectiveness cannot be done in a vacuum. Effectiveness is determined only in the context of relationships between the parts and the processes that lead to the whole. *Always remember that a system cannot be subdivided into independent parts.* A change in one part affects the whole and the other interdependent parts or processes.

This relates to Systems Question #4: *What is the relationship of X to Y?* (And how do they contribute to the overall objective of the whole system and its desired outcomes?)

For example: Has your change process considered its impact on other changes that the enterprise is undergoing at the same time, such as a cultural change and a team-building effort? Have you considered how other changes going on in the entire organization fit with any large-scale complex change you are undertaking?

⊃ THINK DIFFERENTLY

A global tech organization, whose growth strategy has been the acquisition of organizations and keeping them intact to focus on their specialized niches, decided to install an ERP (enterprise-wide resource planning system) through an EWC process. Being a tech organization, they did an excellent job on the technical aspects of the ERP but failed in the implementation. They did not spend time understanding how each of the member organizations uniquely contributed to the overall organization and failed to see the impact on the over-all health and success of the organization of breaking apart the content, processes, and infrastructures of the acquired organizations.

Principle #5: Focus and Strengthen the Basic Units/Systems of Organizations (Holism)

The basic unit of enterprises is not just the individual. It also includes individual relationships. The basic units are (1) individuals, (2) individuals to individuals, (3) teams, and (4) cross-functional teams.

We need to counter-balance our strong Western tendency to glorify the individual at the expense of the team and enterprise. (Asian, First Nation, and indigenous societies around the world often are the opposite.)

This relates to Systems Question #5: *Are we dealing with means or ends?* What is the purpose of each level of the system and how does it relate to the system as a whole?

For example: When a group seems to have a conflict, what are they fighting over? Is it about the next steps or about the desired outcomes?

Principle #6: People Support What They Help Create; There Are Many Different Ways to Achieve the Same Desired Outcomes; Involvement of the Right People in Planning and Implementing the Solutions and Actions Is Key (Equifinality)

It follows that decision making should be as close to the actions as possible. People have a natural desire to be involved and provide input into decisions that affect them *before* the decision is made. For leaders, this is called *participatory management*. It is one of our core values in the OD field.

This relates to Systems Question #6: *What do we need to do to ensure buy-in, stay-in, and perseverance over time (to reverse the entropy)?*

For example: What ongoing involvement methods have you set up for regular "booster shots" with all key stakeholders?

Principle #7: The Steady-State Equilibrium We All Want Can Kill Us—In a Rapidly Changing Society, the Biggest Risk Is to Stay the Same (Steady State, Entropy)

Change keeps us creative, even if it is awkward, uncertain, ambiguous, and even painful. Our natural inclination is to maintain the status quo and its comfortableness. Change requires us to (1) admit we need to change and *will* it to happen and (2) acquire the new skills and abilities needed to function more effectively.

Knowledge and information are inputs into a system. By themselves, they are not enough to make change happen. New skills need to be developed if we want to learn, grow, and change. Short-term creative destruction can sometimes be key to long-term advances. *Today's steady state is one of constant change.*

This relates to Systems Question #7: *What are the new structures and processes we are using to ensure successful Enterprise-Wide Change?*

For example: Have you set up a Change Leadership Team structure that meets regularly? Does it conduct checkups (monthly at a minimum) for your Enterprise-Wide Change? Does it bring all the leadership together to review all sub-changes involved in the larger change?

 THINK DIFFERENTLY

A colleague received a call from an internal OD practitioner within the last year. He worked for an oil company in the southwestern United States and had been asked to help them figure out what to do next in the EWC effort.

The organization had done an excellent job of analyzing its current issues and was problem solving them. However, the CEO was frustrated. The enterprise seemed to be going nowhere.

He was right, as the consultant soon found out. They were solving many of today's problems, but had not focused as a group on a huge gap between *A* (their positioning) and *C* (their current-state assessment of today—their current strengths, weaknesses, opportunities, and threats).

The reason was that the CEO knew what positioning he wanted for the organization but had not clearly articulated it to *anyone*. The change leaders, then, had not answered Systems Thinking's first question (Phase A—*What is your desired outcome?*). As a result, no real future-oriented gap assessment was possible.

Principle #8: Systems Within Systems Within Systems Are Too Complex to Fully Understand and Manage Centrally (Internal Elaboration, Complexity)

Liberation from regulation, shaping corporate bureaucracies into smaller units, privatization, and free market economies are generally more efficient and effective than government or big business can ever be in understanding the complexities of systems. Thousands of little decisions we all make each day in our businesses are what shape and meet market needs, not central government regulations. Big government and big corporations have roles to play in today's society, just not all-encompassing ones.

This relates to Systems Question #8: *What do we centralize (mostly ends) and what should we decentralize (mostly how's and means)?*

 THINK DIFFERENTLY

A colleague worked with medical staff for one Canadian federal department under a supplier contract. As the contract unfolded, the services were being provided directly to the *client department*. However, the corporate purchasing department, which acted on behalf of the total federal government, was really calling the shots. Purchasing's internal regulations and contract requirements added an unexpected compliance burden to the project that was not evident during the contract bidding process. This resulted in an additional cost of close to $750,000 on a project that had a very lean margin to begin with. This created significant financial pressures for the supplier, who was still expected to deliver all services as promised, despite the unexpected additional compliance requirements.

Principle #9: Root Causes and Effects Are Usually Not Linked Closely in Time and Space (Open Systems and Systems Boundaries)

Simplistic cause-effect analyses and the desire for quick fixes often create more problems than solutions. Because our world is composed of levels of complex and interdependent systems, multiple causes with multiple effects are reality, as are circles of causality-effects.

For example: What effects on a farmer and his crops do the ocean—clouds—sun—rain—wind—plants—food play? What causes what?

Delay time—the time between causes and their impacts—can have enormous influences on a system. The concept of "delayed effect" is often missed in our impatient society. It is subtle, and almost always underestimated. When we feel results aren't happening quickly enough, unnecessarily "knee-jerk" reactions can result.

Decisions often have long-term consequences, even years later. Mind mapping, fishbone diagrams, and all sorts of creativity and brainstorming tools are useful here.

However, *the complexity encountered is often far beyond our human ability to fully assess and comprehend intuitively.* For this reason, it is crucial to anticipate delays, understand them, and learn to work with them, rather than against them.

This relates to Systems Question #9: *What are the root causes? Caution:* Dig deep, and dig again. The root causes are rarely obvious.

For example: When a group seems to have a chronic and complex problem they cannot solve, ask the "Why" question again, just slightly differently: "Why does this situation exist?" Ask the same question over and over until you get to deep, root cause(s).

Principle #10: The KISS Method Is Best—Reverse the Entropy!

Systems increase in complexity until they become bureaucratic and ossified, ultimately resulting in death of the system. All living systems require constant energy and inputs (feedback and booster shots) if they are to reverse the process of entropy. Otherwise, all living systems eventually run down and die.

While human beings and families obviously have a finite lifecycle, it doesn't have to be this way for neighborhoods, communities, and organizations. For them, the renewal process is key to long-term success. As Wheatley and Kellner-Rogers

(1996) discuss, chaos and disorder are often precursors to renewal and growth at a higher level.

This is the good news. We now have a virtually limitless supply of constant feedback, which provides us with new inputs for change. On the reverse side, however, we can get information overload and feel that life is becoming too complicated.

We need to eliminate the waste that complexity brings. The KISS method is often more powerful than economies of scale. Focus on the fundamentals, not the fads. The virtual corporation may become more effective than more traditional, vertically integrated complex organizations.

This relates to Systems Question #10: *How can we go from complexity to simplicity, and from consistency to flexibility, in the solutions we devise?*

For example: Simplicity and flexibility are two criteria for success. They must be explicit in the process on a regular basis or they will not occur (they go against natural system characteristics). Simplicity wins the game every time!

Principle #11: Change Is an Individual Act (Seven Levels of Living Systems)

Organizational change is a myth. Organizations and institutions change only when people change. Processes and procedures change when people change their behaviors. Accepting responsibility and accountability for your actions is key.

This *interdependence* is the highest order in terms of wisdom and maturity, coming after dependent and independent growth stages. Independence is really a myth! Focusing on assisting individual change within the family, team, or unit (as a system) is the best way to assist individual change.

This relates to Systems Question #11: *What do I contribute to the problem and what can I change to be a positive and proactive leader on this?*

For example: Each member of a Change Leadership Team should look at his or her own behavior first. They should do it as a group as well to promote openness and teamwork.

⏵ THINK DIFFERENTLY

While working in an executive role in a public-sector organization, a colleague was leading a major EWC process to develop and strengthen a corporate culture of employee empowerment. One staff member who had transferred from another department was having difficulty adjusting to the hectic pace of her new department.

After many months of work trying to make the transition a good one, they were faced with the prospect of having to let this employee go because of her inability to adapt. A critical performance assessment meeting was held to clarify once again what was expected and why it was such an important part of the corporate change initiative.

With a clear understanding of the consequences that lay ahead if she was not able to handle the transition, the employee changed her attitude and she became motivated to succeed. Within months, her performance showed a dramatic improvement and she went on to become a key team leader within the organization.

Organizational change occurs one person at a time.

Principle #12: Problems Can't Be Solved at the Level at Which They Were Created (Albert Einstein)

In many of your change projects, you will need to go to the next higher systems level and its desired outcome in order to succeed—the *helicopter view* of the world.

This relates to the Ultimate Systems Tool and System Question #12: *What is our common superordinate goal here?*

For example: If you are having differences and conflict as a group, can you get the team to agree on a higher-level goal—get them up in a *helicopter* for a higher-level, 5,000-foot view?

 THINK DIFFERENTLY

At what level does the set of problems below need to be solved?

A large middle school in the eastern United States hired a new principal because of the low-performing nature of the school's students. His predecessor had set in place a series of projects to improve the school and ensure "no child is left behind," as President Bush's mandate goes. As a result the first principal had the following complex, fragmented structures in place:

⊃ A senior cabinet of department chairs to run the school

⊃ Separate consultant teams in the school to improve

  • Student math scores

  • English-language speaking skills

- Reading and writing skills

- Teacher development for low-performing teachers

- Serious, disruptive attendance and discipline problems

⊃ A school site council with 50 percent representation from parents and teachers which had been making strategic decisions about the school

⊃ A Parent Teachers Association

⊃ A school audit and intervention team due to the low-performing test scores

⊃ Traditional categorical grant funding by the state for certain other learning program improvement projects

⊃ A union flexing its muscles and causing more problems

⊃ A Total Quality Education Baldrige Award criteria study

⊃ A structure of three *learning communities* overlaid on the traditional grade-level structure

⊃ Design teams to assist learning composed of teachers, parents, classified employees, and administrators

Question: What are the chances of real progress and improvement by the students with all these well-meaning, overlapping, silo approaches? The answer is obvious.

At what level of thinking is the solution even possible?

Principle #13: Paradigm Shift—The World Continually Evolves, Often in Discontinuous Ways, Leading to Breakthroughs Occurring on a Regular Basis

Just as the world has undergone a series of *ages* on Earth over thousands of years, so do the views we have about *What Is the Truth?* A key to change is letting go of the current "truth" for the new one replacing it.

This brings forth Question #13: *What today is impossible to do that, if it could be done, would fundamentally change what we are?*

For example: If your team seems unable to get "out of the box" in their thinking, brainstorm answers to this question, even to the point of being silly or unrealistic.

Principle #14: We Are Holistic Human Beings in Search of Meaning (Multiple Goal Seeking)

The search for meaning in our lives is crucial to our successes and failures. It only comes from the *desired ends* and *whom we want to serve* outside of ourselves. This requires that we understand our own interdependence with others.

The more we can balance ourselves in body, mind, and spirit, the better we can serve others. Starve any of these essential human elements and we starve as human beings. Dehumanize us in our work settings and we don't perform anywhere near our potential.

This brings up Systems Question #14: *What are the multiple goals for this project?* (WIIFM is always present.)

 THINK DIFFERENTLY

A colleague recently conducted an in-house seminar on Systems Thinking. In it she asked participants what their personal *wants* were for this session, thereby legitimizing and surfacing hidden agendas. She adjusted the seminar on the fly and needless to say achieved a much better result for the executives of the insurance company.

Principles #15, 16, 17, 18: You Tell Us . . .

Above all in Systems Thinking is the understanding that we learn about our systems and ourselves as we evolve and grow and change. The learning never stops, nor should it.

The principles and key systems questions just described allow us to discuss organizations of all types using the same language. It allows authors to write books such as this.

Think about it . . . without a set of standard and predictable dynamics and common principles of how individuals, teams, and organizations function, the field of management as a discipline would not exist. See the Chapter Recap for a summary of the systems questions presented here and Table 3.2 for a quick outline.

Currently, there is a worldwide revolution taking place in management thinking and practice, and Systems Thinking and organization learning are becoming one front of the revolution.

Peter Senge, The Fifth Discipline

Questions to Ponder

- Which three Systems Thinking principles seem most useful to you?

- Which of these principles and/or questions are not yet clear or useful to you?

- Can you think of any other key principles of Systems Thinking? What are they?

Table 3.2. Systems Thinking

A new way to think about

- The Environment (and opportunities)
- The Outcomes (and results)
- The Future (and direction)
- The Feedback (and learning)
- The Goals (and measures)
- The Whole Organization (and helicopters at 5,000 feet)
- The Relationships (and patterns)

Stop thinking only about:

• Issues and Problems	• Single Change Initiatives
• Parts and Events	• Defensiveness
• Boxes/Silos/Separateness	• Inputs and Resources

How we think . . . is how we act . . . is how we are!

Think about A-B-C-D-E—All five phases in a totally integrated Enterprise-Wide Change process.

Chapter Three Recap

1. There are four core concepts in Systems Thinking:
   - Seven Levels of Living Systems
   - Natural and predictable cycles of change
   - Systems Thinking is *Backwards* Thinking
   - Twelve characteristics of living systems

2. Four of the Seven Levels of Living Systems and the relationships among them form the Seven Natural Rings of Reality:
   - Self
   - One-to-one relationships
   - Work teams
   - Interdepartmental relationships
   - Total organization
   - Organization–environment interactions
   - Communities and society

3. The Rollercoaster of Change is a useful way to understand the predictable cycles of change.

4. The ABCs of EWC are the core Systems Thinking technology that can bring clarity and simplicity to large-scale organizational change.

5. There are five key strategic questions to ask in dealing with the ABCs of Enterprise-Wide Change:

   Phase A: Where do we want to be? (Our ends, outcomes, purposes, vision)

   Phase B: How will we know when we get there? (The customers' needs and wants connected into a quantifiable feedback system)

   Phase C: Where are we now? (Today's issues and problems)

   Phase D: How do we get there? (Close the gap from C to A in a holistic way)

   Phase E: What is changing in the future environment that we need to consider? (An ongoing question)

6. Consultants and executives should learn the guiding principles of Systems Thinking for EWC.

7. There are twelve characteristics of living systems:

- Living systems exhibit *holism*
- Living systems are *open* systems
- Living systems have *defined boundaries*
- Living systems *transform inputs into outputs*
- Living systems *require feedback* to continue
- Living systems *pursue multiple outcomes*
- Living systems display *equifinality*
- Living systems are *subject to entropy*
- Living systems live in a *hierarchical relationship* with each other
- Living systems require *balance of interrelated parts*
- Living systems have a *dynamic equilibrium* that makes them resistant to change
- Living systems produce *internal elaboration*

Table 3.3 summarizes the best practices for managing these twelve characteristics.

Table 3.3. Best Practices for Managing the Twelve Natural Characteristics of Living Systems

Characteristics	Best Practices
I. The Whole System	
1. Holism	Ask "What's your purpose?" (the #1 Systems Question)
2. Open Systems	Scan the environment continually (ask for implications)
3. Boundaries	Collaborate across boundaries to seek systems solutions (seek win-win)
4. Input/Output	Use "backwards thinking" to focus on what's needed (learn your ABCs of Systems Thinking)
5. Feedback Is a Gift	Actively encourage feedback/gifts
6. Pursuit of Multiple Outcomes	Acknowledge and plan for both organizational and individual outcomes; cover WIIFM

**Table 3.3. Best Practices for Managing the
Twelve Natural Characteristics of Living Systems, Cont'd**

Characteristics	Best Practices
II. The Inner Workings	
7. Equifinality	Focus on the ends and empower the means
8. Entropy	Build in "booster shots" from the outside
9. Hierarchy	First accept, then flatten/allow flexibility
10. Relationships	Recognize relationships and fit
11. Dynamic Equilibrium	Blast away the ruts that lock up the system
12. Internal Elaboration	Create clarity and simplicity

Primary Systems Thinking Questions

I. Preconditions

Precondition #1: What System?

What entity/system or "collision of systems" are we dealing with?

Precondition #2: What Levels?

Within our identified system, what level(s) of the system are we trying to change and what is our purpose/desired outcome?

II. Systems Questions

Systems Question #1: Desired Outcomes

What are the desired outcomes?

Systems Question #2: Feedback

And how will I know I've achieved them? (for example, feedback loop of outcome measures)

Systems Question #3: Environment

What will be changing in the environment in the future that might impact us?

Systems Question #4: Web of Relationships

> What is the relationship of X to Y?

Systems Question #5: Means or Ends

> Are we dealing with means or ends? Corollary: Ask the "five why's."

Systems Question #6: Booster Shots

> What do we need to do to ensure buy-in/stay-in and perseverance over time (to reverse the entropy)?

Systems Question #7: Successful Change

> What are the new structures and processes we are using to ensure successful change?

Systems Question #8: Flexibility

> What do we centralize (mostly what) and what should we decentralize (mostly how) at the same time?

Systems Question #9: Root Causes

> What are the root causes?

Systems Question #10: Simplicity

> How can we go from complexity to simplicity and from consistency to flexibility in the solution we devise?

The Foundation Tool and Question

> What is it that I contribute to the problem and what can I change to be a positive and proactive leader on this?

The Ultimate Tool and Question: Helicopter View

> What is our common superordinate goal here?

Paradigm Shift Question: Backwards Thinking

> What today is impossible to do, that if it could be done, would fundamentally change what we do?

Multiple Goals Question

> What are the multiple goals for this project (WIIFM)?

Part B
Practical Application
to Enterprise-Wide Change

ON THIS SECTION WE WILL APPLY Systems Thinking to an Enterprise-Wide Change process to help you learn how to achieve superior results. The macro model that follows moves you in a predictable yet circular sequence from Smart Start to Clarity of Purpose (Phases E-A-B) to an Enterprise-Wide Assessment (Phase C) to Simplicity of Execution (Phase D) to Sustain Business Excellence—year after year—and back to Phase A again.

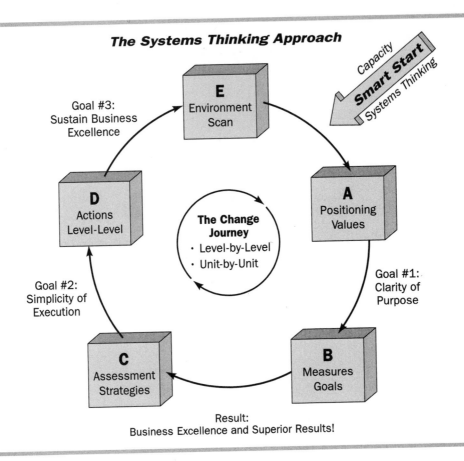

The Systems Thinking Approach

The Change Journey
· Level-by-Level
· Unit-by-Unit

Result:
Business Excellence and Superior Results!

Insanity is doing the same things in the same way and expecting different results.

Steve Haines (with thanks to Albert Einstein and Ben Franklin)

Framework for Part B

The model of Enterprise-Wide Change shown in the figure is the framework for each chapter in Part B. For clarity, the six chapters flow in the same sequence as the model.

 Smart Start is Chapter Four—How to engineer success up-front before formally beginning any changes. Clarity of structure is crucial here.

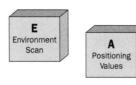 Clarity of Purpose is Chapter Five—
Working *on* the enterprise. Four
missing elements are embedded in
E, A, and B that are crucial to a successful Enterprise-Wide Change:
environmental scanning, positioning, values, and measures/goals.

 Assessing the Enterprise is Chapter Six—How to use the
simple systems framework to successfully assess and guide
the enterprise as a totally integrated living system.

 Simplicity of Execution is Chapter Seven—How to begin
working *in* the enterprise. Leaders must develop and cascade
down the strategies, actions, and work plans that are the *glue*
to overcoming normal and natural resistance to change and involve,
engage, and focus all employees on the specifics of the desired journey.

 Wave after Wave of Changes is Chapter Eight—This is what
is unique about Enterprise-Wide Change. The *glue* in Chapter
Seven must be cascaded down and across the entire organization to achieve business excellence for every single department, unit,
and person. This is a massive task that always involves a cultural change
as well.

 Sustain Business Excellence is Chapter Nine—How to achieve
superior results year after year. Enterprise-Wide Change is
a multi-year journey that requires persistence, long-term
commitment, and focus to sustain the momentum and results, unlike
smaller, more specific time-bound change efforts.

When spider webs unite, they can tie up a lion.

Ethiopian proverb

Smart Start
Engineering Success Up-Front

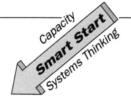

Chapter Purposes

- To explore the Smart Start process as a *planned change* process that can significantly enhance a multi-year EWC journey's probability of success *up-front*

- To understand three different realities present in all human interactions key to the success of Enterprise-Wide Change: Content, Process, and Structure

---

Goal #1: Develop an Enterprise-Wide
Game Plan for Dramatic Change

The ABCs of Enterprise-Wide Change

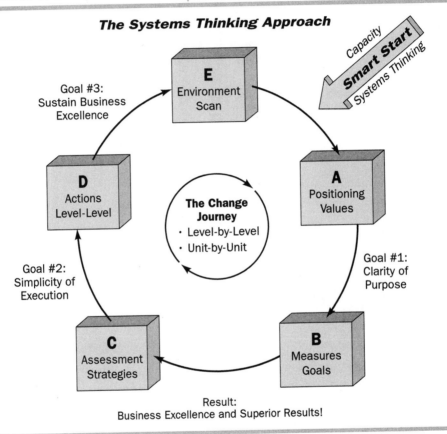

The Systems Thinking Approach

Goal #3:
Sustain Business
Excellence

E
Environment
Scan

Capacity
Smart Start
Systems Thinking

D
Actions
Level-Level

**The Change
Journey**
· Level-by-Level
· Unit-by-Unit

A
Positioning
Values

Goal #1:
Clarity of
Purpose

Goal #2:
Simplicity of
Execution

C
Assessment
Strategies

B
Measures
Goals

Result:
Business Excellence and Superior Results!

Chapter Context

This chapter represents a specific point of view regarding Enterprise-Wide Change; here we introduce two key views that permeate this book:

- Working *on* the enterprise, and
- Working *in* the enterprise.

Smart Start helps to increase your probability of EWC success by using Systems Thinking and analytical thinking in their proper context. Enterprise-Wide Change is an outside–inside–outside sequence that best begins with a Smart Start. Understanding these two key enterprise views is important in this chapter. Keep them in mind as you become educated on change, assess your enterprise, and then tailor and organize the journey. This is what we mean by engineering success up-front in a Smart Start.

Figure 4.1 is a visual way to understand this overall change sequence.

Figure 4.1. Systems Versus Analytic Thinking

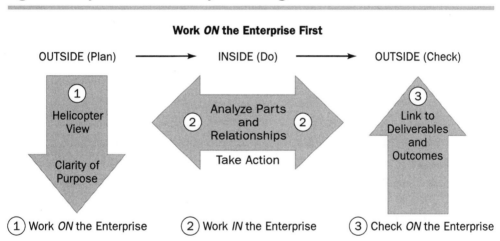

Work *ON* the Enterprise First

OUTSIDE (Plan) ⟶ INSIDE (Do) ⟶ OUTSIDE (Check)

1 Helicopter View — Clarity of Purpose

2 Analyze Parts and Relationships 2 — Take Action

3 Link to Deliverables and Outcomes

(1) Work *ON* the Enterprise   (2) Work *IN* the Enterprise   (3) Check *ON* the Enterprise

Leaders work *on* the enterprise. Managers and project manager offices work *in* the enterprise. Everyone must continually *check on* the enterprise's desired results. Let's begin with a Smart Start.

Smart Start: Engineer Success Up-Front

The ancestor of every action is a thought.

Ralph Waldo Emerson

The Vision of Your Enterprise-Wide Change

Vision is our view of what the ideal future looks like at future time "X." It has dreamlike qualities and represents our future hopes and aspirations, even if they are never fully realized. It is an energizing, positive, and inspiring statement of where and what we want to be in the ideal future.

The very first task in EWC is to answer the number-one systems question: *"What are the desired outcomes?"* Define the ideal future vision that will result from all your change efforts, one that is enterprise-wide in its impact, involvement, and transformation. It may be major growth, expansion, and becoming a global company, or it may be restructuring, redesigning, and building an integrated supply chain. It might be a turnaround of an unprofitable or low-performing business or agency. Perhaps it is a merger, acquisition, new joint venture, or major strategic alliance.

It could also be establishing and institutionalizing a new 21st Century high-performing and employee-oriented culture. It could also be an intense, all-pervasive, customer-focused organization based on high quality, Six Sigma, innovative new products, customer service, responsiveness, or convenience.

Your vision could also be one of operational or business excellence and process improvement, along with low cost and efficiency. It could include installing major new enterprise-wide technologies such as ERP systems.

It could even be creating a new business or executing a radically different strategic or business plan for an enterprise.

Key Factors in Vision-Driven Change

There are four key aspects to vision-driven change:

- Creating and setting the shared vision
- Communicating this vision
- Building commitment to this vision
- Organizing and motivating people and what they do so that they are aligned and attuned to this vision

Whatever your vision, engineer its success up-front by being smart regarding how and when you start your Enterprise-Wide Change. Take a step back, pause, and put in place the education and understanding, the assessments, the tailoring, and the organization of the journey to greatly increase your probability of success. Build an EWC Game Plan *before* you begin, even though it will be changed and adjusted time and again throughout the journey.

The Enterprise-Wide Change *Smart Start* methods are guided by *three main premises* about enterprises and the people who make them *living systems.*

Premise #1   Planning and change management are now the *primary* tasks of senior leadership (see upcoming Players of Change)

Premise #2   People support what they help create (see upcoming Parallel Involvement Process)

Premise #3   Executives and change consultants use Systems Thinking, focusing on outcomes, and serving the customer (our ABCs of Enterprise-Wide Change framework)

These premises are the foundation of the Systems Thinking Approach to Enterprise-Wide Change.

The leaders and drivers of change efforts must understand the Science of Living Systems and how it will impact change efforts in their enterprise. A Smart Start in pre-planning the EWC process is one way for this understanding to occur. Some activities are shown in Table 4.1.

Table 4.1. Four Smart Start Activities

Activity #1   A Smart Start offsite for change leaders and support staff to begin developing the Enterprise-Wide Change Game Plan

Activity #2   A Parallel Involvement Process with all the key stakeholders to test and critique key initiatives of the Enterprise-Wide Change Game Plan

Activity #3   A second, follow-up offsite for the leadership team to finalize the EWC Game Plan

Activity #4   A rollout of training on the principles of Systems Thinking, first to change leaders, and then to all change implementers

A Smart Start Offsite: The First Activity

The probability of completing a successful Enterprise-Wide Change is far greater if the people at the top are first prepared for it through the Smart Start process. The first structured tool change consultants can use for this purpose is an offsite retreat, away from everyday stress and pressures.

The purpose of the initial offsite is to *educate, assess, tailor,* and *organize* the Enterprise-Wide Change effort. Setting the right direction in the right way is critical to success. The consequences of getting it wrong are extensive and expensive. A two-day retreat is strongly recommended to allow for a comprehensive overview of the requirements and prerequisites for success.

In the Chapter Recap, a table of potential tasks is provided for the executives and change consultants to use in tailoring their Enterprise-Wide Change Game Plan to the needs of each situation and purpose.

The final Smart Start task, the definition of an EWC Game Plan and then actually building it, will be discussed at the end of this chapter. The recap includes everything covered in this chapter (and more). It makes a good summary of Smart Start outcomes.

 THINK DIFFERENTLY

In a recent EWC process with a California manufacturer, a colleague proceeded as follows in the two-day Smart Start sessions.

Day 1:

Educate: The first morning included education on the infrastructures and processes of Enterprise-Wide Change. It also included development of a vision of the desired outcomes.

Assess: The results of an Enterprise-Wide Assessment were presented in the afternoon. (An assessment instrument had been completed online by the management team as prework.) The assessment also included some onsite assessment prework to understand where they were in relation to their strategic direction.

Day 2:

Tailor: The actual tailoring of the change process was completed in the morning. It included developing a one-page Yearly Map of Implementation (see Table 4.2).

Organize: The consultant then designed the actual infrastructures required for change. Of key importance were clarifying roles and defining the level of employee involvement desired.

Note: The completion of the full EWC Game Plan had to be finished at a later date. Too much was unclear, even though the client wanted to proceed immediately.

A key outcome from the Smart Start phase is the Yearly Map of Implementation shown in Table 4.2. This simple document is a key element to keep the change process on track in the face of daily pressures encountered throughout the year.

Table 4.2. Sample Yearly Map of Implementation

Date	
June—**Year #1**	1. Begin Enterprise-Wide Change Smart Start (2 days)
July–August	2. Build Clarity of Purpose and EWC Game Plan (3 to 5 days overall)—plus time for the Parallel Involvement Process
September	3. Develop Department EWC Work Plans/Budgets
October	4. Conduct Large Group Dept. Plan Review (1 day)
November	5. Conduct last Smart Start meeting (1 to 2 days)
December	6. Roll out the EWC to the entire enterprise
January—**Year #2**	7. Ongoing Operation of Program Management Office (PMO)
January—Ongoing	8. Monthly Change Leadership Team Review Sessions
As Needed	*Wave after Wave of Change*
	9. Develop 3-Year EWC Business Plans as needed (for Business Units/Major Support Departments)
October	10. Evaluate EWC Game Plan's Year #1 Success
October–November	11. Conduct Annual EWC Strategic Review and Update (3 to 5 days overall) including Parallel Involvement Process—Recycle Department Plans and Budget sharing
December	12. Roll out Enterprise-Wide Changes
January—**Year #3**	Recycle the EWC Process • Continue as necessary • Build overall EWC capacity

Questions to Ponder

- Is building the Smart Start that engineers success up-front important to you? How well do you do it?
- Review the four sets of tasks in the Smart Start offsite. Which are the top three priorities for you in each set of tasks for your Enterprise-Wide Game Plan?
- Do you have an implementation map for your EWC process? What else might be on it?

The Iceberg Theory of Change—Three Realities of Life: Content—Process—Structure

It is crucial in this Smart Start phase to educate the team on the three-dimensional Iceberg Theory of Change.

This is a sub-model, useful for the Smart Start phase. An iceberg metaphor is often used to illustrate the fact that dangers usually loom larger, and run deeper, than they may appear on the surface.

The Iceberg Theory of Change shown in Figure 4.2 suggests that it is the 87 percent of change activities that occur *below the waterline* that sink ships—and enterprises.

Figure 4.2. The Iceberg Theory of Change

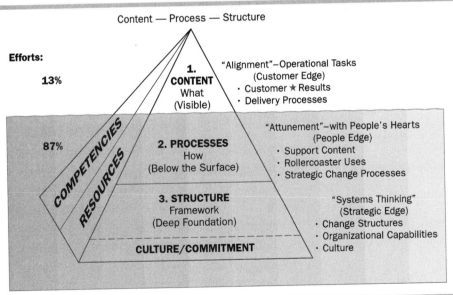

In Enterprise-Wide Change, the 13-percent portion of the iceberg that is visible corresponds to the *content* of change—the obvious tasks and improvements that organizational leadership has *already* identified as necessary that are usually the catalyst underlying an EWC initiative.

Below the surface, however, lies the majority of the work that must be done—the *processes* and *structures* that must be built to support the content of change.

Creating a customer-focused, high-performance organization requires a delicate balance of time and energy among *content, process,* and *structure*:

1. A focus on the *content or tasks* to achieve the desired vision

2. A focus on the *processes* and *how people behave* while working on the tasks

3. A focus on the *structures, infrastructures, context,* or *arrangements* of change below the waterline within which the *content* and *processes* operate, both the day-to-day activities and EWC initiatives

1. The Content of Change: Content Myopia

Content myopia is a tendency to focus mostly on content or business tasks. Content myopia is a normal consequence of the iceberg. People instinctively focus on what they want changed, such as desired growth, marketplace positioning, restructuring, and the like. If content myopia is not remedied early in the EWC process, it threatens to build in failure up-front.

Successful change requires identifying, adjusting, and leveraging organizational processes and structures within a systems framework.

The content of change starts when change leaders start building a Game Plan for Enterprise-Wide Change in the Smart Start retreat.

2. The Processes of Change

Three different kinds of processes are important here.

- *Process consultation* and the content-process dilemma is frequently the reason OD professionals are asked to work with an enterprise. An outside expert is needed because senior management typically cannot focus on both the content of change and the processes of change simultaneously. Most organizations need a neutral third-party facilitator to manage and facilitate the process.

Process Consultation is a set of consultant activities, which help the client to perceive, understand, and act upon [business] process events, which occur in the client's environment.

Edgar Schein, Process Consultation:
Its Role in Organization Development *(1969, p. 9)*

- *Business processes,* on the other hand, are the ways in which business gets done to serve the customer. This is a key distinction. Organizations usually organize and differentiate vertically by functions (HR, legal, marketing, engineering) and achieve business results by integrated horizontal business processes that serve the customer. Such approaches to organizational change as TQM, reengineering, Six Sigma, and so forth deal primarily with business processes.
- *The process of change* is a third process in and of itself, although some executives may not recognize this fact. This process is one of the four main concepts in Systems Thinking, the Rollercoaster of Change.

3. The Structures of Change

Structure influences behavior. Infrastructures are among the most powerful influences on behavioral change there are and, ironically, the least recognized and utilized by executives in Enterprise-Wide Change. The structures (or infrastructures) of change can be physical (process or project teams), mental (what roles to play), or even behavioral (culture is a strong infrastructure).

Room setup, for example, is a basic infrastructure that trainers and facilitators look at carefully, because this is the environment in which learning must take place. If the temperature is too hot or too cold, ambient sounds are distracting, or the tables and chairs are arranged in rows rather than in a circle when group interaction is critical to learning, the trainer or facilitator makes immediate adjustments to create the infrastructures needed to support the particular change process (learning).

Here is a list of key principles about how *structure influences behavior*:

1. Having the right structures in place to begin a change is critical.
2. Desired behaviors need desired structures—both physical and mental/emotional/cultural.

3. Even colors and shapes and visuals are effective structures.

4. Structures create chain reactions—slow at first, faster later on.

5. Structures need flexibility. Either too rigid or too soft are both usually bad.

6. Too many structures will create bureaucracy.

7. The linkages of the structures to each other are key.

8. Without change structures, complacency and chaos rule the day.

9. Persistence with the structures is key to change.

10. Leverage off the naturally emerging structures for change.

11. Organizational structure is designed to run today's business, not create the future. It is resistant to change.

In EWC efforts, it is not unusual for major organizational structural components and contexts to be ignored. Our experience has shown that clients are usually even *less* aware of the impact of infrastructure than they are of the organizational context. Clients' typical view of structure is the organization chart—usually a work of pure fiction that displays how work is thought to be organized and accomplished in the enterprise.

EWC structures go much deeper than just an organizational chart. A key infrastructure starts with roles for the key players in the Enterprise-Wide Change process.

The Structures of Change Expanded: Tailored to Your Needs

This last and deepest part of the iceberg is structure, crucial to EWC success. The day-to-day running of a business has an organizational chart (structure). EWC also needs a structure—one that is more subtle and is a set of infrastructures tailored to your needs in the Smart Start phase. If we want our change process to succeed, we must be clear about who is involved. Just as we have an organizational chart to run day-to-day operations, what are the guiding structures and infrastructures to lead the EWC effort? It starts with knowing the various *players of change* and their roles.

We also need to be able to assess the skills of the individuals involved. Managing EWC is a complex core competency that leaders and change consultants must define, understand, sharpen, and then master.

Ineffectiveness of the Hierarchical Cascade of Implementation alone: This normal cascade strategy for implementing change is usually ineffective, because memories remain embedded in the way the organization works after the change. This applies particularly if the change relates to the culture rather than to work practices or systems.

Richard Beckhard and Wendy Pritchard, Changing the Essence: The Art of Creating and Leading Fundamental Change in Organizations *(1992)*

In this book we present a new way to run your business, giving equal weight to (1) managing desired future Enterprise-Wide Change and to (2) the ongoing daily management of the business.

CEOs have four choices to structure their overall EWC efforts:

1. Do it ourselves

   - Failure model (a fool for a client)

2. Facilitation of the Change Leadership Team meetings, and do the rest ourselves

   - Powerful neutral external facilitator (with internal coordinator)

3. Set up separate internal project managers for each project

   - External consultant works with internal project managers

   - Content/process experts used as needed

4. Set up a Program Management Office for multi-projects, processes, and overall day-to-day coordination of change

   - Joint accountability and responsibility by executive and external systems consultant

   - Program Management Office set up for daily functioning

   - Analysis and support cadre available

   - Rewards and incentives support the EWC

The fourth choice makes the most sense for EWC. The roles and structures of the *players of change* in Figure 4.3 help us understand why some change initiatives do not work and why others achieve the desired changes.

Figure 4.3. Essential Structures and Players in Enterprise-Wide Change

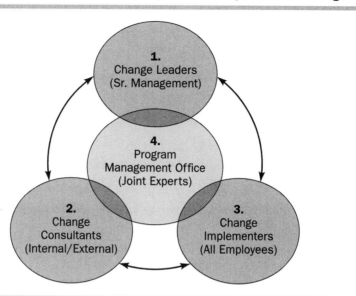

The two-way arrows in the figure demonstrate that the working relationships and structures among all change players are reciprocal. The areas of overlap with the Program Management Office by all change players show how the PMO occupies a central position in the change team effort, integrating the players into a systemic Enterprise-Wide Change process.

Effective change depends on mutual respect, communication, and teamwork with all parties, their roles, and their contributions.

Structure and Player #1: Change Leaders

Our number-one premise is that planning and change management are now the *primary* tasks of senior leadership. We have learned that it is a waste of time and effort to work with clients on Enterprise-Wide Change if they are not willing to install an Enterprise-Wide Change Leadership Team led by the CEO and senior management. This group must accept responsibility for initiating and leading change and guiding the overall dynamic, strategic, and complex process.

Change leaders must be highly committed to the change initiatives and develop and exercise their leadership skills to bring about the desired change. Change leaders also must show concern for the individuals who will implement the change and the impact it will have on their lives. They must lead the EWC Leadership Team on a continuing basis.

Essential Skills of Change Leaders

- A deep understanding of the Enterprise-Wide Change process and the four main concepts of Systems Thinking
- Discipline and courage to ensure consistency, integrity, and focus of the entire enterprise to its strategic positioning in the marketplace, year after year
- Persistence and energy over the long term to ensure superior results through a focus on both *economic alignment* of delivery and the *cultural attunement* with people's hearts and minds

Structure and Player #2: Change Consultants

Typically constituting both staff leaders and OD professionals, change consultants are experts in the processes and structures of change, as well as the content of specific staff functions. "Outsiders" contribute in-depth expertise, objective viewpoints, and experience that the organization often cannot afford on a full-time basis. Internal consultants and support team members best understand the various functions under their purview.

Support for the Enterprise-Wide Change efforts and the Program Management Office usually requires a combination of both internal and external support, shown in Table 4.3.

Table 4.3. Examples of Support Areas

Instructions: Fill in the names of your needed support cadre.

Support Cadre Type	Typical Tasks	Names Chosen
Change Consultants (Internal and External)	Facilitating groups/projects	
	Coaching executives and managers	
	Planning business unit change	
	Supporting organizational assessment	

Table 4.3. Examples of Support Areas, Cont'd

Support Cadre Type	Typical Tasks	Names Chosen
Finance and Budget	Coordinating key success measures	
	Analyzing ROI/economics	
	Budgeting	
Human Resources	Facilitating employee relations	
	Managing performance/rewards	
	Coaching support	
	Training and development	
Communications	Planning and executing communication	
	Distributing updates after each meeting/event	
	Preparing final Enterprise-Wide Communication Plan	
Administrative Assistant	Managing logistics and follow-up	
	Taking minutes on laptop	
	Revising documents	
	Producing drafts of EWC Game Plan	

Change consultants, like any professionals, potentially move through four stages of growth in their careers:

- *Dependence*—Trainee/apprentice (our estimate is 40 percent of the field)
- *Independence*—Technique-driven/colleague (40 percent of the field)
- *Interdependence*—Model-driven/mentor but still eclectic (15 percent)
- *Mastery*—Wisdom/sponsor with strategic and Systems Thinking orientation (5 percent)

The tasks each change consultant and support cadre member undertakes should be appropriate to his or her stage of growth and desire to learn. It does no good to put someone in a task *over his or her head.*

Structure and Player #3: Change Implementers

The change implementers, including all employees and managers, must accept and commit to the need for change and implement it within their daily work and behaviors. This group also always includes the change leaders, change consultants, and the Program Management Office. They must also ensure that change implementers *buy in* and *stay in* throughout the Rollercoaster of Change.

Parallel Involvement Process for Change Implementers

People support what they help create is our second main premise. It follows that building enterprise-wide participation for the change implementers in Enterprise-Wide Change is essential, not just an option.

Today's realities must be taken into consideration in Enterprise-Wide Change. It makes the leadership job more difficult than the old D.A.D. technique ("Decide—Announce—Defend") of the *command-and-control* past. Involvement and participation of key stakeholders is no longer "if," but how, when, and for what purposes. A number of methodologies and practices are now available to executives and change consultants to involve and engage all the key stakeholders. Options include

- The *Whole Systems Approach* to large group participation, which includes the presence of many employees of the organization in the room at one time to plan and execute change. Dannemiller Tyson and Associates are the pioneers of this process (www.dannemillertyson.com).
- The *Future Search Method* from Marv Weisbord and Sandra Janoff (www.futuresearch.net).
- The *Parallel Involvement Process* methodology (www.csmintl.com).
- Public Consultation in government.

The overarching objectives of these participation processes are to

1. Improve the quality of the Game Plan and
2. Increase understanding and buy-in for successful execution.

It is not our intention to detail these processes here, but only to reinforce the importance of commitment-building events and processes as major components of Enterprise-Wide Change.

Stakeholders are those—both internal and external to the enterprise—who are most affected by the success or failure of Enterprise-Wide Change. Involvement of key stakeholders is crucial to buy-in—*people support what they help create.*

The fundamental point is simply that people in an organization will naturally want to have input and involvement in the process of decision making on matters that affect them—*before* the final decision is made.

Strategic thinking about clarity of purpose and marketplace positioning requires a high level of understanding, discipline, and critical thought. Difficult tradeoffs have to be made. Most people in enterprises have enough common sense to know that *all* decisions cannot be open to a broad consensus, because not everyone has the requisite skills and business acumen to make strategic decisions. Two related involvement definitions we frequently use are key here:

Skeptics are my best friends is a crucial concept executives and change consultants should internalize. It is a way to encourage feedback. *Skeptics* want the organization to be successful. They just have information about ways it can fail. *Cynics,* on the other hand, are bitter and have no suggestions for improvement.

Actively support is the essence of consensus decision making. Ask for the commitment to *actively support* a decision (win-win) to ensure you really have consensus, not just deference to authority such as, "I can live with it" (a win-lose view).

 THINK DIFFERENTLY

In helping a fundamental transformation of a large K-12 school district in California, a colleague ran into a brick wall. The district's students were not performing well on their test scores. This had caused a serious rift in the community along racial lines. In particular, two elected members of the board of education had gone public with their concerns.

The long-term, highly respected superintendent tired of dealing with this and retired, causing even more problems. Into the void, the consultant was asked to help build an EWC process that had credibility in content, process, and organization infrastructure.

The development of the vision, Game Plan, and clarity of purpose phases were quite extensive. Over one hundred Parallel Involvement Processes were conducted by the consultants and staff (once trained).

As a result, the Game Plan had the backing of both the community as well as the two concerned board members, since they were the architects.

Structure and Player #4: Program Management Office

You cannot chase two gazelles.

Zulu saying

It is almost impossible for senior management to *chase two gazelles*: the day-to-day and also the EWC process. Hence, the need for a Program Management Office (PMO).

Program is the term often used for a multi-faceted set of processes, projects, and complex initiatives that must be coordinated and integrated to achieve Enterprise-Wide Change.

A PMO consists of a joint group of internal and external senior-level experts in the content, processes, and structures of successful Enterprise-Wide Change efforts, as well as the business itself. This is analogous to the PMO in large-scale defense, aircraft, and shipyard projects. Failure in any of these offices to integrate multiple projects and processes and ensure close coordination will result in planes that won't fly and ships that sink.

Ideally, the PMO is jointly led by an organizational executive and a master-level external consultant, both of whom are well-respected, have high credibility, and report directly to the CEO. The executive must have no day-to-day responsibilities except for the Enterprise-Wide Change effort. Working through the structure of a PMO, the external consultant becomes an enterprise-wide *systems consultant*, working both economic alignment and cultural attunement issues and potential failures.

Large consulting firms such as Booz-Allen and McKinsey regularly use Program Management Offices in their consulting initiatives. However, the PMO structure is a departure from the approach used by many change consultants and OD practitioners. It moves well beyond process consultation and subject-matter experts. Through the PMO, an external consultant forms a *team of two* with an internal executive, and both have shared accountability for actual results. (It goes without saying that the PMO also needs support staff, a financial analyst, space, and a budget.)

This places the external consultant role in a new light. The external consultant in the Program Management Office is playing a leadership role in the change and OD field—a *systems consultant*.

In business there are *systems analysts* and *systems integrators*. The IT world has *systems consultants* who focus on technological systems, rather than human organizational systems. So do *systems engineers*. Change and OD consultants can become competent enterprise-wide *systems consultants*, covering both alignment and attunement issues.

> ### ⟩ THINK DIFFERENTLY
>
> A client asked a colleague to conduct a strategic planning workshop for their high-potential executives. However, they insisted on also hiring a different consulting organization to run a second workshop on change management.
>
> Predictably, the mental models proposed for each workshop were in conflict. Suddenly, the client was very concerned about their analytic approach to a systems problem. Teaching two different mental maps to the same executives led to confusion, failure, and the firing of the client's executive in charge of the program.
>
> The two workshops, considered separately, went just fine. But from a Systems Thinking perspective, the predictable results were disastrous: a piecemeal approach caused by the first of the "big three" failures (multiple mindsets and mental maps).

The External Systems Consultant Role in the PMO

- Develop and support EWC structures and processes to coordinate integration across multiple projects
- Facilitate the development of the EWC Game Plan
- Act as a devil's advocate by
  - Modeling core values in the process
  - Pushing for concrete decisions, directions, and priorities
  - Challenging executives about issues they may be backing away from
  - Supporting the decision-making process on difficult issues
- Contribute mastery-level expertise in both content areas (business and people)
- Lead the internal staff support team in their respective roles
- Lead in developing an overall leadership development system tied to the strategic direction and Enterprise-Wide Change
- Ensure development and installation of a strategic management yearly cycle
- Coordinate the implementation of the results of an organization-wide best practices assessment to ensure integrity to the vision, values, and positioning

Skills of the Systems Consultant

- In-depth knowledge and set of skills in Systems Thinking applied to all levels of an enterprise
- A strong business, economic, and industry sector orientation
- Knowledge and skills in large-scale, Enterprise-Wide Change
- Expertise in strategic thinking and multiple project management
- A well-developed mental map of overall organization design, fit, and functioning
- Skills in human and interpersonal behavior, group dynamics, process facilitation, and teamwork
- Skills in the consulting process, executive coaching, and meeting management
- A strong internal sense of self-esteem tempered by humility and courage

---

Note: For purposes of simplicity in this book, when we use the term "change consultants," we include systems consultants as well.

Questions to Ponder

- Are the roles and structures of each of the players of change clear?
- What would you add or subtract?
- Do you agree that there is a need for a PMO? Why or why not?
- What other support staff might you need in Enterprise-Wide Change?

A Menu of Additional Change Infrastructures

One essential aspect of the Iceberg Theory of Change is building the appropriate structures or infrastructures to guide the change tasks and processes. The four different roles of the players of change constitute one set of infrastructures. There are many more to choose from on the *change menu* in Table 4.4.

The menu of possible change infrastructures is a flexible one. It might be added to or pared down over time, depending on the scope and scale of change efforts. Only those structures that are actually required for success should be installed, because too many temporary structures can strangle change efforts.

Of all the change infrastructures, a strong EWC Leadership Team and the PMO are an *absolute necessity for successful change*. The leadership team tracks and adjusts everything else throughout the EWC process. They follow through on the Yearly Map and lead implementation of the EWC Game Plan.

The CEO must frequently communicate the vision and reasons why the change is necessary. The rest of the senior management team must support the CEO as additional *structures* (yes, people can be considered structures too).

Table 4.4. A Menu of Change

Main Infrastructures: Senior Leadership and Support Structures

Infrastructure:	Purposes:
Player #1 Change Leaders: CEO/senior executives with personal leadership plans who are the change leaders	For repetitive "stump speeches" and reinforcement To ensure fit/integration of all parts and people toward the same vision/values
Player #1 Executive Committee	For weekly meetings and attention To ensure follow-up on the top 15 to 25 priority yearly actions from the strategic plan
Player #1 Enterprise-Wide Change Leadership Team	For monthly follow-up meetings to track, adjust, and refine everything To ensure follow-through via a yearly comprehensive map of implementation
Player #2 Change Consultants: A cross-functional support team, including change consultants	For coordination of the implementation process To ensure the change structures and processes don't lose out to day-to-day issues and concerns
Player #3 Change Implementers: (Parallel Involvement Process)	For input and involvement of all key stakeholders before a decision affecting them is made To ensure a critical mass in support of the vision and desired changes
Player #4 Program Management Office	Joint internal and external experts for Enterprise-Wide Change requiring management of multiple change processes and projects on a day-to-day basis To ensure fit, support, and integration with vision, positioning, and values

◗ THINK DIFFERENTLY

A California telephone company making technological changes cut over to a new wireless system on a Wednesday which then failed. Their cellular telephone system went down for eighteen hours, resulting in the loss of many customers. Why didn't they switch it over on a Saturday or a Sunday rather than a business day? Why didn't they have people trained, ready, and in stand-by mode for any problems that were bound to ensue? Structures, structures, structures (like many listed in Table 4.5) were missing—with no link to a Change Leadership Team. Cleaning up the problems from this analytical approach required major effort.

Table 4.5. Substructures of an Enterprise-Wide Change

Main support structures must be created at the highest level of an enterprise, while others are effectively subcommittees (or projects/processes) of the Change Leadership Team. Each subcommittee must include a member from the leadership team for best integration. In addition, subcommittees are often assigned projects/processes that more junior change consultants are effective at facilitating.

Substructures	Purposes
Project or Process Teams	For each change strategy and/or specific change initiative
	To ensure achievement of each one
Employee Development Board (Attunement of People's Hearts)	For succession, careers, development, core competencies, performance management
	To ensure fit with the desired culture and employees as a competitive edge
Technology Steering Committee	For computer, telecommunications, software fit and integration
	To ensure "system-wide" fit/coordination around information management
Strategic Communications System (and Structures)	For clear two-way dialogue and understanding of the plan/implementation
	To ensure everyone is heading in the same direction with the same strategies/values

Table 4.5. Substructures of an Enterprise-Wide Change, Cont'd

Substructures	Purposes
Measurement and Benchmarking	For collecting and reporting of key success factors, especially customers, employees, and competitors
	To ensure an outcome/customer focus at all times
Accountability and Responsibility System (all levels)	For clear and focused three-year business plans and annual department plans that are critiqued, shared, and reviewed, as well as individual performance appraisals
	To ensure a fit, coordination, and commitment to the core strategies and annual top priorities
Rewards and Recognition	For recognizing and paying people for strategic management accomplishments
	To ensure reinforcement of the accountability and responsibilities system
Organization Redesign Team	For studying and recommending what redesign of the organization is needed
	To ensure synergy of the strategies, structures, processes, policies, values, and culture
Environmental Scanning System	For collecting data from the environment
	To ensure advance awareness of coming changes to the environment

Further Elaboration on Key Structures

Some further points on two more key structures from the "menu" of infrastructures for change are in order. Others are self-evident and should be used where necessary and appropriate.

Employee Development Board: Invest in Your People First

The people management practices in every organization should be viewed as a system of people flow, from hiring through to retirement or termination. Making all this happen is the responsibility of senior management. It is usually best done through an Employee Development Board that focuses solely on *creating people as a competitive business advantage,* a key leverage point in any EWC effort.

The employee development board reinforces senior management's responsibility for carrying out organization-wide *stewardship*. The best way to accomplish this is to create a strategic *people edge*/HR plan that fully defines and implements the people side of the EWC Game Plan.

 THINK DIFFERENTLY

Since the people side of the change effort is often undervalued and understaffed, a board is usually needed. One of the authors was responsible for an employee development board at an Exxon division, a Sunoco division, and later in his career, for all of MCI's succession planning and development in its heyday of growth. Each time, having such a board made a significant difference in focusing on the people side of the business while keeping it tied to the strategic direction.

Innovative Process or Project Teams

Process or project teams are the main vehicle for implementing major elements of these complex change efforts. Building accountability and innovation into each team's operation increases the probability that tasks are done well and goals are achieved. It is the responsibility of the PMO to coordinate all these efforts.

Questions to Ponder

- Do you agree with the three premises of Enterprise-Wide Change presented thus far in this chapter? Why or why not?

- Is the Iceberg Theory of Change clear to you? Do you agree with the premise? Why or why not?

- What structures are most important to your own EWC process? Why is that?

The Game Plan for Enterprise-Wide Change

The ultimate goal of Smart Start is to develop an intelligent, research-based, highly specific vision and EWC Game Plan. It will increase the probability of success of your EWC journey compared with the usual 25-percent success rate for this type of transformation.

The Enterprise-Wide Change journey requires its own EWC Game Plan. This chapter and the next one have as their outcomes building a coherent, integrated Game Plan of all the key points discussed under the Iceberg Theory of Change topic.

The Game Plan is extensive and includes

- The content and vision of the change (further explained in Chapter Five)
- The infrastructures for change (explained earlier in this chapter)
- The process for change (further explained in Chapter Eight)
- Competencies, commitments, and resources for change (further explained in Chapter Nine)
- Yearly Map of Implementation for change (explained in this chapter)

Please see the specific details of the Enterprise-Wide Change Game Plan in the Chapter Recap after the following case study.

▶ COMPREHENSIVE CASE STUDY

For the rest of this book we will work through an ongoing story of an actual Enterprise-Wide Change situation. At the end of each chapter, we will detail the ideal EWC activity sequence compared to reality. The activities are applied in a practical way so that you can see the messy reality versus the ideal of the model. The case serves as a more comprehensive example of Enterprise-Wide Change and ties the book together in a practical way.

East Coast Federal Credit Union Enterprise-Wide Change: Part 1

This case is of a medium-sized, U.S. east coast credit union. We have changed its name and true identity, as it is an ongoing organization. We will call it *East Coast Federal Credit Union*, ECFCU for short. While the company's name is disguised, the pertinent facts in this story are accurate. It is a multi-year story of a real transformation of an enterprise near bankruptcy to one with a viable future.

A credit union was chosen as a universal case because credit unions are a worldwide movement. They are nominally in the not-for-profit sector and publicly regulated. Yet because credit unions must be profitable and have reserve capital, it is easy for the private sector to relate to this story. Credit unions are in a highly competitive marketplace, competing against all types of for-profit financial services firms, including local, community, and multinational banks, non-banks, and insurance companies.

ECFCU has multi-state retail service branches providing a full range of consumer financial services, including checking, savings, ATM, credit cards, certificates of deposits, and loans of all types, such as home mortgages, second trust deeds, and car and boat loans.

ECFCU is organized in a typical functional structure with a CEO, COO, and VPs of Operations, Finance, HR, Loan Origination, and Marketing (an open position).

ECFCU was formed many years ago to support a major corporate sponsor. They grew steadily under the leadership of a long-term CEO and a very uniform and stable board of directors.

In the mid-1990s, they got into deep trouble and were in danger of going bankrupt. Some problems that cropped up included

- Their corporate sponsor moved out of their geographic region and merged with another organization.
- They had an information systems outsourcing contract with *IT International* (fictitious name) that was too expensive and had prolonged downtime.
- They outsourced their car loan originations and servicing to *CarLoan, Inc.* (fictitious name) with disastrous results, including high delinquencies and charge-offs.
- Expenses were out of control and no real plans and budgets were in place.
- Their supervisory (audit) committee was functioning minimally. The board of directors was passive and submissive to an autocratic CEO.
- Market share was minimal and many customers were paycheck cashers only.

By the late 1990s, ECFCU was losing money with no EWC Game Plan for recovering. In 2000, the CEO was given early retirement, while under a serious investigation. The federal regulatory examiners (National Credit Union Administration, or NCUA) were deeply involved, had issued a "cease and desist" order, and were prepared to take over ECFCU if necessary. A brand-new VP of Operations was selected and thrown in as the next CEO.

Activity #1. The CEO quickly evaluated the situation and called *Systems Consultants, Inc.* (a fictitious name) for help. Initial scouting revealed serious problems. After intense consultant-CEO discussions, they met with the board chairman, who agreed, with reluctance, to undertake an Enterprise-Wide Change process that the NCUA agreed with and supported. At that point Smart Start began.

Activity #2. A one-day Smart Start offsite meeting for senior management was conducted in July. A critical issues list was developed. Their regulatory rating code was a 3 (on a 1-to-4 scale, 4 being a takeover by the NCUA). A number-3 rating had resulted in a PCA ("Prompt Corrective Action"), an official letter, as they were failing and did not have a Game Plan to reverse the situation. The only reason the NCUA had not given them a 4 was their budding confidence in the new senior management team and the initial small progress that was being made. Senior management recognized the reality of the situation and was determined to persevere and succeed.

Activity #3. Systems Thinking was introduced during the offsite, as was the ABCs of Enterprise-Wide Change Model. It was agreed they were in a survival mode, yet they were in serious conflict with their board over their future direction. A new clarity of purpose and direction that both groups supported was needed.

In effect, a de-facto Program Management Office was set up with the CEO (due to the firm's survival situation) and one of the Systems Consultants, Inc., partners leading it. The CEO needed to devote almost full time to the needed transformation. The COO would run the day-to-day Phase I of this Enterprise-Wide Change process, viewed as *survival*. Another consultant and the VP of HR were designated as the change consultant cadre to assist the PMO.

At that time, it was decided NOT to involve the rest of the employees. This would only aggravate the situation. Nor was it time to introduce the employees to Systems Thinking. The KEY issue was board and senior management agreement to restructure and transform the credit union into an entity that had a chance to survive.

Activity #4. It was decided that a two-day retreat offsite with management and the board was required. The goals were

·   To both build the relationships and define the Clarity of Purpose and

·   To define and decide the actions to move toward profitability and a sustainable future

The Game Plan had to be jointly developed (*People support what they help create*). This approach was presented, reviewed, and agreed to by the board with the NCUA's help at a special board meeting in August.

To be continued . . . ◀

Chapter Four Recap

1. Three premises for successful Enterprise-Wide Change are

    • Planning and change management are the *primary* tasks of senior leadership today

    • People support what they help create

    • Use Systems Thinking to focus on outcomes and serve the customer

2. The four activities of the Smart Start sequence are

    • The initial offsite for the EWC Leadership Team to develop the first draft of the EWC Game Plan

    • A Parallel Involvement Process to test and critique the EWC Game Plan

    • A follow-up second offsite for the Change Leadership Team to finalize the Game Plan

    • A rollout of training on the principles of Systems Thinking, first to change leaders and then to all change implementers

3. The Iceberg Theory of Change is a reality of life. Honoring and balancing content, process, and structure is critical for successful Enterprise-Wide Change.

4. A two-day Smart Start process is an essential first step in Enterprise-Wide Change. It serves four key purposes:

    • Educate executives

    • Assess the organization

- Tailor the Enterprise-Wide Change Game Plan
- Organize the Enterprise-Wide Change Effort. Clarify roles of the players of change

5. A Yearly Map of Implementation is essential to guide each year-long complex set of tasks and processes.

6. You can move beyond content myopia by selecting from a menu of the infrastructures for change. Structure influences behavior.

7. Three absolutes for success include

- Regular meetings of the Enterprise-Wide Change Leadership Team
- A PMO to guide the day-to-day change efforts that build the future business
- Knowledge, skills, and capabilities in Systems Thinking as a new orientation to life

8. Develop a clear ideal future vision and a Game Plan for Enterprise-Wide Change by building a Smart Start (see Table 4.6) before beginning the actual changes.

Table 4.6. Smart Start Sample Tasks

Purpose #1: **Educate**	Educate change leaders about . . . · The goals and premises of change · Why change often fails · The Iceberg Theory of Change · The needed infrastructures and Rollercoaster of Change · Levels of maturity needed, and capabilities and readiness for change
Purpose #2: **Assess**	· Assess the organization's current performance vs. best practices · Clarify enterprise-wide organizational reality and gaps · Identify gaps in capabilities, competencies, and talent · Assess multi-year cultural change education needed by the collective leadership and management to successfully carry out EWC · Assess management and employee knowledge and skills regarding EWC best practices

Table 4.6. Smart Start Sample Tasks, Cont'd

Purpose #3: **Tailor**	• Clarify your vision of desired outcomes of the Enterprise-Wide Change Process
	• Develop core strategies and action plans/key initiatives
	• Create and tailor performance and rewards systems to reinforce the desired change
	• Create strategic marketing, sales, and product development plans
	• Create strategic HR plans
	• Build a single-page, yearly map of implementation
	• Set up one agenda—one-day meetings on key nuggets (chronic strategic or systemic change issues)
	• Decide how and when to tailor an overall Enterprise-Wide Change Game Plan (and list of desired major changes) from all the above
Purpose #4: **Organize**	• Organize the Enterprise-Wide Change effort
	• Organize the Change Leadership Team, a program management office,and needed systems consultants
	• Organize internal and external facilitators, subject-matter experts, and change consultants as a support team
	• Set up innovative project teams for major initiatives
	• Establish an employee development board for cultural attunement issues
	• Establish a key success measure tracking and reporting system

Enterprise-Wide Change Game Plan Template (Based on the Iceberg Theory of Change Framework)

Content

1. EWC vision (including both economic alignment and cultural attunement issues)

2. Any missing elements from your clarity of purpose (covered in Chapter Four, regarding Phases E, A, and B of the simplicity of systems thinking)

Infrastructures for Change

3. Main EWC infrastructures (including the PMO, change consultants, and the support cadre, plus the Change Leadership Team)

4. EWC substructures (such as an Employee Development Board, Rewards Team, Innovative Process/Project Teams, Technology Steering Committee, and so on)

5. Clear roles for the players of change (all four roles, plus personal leadership plans for all executives, and the Parallel Involvement Process with all employees)

Processes of Change

6. Leading, managing, and re-creating the change processes (including the Rollercoaster of Change's six stages, the waves and waves of change, and the HR/people processes to support them)

Competencies, Commitment, and Resources for Change

7. Change competencies (for executives, change consultants, and all employees, including Systems Thinking)

8. Commitment to the perseverance required (by the CEO, senior management, the board of directors, and change consultant cadre)

9. EWC resources (all types of resources needed are committed to and funded)

Yearly Map of Implementation for Change

10. The detailed map (including all Change Leadership Team meetings, the EWC annual strategic review [and update], and an EWC capacity review)

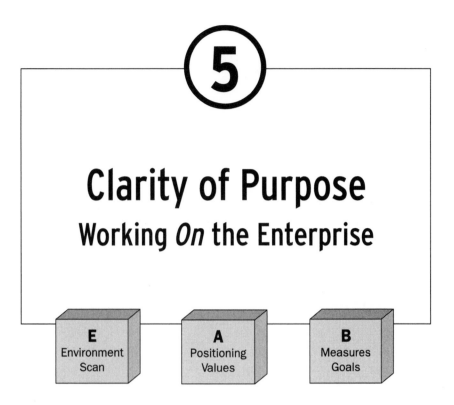

Chapter Purposes

- To provide a process for clarity of purpose for Enterprise-Wide Change through Systems Thinking (the *content* and desired outcomes)

- To clarify and simplify—clarify and simplify—clarify and simplify

- To examine four elements often lacking in Enterprise-Wide Change

  The Environmental Scan (Phase E)

  Outcomes: Positioning (Phase A)

  Outcomes: Core Values (Phase A)

  The Quadruple Bottom Line (Phase B)

The ABCs of Enterprise-Wide Change

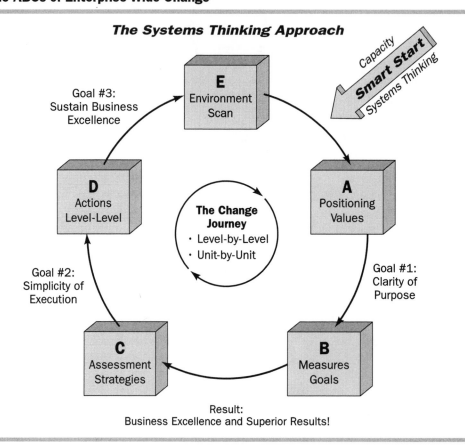

The Systems Thinking Approach

Result:
Business Excellence and Superior Results!

To chop a tree quickly, sharpen twice, cut once.

Chinese proverb

Chapter Context: Working *On* the Enterprise

Enterprise-Wide Change: An enterprise is a system—a complex network of inputs, processes, outputs, and feedback from suppliers, employees, and customers.

Management therefore needs a set of concepts and tools for wiring and aligning those components together, with the integrity needed for improving quality and service, reducing time and costs, and implementing strategies.

Goal #1, the "clarity of purpose" in this chapter, is the visible part of the iceberg—the content of the desired outcomes from an Enterprise-Wide Change process.

In this chapter we focus on four elements of the *content* and desired outcomes from the Enterprise-Wide Change process—the visible part of the Iceberg Theory of Change—with the goals of constant growth, business excellence, and superior results. These elements are often missing, leading to a confused, chaotic, unclear change effort.

Our "helicopter view" means working *on* the enterprise first, before working *in* it. Working on the enterprise means clarity on four key elements, which are often missing:

- Element #1: Environmental Scanning
- Element #2: Vision and Positioning
- Element #3: Core Values
- Element #4: Measures and Goals

If you already have these elements (and we hope you do), this chapter may be just reinforcement.

The future exists: First, in the imagination, then in the will, then in reality.
Robert Anton Wilson, Prometheus Rising

What's changing in the environment that could affect us?

Missing Element #1: Phase E
The Helicopter View: An Environmental Scanning System

Scanning the environment and creating organizational strategy as a context for daily strategic thinking is *the most important thing* a leader can do.

Scanning the global environment and making future projections of several variables at once makes it possible to see how they might impact your organization and change effort. Some examples of questions to ask include

- Will shifting or emerging country markets, international affairs, monetary movements, or government interventions drive sales up or down?
- How might they impact advertising and sales?
- How are the demographics of Generations X and Y impacting your enterprise?
- If the dollar is cheaper in China, what does that mean for your product in North America?
- If the world population is aging and they have more money, how will this change buying patterns for your products?
- How are new world trade agreements affecting your business?
- As the world is globally interconnected, how does the variable of speed impact demand, volume of work, and distribution?

The challenge for executives is learning how to become savvy about the global environment.

Environmental scanning is a standard tool that has been employed in establishing strategic direction and complex change efforts for some time. However, Systems Thinking has two differentiations.

1. The environment to be scanned is not today, but the future timeframe extended out to the end of the Enterprise-Wide Change horizon. The idea is to become a futurist and try to understand and predict, as much as possible, what the future holds for your enterprise at least three years from now.

   Contrast this approach with the standard SWOT technique, which looks at opportunities and threats in the environment as they exist today. This SWOT technique is important to use each year as a part of the planning, change, and updating processes, but it is fundamentally different from a detailed, future-oriented environmental scan.

2. Environmental scanning can no longer be conducted once a year as part of a planning or strategic change process. We recommend performing an environmental scan at least quarterly as part of a leadership team meeting that

guides Enterprise-Wide Change. The world is changing too fast to only look at it once a year.

When the rate of change outside exceeds the rate of change inside, you are in serious trouble.

In the Systems Thinking Approach, we employ the SKEPTIC acronym to guide a comprehensive environmental scanning process. Table 5.1 shows how this approach can serve as the content framework and *grounding* for the EWC process.

Table 5.1. Environmental Scanning SKEPTIC

	Variable	Watch for Changes in . . .
S	**Socio-Demographics**	Health, skills, mobility of labor force, infrastructure, level of literacy, population growth, age and cultural diversity, migration of workers, aging workforce
K	**(K) Competition**	Reputation, pricing strategy, core competencies/capabilities, product or service positioning, market share, niches
E	**Economics**	Inflation, standard of living, availability of resources, capital flows, taxation, business confidence, GNP/GDP, productivity, international finances
	Ecology (2nd E)	Adverse weather, pollution, natural disasters, ozone layer impact, regulations, business opportunities, and discovery of natural resources
P	**Politics**	Regulatory issues, tax climate, distribution of wealth, corruption, strength of political institutions, quality and direction of leadership, wars, trade laws, common markets
T	**Technology**	Technical systems, wireless applications, telecommunications, satellites, biotech, new materials, and enterprise-wide resource planning systems
I	**Industry**	Size, profitability, mergers and acquisitions, substitutes, forces of competition, numbers of players, recent entrants, taxation, state of industry lifecycle
C	**Customer**	Values, needs, demographics, wants, expectations, perceptions, experience, and demands.

It is best to assign a team to each letter. It also helps if a senior management member sponsors each team, using the natural roles the various functional executives play; for example, S (socio-demographics) sponsored by the VP of human resources, E (economics) by the CFO, and so forth.

Build each team by asking for volunteers. Middle managers are a crucial part of successful environmental scanning, but they should volunteer based on their expertise and interests (it is a great developmental tool as well).

The key point to remember in conducting this future environmental scan is to be able to understand the potential impact of these changes on your business. Will they be helpful? Will they create a problem for you? Is the impact neutral?

Change consultants can assist the organization in setting up an environmental scanning process by doing the following:

1. Identify the environmental scanning framework (SKEPTIC).

2. Form teams around each SKEPTIC letter and assign scanning tasks to each team.

3. Identify people who will participate in the environmental scanning process (not just members of the senior management team).

4. Help the team generate a list of information sources (trade shows, publications, technical meetings, customers, and the Internet).

5. Have teams collect data on a regular basis.

6. Disseminate information in a large EWC group meeting on a quarterly basis.

Questions to Ponder

- What sources might you scan to get a better view of the changing environment?

- A longer-term view—five years or more?

- A medium-term view—one to three years?

- What Internet sources are best for your industry or business sector? (Government is a business too.)

Where do we want our positioning in the marketplace to be?

Missing Element #2: Phase A
Backwards Thinking from Your Positioning

You may have heard marketing gurus use the word *positioning*. It is usually used with respect to positioning the organization or strategic positioning or your *value proposition*.

Positioning, simply put, is the act of carving out a unique and better reputation in the marketplace, in the eyes of the customer, that sets you apart from the competition and that motivates customers to do business with you.

It is also called the driving force, strategic thrust, grand strategy, strategic intent, reputation, image, *Strategy* [capital S], brand, competitive edge or advantage, customer value, provider of choice, or providing value. The proliferation of words is a problem because executives and change consultants often don't share a common language to discuss the issue. We prefer the term *positioning* because it is the most common, and most descriptive, in the field.

"What's your positioning?" is the final "Who Wants to Be a Millionaire?" question for an enterprise. Finding the answer is far more difficult, and the potential payoff, in economic consequences, is far greater than a million dollars. Unfortunately, there are many different options for the right answer for each organization.

Positioning is also the single most important guidepost for an enterprise's vision, strategic direction, and Enterprise-Wide Change. It is the one decision around which your organization should be uncompromising in building everything else to support it.

Positioning is the essence of your vision. Vision is your view and image of an "ideal future." It is aspirational and idealistic, a guiding star with dreamlike qualities. A *shared vision* is a prerequisite to successful Enterprise-Wide Change.

Positioning is also called "the mother of all core strategies," as it defines "how we are driven" as an organization.

Clear and unique positioning

- Is the central issue to which all other functions, directions, decisions, and criteria must be subordinated

- Is your organization's core (or distinctive) competency—the thing that makes an enterprise unique and better than all the competition
- Will sustain a competitive edge over a period of years
- Cannot be easily duplicated
- Is either a current reality, or can become a reality within the period of time for which the EWC is planned

Consumers, Costs, and Positioning

Thanks in part to the Internet, consumers today are more demanding, more aware of products and services available, and more able and willing to compare products and prices. Product and service loyalty is at an all-time low. Fierce price competition is becoming the norm as once high-end products and services become increasingly perceived as commodities.

You lower your price and I'll do the same. What kind of positioning is that? Who wins?

No one in the industry wins—just the customer.

In *The Discipline of Market Leaders*, Michael Treacy and Fred Wiersema (1997) discuss how yesterday's stars often turn into today's has-beens. Praiseworthy companies fall into decline if they fail to maintain their positioning. They let it erode, day after day. Remember when GM had 50 percent market share? 40 percent share? 30 percent share? What is it today?

➤ THINK DIFFERENTLY

The U.S. auto industry is in danger of killing itself with large cash-back offers such as zero-percent financing for three to four years.

The message to the consumer is clear—*never* buy a car, truck, or SUV unless there's a drastic sale in progress. If no sale is going on, just wait; there will be another. Buy then.

While consumers love this, much lower profits for the auto industry have resulted.

You can imagine other automakers muttering, "Thanks, GM and Ford."

Commoditization is happening to AT&T, Westinghouse, American Express, and Kodak. Having attained positions of market leadership with strong positioning, some firms have succumbed to the temptation to celebrate victory, admire their operating model from within, and rest on their laurels.

These companies violate a central rule of market leadership: Successful enterprises dominate their markets by improving their positioning, year after year. Competitors are working to knock off the leader and claim the top of the hill for themselves.

To stay ahead, you must dedicate your full energies to continuously creating major improvements in positioning. Otherwise, it is impossible to retain a lead.

Sustaining market leadership is a full-time Enterprise-Wide Change effort.

How to Raise Your "Strategic IQ" by 50 Points

In our practice, we have experienced up to 50 percent of all senior executives in our Enterprise-Wide Change efforts not understanding and/or developing a strong, unique positioning. Without it, daily Strategic Thinking is much more difficult, if not impossible.

Clarifying and committing to one unique position across an entire enterprise effectively demands a master's degree level of understanding in Strategic Thinking. Senior management who try to be all things to all people don't focus clearly on this concept.

Positioning is difficult. It involves difficult tradeoffs and choices. It requires investing fully in where to focus and build your reputation. It is a conflict-ridden process that requires the best *advocacy, inquiry, and facilitation* skills of all involved.

Being clear on your organization's positioning is like raising your Strategic IQ by 50 points.

Positioning Specifics: Five Unique Factors

In researching this topic, we have found five key factors that consumers look at when they buy. We interpreted and translated this research into a visual representation as a five-point star, shown in Figure 5.1, to make it easier to remember.

The five core potential positioning factors are

- Responsiveness/convenience
- High quality
- Caring customer service
- Personal choice
- Total cost

Organizations need to decide how they want to position themselves to deliver to these customer wants. In how many of these factors should an organization try to excel? A successful enterprise can't be all things to all people. According to our research, an organization should try to excel in only *one* of the five factors.

It's difficult to achieve even one singular and unique position over *all* competition. An organization will fail to develop even that singular advantage if it seeks too many positions.

Does this mean that an organization does not have to compete on the other four factors? The answer is *emphatically no*—even with the best possible quality, for example, an enterprise won't be competitive if its customer service is shoddy, its responsiveness is nil, and its cost is outrageous. Successful positioning simply draws consumers' attention to how the enterprise *excels* in one of the five factors. Successful companies must also be competitive in the other four points on the star, or they will find themselves at a competitive *disadvantage*.

Figure 5.1. World-Class Positioning

Your Competitive Business Edge—Creating Customer Value

C = Personal Choice
Fashion, Control, Self, Customized,
Tailored, Variety, Individuality,
My/Me, Comprehensive Choices,
Mass Customization

R = Responsiveness
Past Delivery, Convenience,
Methods, Timing, Distribution,
Flexibility, Access,
Ease of Doing Business,
Support Services, Cooperation

S = Caring Service
Personal Service, Values,
Feeling Important,
Customer Relationships,
Respect, Caring, Emotions,
Recovery Strategy, Integrity,
Empathy, Sensitivity, Familiar,
Trust, Cultural

Customer   Service

Creating Customer Value

T = Total Cost
Psychological Cost, Price,
Life Cycle, Risk,
Opportunity Costs,
Waste/Environment,
Working Conditions,
Product/Services Cost

Q = High Quality
(Products and Services)
Features, Authenticity, Simplicity,
Information, Technology, Accuracy,
Knowledge, Performance, Reliability,
Functional, Durability, Uses,
Consistency, Stability, Soundness,
Unique, Experiences, Innovative

Positioning Factor #1: Responsiveness/Convenience

Today's busy consumers almost always appreciate anything that makes life or work easier and faster. Thus convenience almost always improves an organization's competitive edge in the eyes of its customers.

For example, Wells Fargo Bank has increased its responsiveness in California by setting up branches and ATMs inside grocery stores, making them more convenient and safe for customers.

Positioning Factor #2: High quality

High quality is also a great way to achieve customer loyalty. For example, Eagle Creek Travel Gear, Inc., is known for the quality and durability of its products (outdoor luggage, backpacks, and accessories).

Positioning Factor #3: Caring customer service

Good customer service is the third factor. Nordstrom Department Stores are widely known for service. So are the Ritz Carlton Hotels.

Positioning Factor #4: Personal choice

Sometimes, customers like a lot of choices. Dell Computers is known for the variety of choices offered to the consumer in terms of their computer needs. So is the Container Store.

Positioning Factor #5: Total cost

This factor is different. Total cost is what consumers must *give* to get their desired products or services. Based on more than just what a consumer pays for a given product or service, total cost also includes the negative psychological side to service, reputation, the product's life cycle, production waste, and working conditions, as perceived by the customer.

In sum, cost is always an issue. Cost is not value. Value concerns the ratio: *what do I get for what I give* (outputs/inputs). Only those firms that can build a lower cost structure than their competitors can dominate here. For example, Costco's bulk volume purchases and sales warehouse means lower operating costs.

Use the five-point star factors to determine what positioning means to your organization. The details under these five factors will be different for each industry and firm.

Questions to Ponder

- Which positioning factor does Blockbuster Video share with Office Depot?

- In which of the five positioning factors do Hertz and Marriott Hotels distinguish themselves?

- What do Southwest Airlines and Wal-Mart have in common regarding positioning?

- As change consultants and senior executives, do we understand the concept of positioning? Do we also know and understand the stories of the above firms and others like them? Do we read (or at least browse) *Business Week, The Economist, Harvard Business Review, Red Herring,* and *Fast Company*? Clients and competitors do.

- As change consultants and senior executives, do we have the clarity of purpose and courage to make the difficult tradeoffs and choices? Not choosing is a choice in and of itself—a choice *not* to have clear positioning.

▶ THINK DIFFERENTLY

Some answers to the questions above:

- ⊃ Choice, or selection, is what Blockbuster and Office Depot pride themselves on. Each of these companies is committed to deliver more choices in the marketplace. Each has positioned itself to sustain its lead in dominating its specific market.

- ⊃ If you guessed customer service, you're right about Marriott and Hertz. Compared to their competitors, their prices, quality, and choices are competitive. Service is why they stand out.

- ⊃ Southwest Airlines and Wal-Mart have built a competitive edge when it comes to price/cost. Why is this successful, since we said there is a danger in focusing on costs alone? Do you understand exactly what factors provide companies with a lower cost structure and way of doing business that their competitors cannot duplicate?

⊃ Southwest has unique ways of doing business that make it almost impossible for competitors to match them on price/cost without losing money—among them, their strategic decision to fly only one type of aircraft, the 737. This simplifies their business and streamlines their aircraft maintenance and training costs.

⊃ Wal-Mart's inventory is a *profit center,* not a 70-day inventory cost (like cars at GM).

Do you know these stories well? Can you discuss them? Your competitors in India and elsewhere can and do.

Positioning Pitfalls

Executives and change consultants sometimes are confused about the specifics for finding one's ideal positioning. They

- Don't know the difference between *positioning* and *value*
- Find the definition of the *customer* versus the *stakeholder* unclear
- Don't know about the five-star model options and concepts available to them to achieve their positioning
- Are unrealistic in their expectations of positioning, wanting to excel equally in all five areas
- Don't understand that just being competitive in the marketplace on the other four star points is fine
- Forget that lowest cost is not necessarily *value* in the eyes of the consumer—and can usually be quickly matched by the competitor, unless their cost structure is different
- Don't know their own positioning and are unrealistically positive when comparing themselves to the competition
- Have little customer information (feedback) on the effectiveness of their positioning
- Confuse positioning with *what we do well.* Positioning requires being *better than or unique* from the competition in the eyes of the customer

Questions to Ponder

- What is your organization's positioning? Is it really better relative to the competition?

- Where are you on cost factors? How much do you use it to sell something?

- Are you competitive on all five factors of the star model? Do your customers want them all?

- What does *high quality* stand for in your organization? Is it about product quality or high-quality customer service or quality of experience?

What do we want our core values and culture to be?

Missing Element #3: Phase A
Core Values Revisited: More Essential Than Ever

Core values is a familiar concept to most progressive executives as well as change and OD consultants. (See Hultman, 2001, for a full treatment of this key subject.)

As we saw earlier, a primary focus either on *economic alignment* or on *cultural attunement* leads to failure in Enterprise-Wide Change. Selection and institutionalization of the right core values are crucial to 21st Century success. Research shows that the most successful enterprises have *strong* core values that are articulated and shared throughout the organization. They lead to business excellence and superior results, time after time (Collins & Porras, 1997).

Today, most enterprises are at least partly service organizations depending on their people to satisfy each customer. Thus, the cultural attunement of people's hearts and minds has finally been recognized as crucial to strategic success. Core values are the *social glue* that holds an organization together. People generally want to believe they are working and being treated honorably. It is as important to them as money. Most organizations do not derive honor and integrity directly from their products and services, so the best way to achieve it is by building and sustaining organizational values and the culture that results.

For change consultants who focus primarily on *economic alignment of delivery,* adding core values and *cultural attunement* to their tool kits is especially crucial. Failing to understand and embrace the importance of attunement, in fact, is part of the number-one failure in Enterprise-Wide Change, namely a mechanistic, fragmented, analytic view of a systems problem.

There doesn't seem to be only one set of correct core values for an organization. The Systems Thinking Approach integrates with positioning and strategic direction. In fact, the term *guiding principles* is often used instead of *core values,* which are seen as more personal rather than organizational in nature. These principles should guide the behavior of all employees in the enterprise, reflecting a mix of both the economic alignment and cultural attunement schools of thought. Too often, they are not.

➡ THINK DIFFERENTLY

One of our current clients in the electronics industry in California was updating their EWC Game Plan.

When they reexamined their core values, they discovered that they had no core value regarding performance and accountability. It was a key part of the CEO's values and how they were running the enterprise anyway, so they rectified the situation and added it as a core value.

Without this addition, their core values may have sounded nice, but they were disconnected from their senior leader's values.

In summary, keep in mind these two key points:

First, core values are often developed in large group consensus processes with a typical yet unintended result—a wonderful exercise that may miss the consensus and buy-in of senior management as to how they actually run the business. Without this buy-in, these core values (guiding principles) are just a piece of paper to be used at new-hire orientation—and rarely elsewhere.

Second, some core values (guiding principles) are more effective than others in dealing with our complex and chaotic world. A list of what we personally believe are guiding principles important to enterprise success in the 21st Century is in Table 5.2.

What is on your list?

Table 5.2. Suggested Core Values

Learning and Knowledge Transfer	Holistic and Systemic Orientation
Creativity and Innovation	Flexibility and Adaptability
Relationships and Connectedness	Openness, Sharing, Feedback, and Communications
Courage and Integrity	Accountability and Responsibility
Teamwork and Collaboration	Customer and Service Orientation
Speed and Responsiveness	Parallel Involvement Process and Communications

See the Chapter Recap for a checklist on assessing core values and uses throughout your organization.

How will we measure our vision and goals?

Missing Element #4: Phase B

Key Success Measures

Metrics is a buzzword in the public sector, while in the private sector, we often hear about "The Balanced Scorecard." Understanding measures is easy. Developing them is difficult.

To develop useful organizational metrics, you first need to define your positioning. Once you've defined that, the way to know whether you're reaching your goals is through measurement. That's where key success measures (or measurable goals)—Phase B in the Systems Thinking Model—come in.

Measuring is the first step that leads to control and eventually to improvement. If you can't measure something, you can't understand it. If you can't understand it, you can't control it. If you can't control it, you can't improve it.

This missing fourth element in our view creates three problems of measurement.

The First Problem of Measurement: Metrics

Metrics is a multi-faceted concept, and it is not necessarily the same as *goals* or *key success measures*. We tend to measure what's easy to measure, not what is important.

Many organizations have *comprehensive* activity measures, not *key* success measures. They don't seem to differentiate between *means* (activities) (Phase D) and *ends* (results) (Phase A). Measuring activities (such as how many people attended training) is easy; measuring the *results* of training is much more difficult.

We recommend that organizations focus on only five or six (maximum) overall measurable goals or metrics. Focusing on the outcome success measures requires clarification of your terminology (see Table 5.3) of *means measures* versus *ends measures* that are key in Systems Thinking.

Table 5.3. Clarifying Measurement Terminology

Is It Means (Phase D)?	or	Ends (Phase A)?
Metrics	or	Key Success Measures
Activities	or	Results
How to	or	What
Strategies	or	Measurable Goals
Actions/Tasks	or	Purpose/Vision
Initiatives	or	Positioning
Behaviors (Values in Action)	or	Culture
Linear Thinking	or	Backwards Thinking

It's imperative to take time up-front to develop measurable goals/key success measures/ends (the terms are interchangeable) that senior management wants for the entire organization. In the absence of clearly defined ends, we are forced to concentrate on activities and efforts, but we ultimately become enslaved by them.

In other words, if we have not established quantifiable key success measures/goals for our positioning, how will we know we've achieved it?

The Second Problem of Measurement: Financial Viability Is Necessary, but Not Sufficient

Organizations traditionally tend to focus their measurements on concrete financial areas. This ultimately limits, however, their ability to *grow* and shape the organization in a sustained and balanced way.

We've all seen or experienced organizations that measure success strictly by budgets and ROI forecasts. It's easier to measure the financial side of things than the people or customer side.

What invariably happens in these organizations is that the finance department becomes the driving force of the company. Customers, products, services, and employees are often forgotten in the organization's success equation.

 THINK DIFFERENTLY

A regional, integrated energy company located in the western U.S. merged with an exploration and production company and went public. They began to concentrate on the financial end of their corporate activities. The upshot was that their high-quality customer service—which had been their original positioning and most important measure—lost its importance.

Through Enterprise-Wide Change, the company developed a set of measurement areas to rebalance it:

⊃ Customer service

⊃ Shareholder value

⊃ Strategic/opportunistic growth

⊃ Stable supply of raw materials

⊃ Employee satisfaction/ethical behavior

⊃ Safety

This energy company now employs all these measures to encourage continual focus on their overall customer service vision, rather than on economics alone.

The end result, even during the first year of implementation of their EWC, was a dramatic increase in stock price, along with a high level of favorable press and customer satisfaction.

Although being financially viable prevents failure, it does not guarantee success. Success is driven by how well you serve and keep customers. The most important metric to measure is the status of your positioning.

The Third Problem of Measurement: The Quadruple Bottom Line

Measurement needs to somehow encompass a holistic balance of desired outcomes. We call this the "Quadruple Bottom Line."

We recommend that organizations planning their EWC journey define their Key Success Measures up-front, in four broad categories, to fully define and measure success.

Key Success (Outcome) Measurement Areas

1. Customer satisfaction (with products, services, and your overall *positioning*)
2. Employee satisfaction (with core values)
3. Shareholder/owner satisfaction (with financials)
4. Contributions to society and community with stakeholders' feedback

By looking at all four of these bottom lines, organizations can fully see, track, and understand their successes, failures, and long-term sustainability in a world of dynamic change. Keep in mind that identifying, developing, and sustaining your positioning in the marketplace is THE most important multi-million-dollar question. Without customers, the other measures and, in fact, your whole enterprise won't exist. *Do you measure customer satisfaction regularly?*

In addition to the Quadruple Bottom Line outcome measure of success, we recommend you also focus on a fifth measure—*key operational indicators (how to's)*—the difference between theory and practice. In real-world enterprises, most senior executives know two or three key operational indicators that are leading indicators to the Quadruple Bottom Line results they want. In addition, some key success measures are not easily quantified, so the one to three *key operational indicators* help keep a daily focus on the key outcomes of superior results.

 THINK DIFFERENTLY

Southwest Airlines knows that the percentage of airplane seat occupancy is a key operational variable that leads to profits and losses. By the same token, Best Western Hotels knows that the daily census is the key operational variable (the percentage of occupancy of their hotel rooms).

It is important to be creative about translating these results into specific and quantifiable measures on which each of these Quadruple Bottom Line categories focuses. Key success measures, not comprehensive activity metrics, is the difference.

⟩ THINK DIFFERENTLY

⊃ A large California credit union developed an entire EWC process called M1C (Members 1st Commitment). In two years, their positioning and reputation have been greatly enhanced by this total enterprise-wide focus on members first. All departments have yearly change work plans on what they can do to ensure this outcome.

⊃ Marriott Corporation has its corporate managers become mystery diners at their restaurants. This creates feedback on their services from the customer's perspective (plus free meals as an employee benefit).

⊃ FedEx uses its on-time delivery for overnight, two-day, and three-day deliveries, as well as 10:30 a.m. delivery guarantees. It is their way to respond to customers and achieve desired marketplace positioning.

⊃ A credit union in the San Jose, California, area gives employees time off to work in the community. They measure their influence in the community by the number of employees in leadership positions in community organizations.

⊃ Some large corporations have annual *corporate social responsibility* reports, including General Electric, Exxon, IBM, Royal Dutch Shell, BC Hydro, and Unilever.

It's important to focus on a small number of the most important *success* areas. The best measures for all enterprises are the ones that can be stated in simple, clear language. Having more than five measures tends to confuse matters and takes the leadership team's eye off the ball. Therefore, a good question to start with when evaluating possible measures is: "Is the proposed measure a key result for the organization's EWC?"

In the private sector, the most common tendency is to commit to only financial goals. The result is that organizations forget about positioning, experience confusion, ignore people and customer issues, and lack a clear sense of purpose. The narrow, financial-only view of the world is an analytic approach to a systems problem and one of the "big three" failures in EWC.

The public sector, unfortunately, is even more vulnerable to missing the bigger picture. Because the public sector often does not focus on the customer and other outcome measures, they can become slaves to activities and budgets. *Metrics in the public sector often is shorthand for measuring comprehensive activities,* rather than focusing on key success measures/goals.

 THINK DIFFERENTLY

Although a large California school system did a great job in developing ownership and commitment to their Enterprise-Wide Changes, they never reached consensus on a set of key success measures. As a result of internal problems with their board of education, the superintendent resigned. His replacement lasted little more than a year, symbolizing how they failed to establish and use a set of clear, agreed-on success measures.

Questions to Ponder

- What are your outcome measures of success? How many do you have?
- Do you limit yourself to financial measures alone?
- What else should be included as your success measures?

 THINK DIFFERENTLY

Typical results from seriously and successfully executing an Enterprise-Wide Change process over a multi-year timeframe has shown the following from internal client working papers of our Centre for Strategic Management:

Employee Satisfaction

- Cross-functional teamwork and cooperation greatly improved
- Cross-functional conflict much lower

◯ Core values—culture modified and employee satisfaction improved over time—less turnover

◯ Accountability—clear and higher performance

Key Operational Indicators

◯ Chronic issues—two to three identified, broken down, solutions developed, and results achieved

◯ Technology infused into the organization—all-pervasive

◯ Three-year business plans developed and successfully executed for business units and major support functions (HR/Marketing/IT)

Customer Satisfaction

◯ Organization-wide focus—much more "customer driven"

◯ Customer satisfaction ratings tracked and measured with significantly increased satisfaction

Financial Return

◯ Revenue growth: double in size over five years (14 percent/year compounded)

◯ Profits grow 10 percent per year routinely

Community and Society

◯ More focused involvement and increased employee participation

◯ More visibility and return to client's brand image

Summary: Clarity of Purpose

Defining these four missing elements requires a clear process in EWC. Be sure to work *on* your enterprise before working *in* it. We recommend the activities in Table 5.4 if you have not already established them.

Table 5.4. Process to Establish Four Missing Elements

Activity #1	A two-day retreat by the Enterprise-Wide Change Leadership Team to provide clarity of purpose
	The topics to develop include all four missing elements as needed:
	#1: **Phase E**—Get the Helicopter View: An Environmental Scanning System
	#2: **Phase A**—Use Backwards Thinking: Positioning in the Marketplace
	#3: **Phase A**—Core Values Revisited: More Essential Than Ever
	#4: **Phase B**—Key Success Measures: The Quadruple Bottom Line
Activity #2	One-Day Large Group Parallel Involvement Process with All Possible Key Stakeholders to Review, Critique, and Add to the Clarity of Purpose
Activity #3	A Second Enterprise-Wide Change Leadership Team Offsite to Review Feedback and Finalize the Elements and Your Clarity of Purpose
Activity #4	A Parallel Involvement Process for the Key Stakeholders to Share the final Clarity of Purpose and Obtain Their Commitment and Buy-In

▶ COMPREHENSIVE CASE STUDY

East Coast Federal Credit Union Enterprise-Wide Change: Part 2

Activity #1. While *Phase I Survival* and day-to-day problem solving were going on, the board-management retreat was scheduled. It was to be in a different city so the necessary conflict and focus could be confronted and resolved, and a direction established. It was not held until October, reflecting the lack of urgency of the board, as they still wanted the strategic planning session to be a two-hour meeting, not a focused and facilitated two-day retreat.

Management's goal was a *Phase II Transformation.* The next steps were to gain agreement and kick off an Enterprise-Wide Change process. It would first get them out of their survival mode, and then give them a chance for future success as a viable entity.

Activity #2. In preparation for the retreat, the consultants met with management in September and shared more on the *enterprise as a system* concept. As a result, they developed an internal Current State Assessment in advance of the retreat. Further, the CFO, with the help of the others, developed a complete economic set of historical and current documents he called *Reality Documents,* to ensure the survival issue was clear to the board.

Activity #3. The retreat was held in October. The consultants facilitated an agenda, including the EWC ABCs Systems Model, the critical issues, and roles of the different players of change. At the same time, they wove in and honored the history and growth of the credit union, which was extremely important to the board.

A future environmental scan (Missing Element #1) was also conducted at the retreat. A surprising consensus emerged on the future vision. It was decided that long-term success must focus on only their home state (despite three branches in other states). This turned out to be the trump card in the entire process with the board.

Despite the conflict and disagreements, the planning retreat ended with an initial vision and Game Plan, a consensus action plan, and an overt acknowledgment, including five points of agreement on the ominous reality. The board recognized that their unprofitability and lack of clear positioning (Missing Element #2) would not change for the next nine months—until July of the second year.

As a result, the board decided to reconsider their positioning in July only IF the main *consensus action plans* of ten key decisions was implemented. If accomplished, these ten key decisions held out the distinct possibility to actually transform the credit union into a new entity.

The board reluctantly agreed to a set of measurable financial goals (Missing Element #4) as imposed by the NCUA—in July of year two they must be profitable and have a positive trend. This was necessary to keep the NCUA supportive of the credit union's effort, even though they did not yet know how to do so. This list also included a management action to work with the employees to develop a set of core values (Missing Element #3).

They agreed to meet and finalize all this in a December board meeting.

To be continued . . . ◀

Chapter Five Recap

1. Enterprise-Wide Change requires working *on* the enterprise and taking a helicopter view *before* working *in* the organization.

2. Clarity of purpose is the first job of Enterprise-Wide Change—clarifying four elements that might be missing (environmental scanning, positioning, values, and success measures).

3. Environmental scanning is not new, but within the SKEPTIC framework, a future focus, involvement of many employees, and increased frequency of scanning are new (Phase E).

Note: *If these four* elements *are already established in your organization and* not *missing, then this chapter has been a refresher/reinforcement.*

---

4. The first requirement for EWC success is clear positioning that is unique, different, and better than the competition in the eyes of the customer (Phase A).

5. Change consultants have long recognized the importance of core values and culture in the OD field. Values are more important than ever to achieving an organization's positioning, business excellence, and superior results year after year (Phase A).

6. Two major failures made in many Enterprise-Wide Change efforts were listed in Chapter One: (1) focusing mainly on the *economic alignment* of delivery or (2) focusing mainly on *cultural attunement* and involvement with people. The Quadruple Bottom Line measurements of key success measures/goals prevent each type of failure by ensuring that both are regularly monitored and measured (Phase B).

7. Four key success measurement categories that assess both economic alignment and cultural attunement results are

   - Customer Satisfaction
   - Employee Satisfaction

- Financial Satisfaction

- Contribution to Society

8. You can increase your strategic IQ by 50 points in Enterprise-Wide Change by keeping strategic thinking focused on your positioning and its watertight integrity.

9. There are four main activities in clarity of purpose:

   - *Activity #1:* Two-day retreat by the Change Leadership Team to develop clarity of purpose

   - *Activity #2:* One-day large group key stakeholder Parallel Involvement Process

   - *Activity #3:* A second Change Leadership Team offsite to finalize the clarity of purpose

   - *Activity #4:* A Parallel Involvement Process for the key stakeholders to share the final clarity of purpose and ask for the buy-in commitment to the desired results

ATTUNEMENT WITH PEOPLE'S HEARTS AND MINDS: CORE VALUES ASSESSMENT

The following are typical categories where core values should appear and be reinforced within an organization. Where else should they appear and be reinforced in your organization? Make notes on the sheet.

1. **Strategic Plan (Phase A)**

   - Explicit corporate philosophy/values statement—visuals on walls; in rooms

2. **Feedback (Phase B)**

   - Using this analysis assessment tool

   - Employee survey

   - 360-degree feedback

3. **Links to Strategies (Phase C)**

   - Annual departmental plans

   - Performance evaluation; appraisal forms (assess values adherence); team rewards

Alignment of Delivery Processes (Phase D)

4. **Operational Tasks/Processes**

   - Corporate and product advertising

   - New customers and suppliers vs. current customer and supplier treatment and focus (vs. values)

   - Operational processes resulting in quality and service

5. **Structure**

   - Dealing with difficult times/issues (layoffs, reorganizations)

   - Organization and job design questions

6. **Resources/Technology/Communications**

   - Internal communication (vehicles/publications)

   - Press releases, external publications/brochures

   - Image nationwide (as seen by others)

   - Resource allocation decisions

(Continued)

ATTUNEMENT WITH PEOPLE'S HEARTS AND MINDS: CORE VALUES ASSESSMENT, Cont'd

Attunement of People's Hearts and Minds (Phase D)

7. Leadership

- Flow of orientation and assimilation versus sign-up

- Job aids/descriptions

- New executive start-up

- To whom and how promotions occur (values consequence assessed); criteria

- Executive leadership ("walk the talk"); ethical decisions; how we manage

8. HR Processes and Practices

- Recruiting handbook; selection criteria

- How applicants are treated (vs. values)

- How "rewards for performance" operates (vs. values), especially non-financial rewards

- Role of training; training programs (vs. values)

- Policies and procedures (HR, finance, administration); day-to-day decisions

9. Teams

- Cross-departmental events, flows, task forces/teams

Strategic Change Management Process (Phase D)

10. Macro

- Managing change (according to values)

- Stakeholder relationships (vs. values)

Assessing the Enterprise as a Living System

C
Enterprise
Assessment

Where are we now?

Chapter Purposes

- To learn how to use a new, best practices Enterprise-Wide Assessment framework to successfully assess and guide the enterprise as a totally integrated living system.

- To avoid the Big Three Failure Issues described in this chapter (no more piecemeal approaches to Enterprise-Wide Assessment!).

The organization is a complex living system. How can we understand its fundamental simplicity instead of its daily complexity?

The ABCs of Enterprise-Wide Change

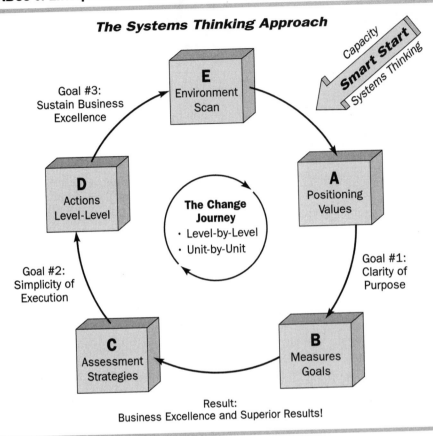

The Systems Thinking Approach

Goal #3:
Sustain Business
Excellence

E
Environment
Scan

Capacity
Smart Start
Systems Thinking

D
Actions
Level-Level

**The Change
Journey**
· Level-by-Level
· Unit-by-Unit

A
Positioning
Values

Goal #1:
Clarity of
Purpose

Goal #2:
Simplicity of
Execution

C
Assessment
Strategies

B
Measures
Goals

Result:
Business Excellence and Superior Results!

Chapter Context

C
Enterprise
Assessment

Current state assessment or organizational assessment is a time-honored way to begin any change efforts. There are two methods familiar to readers of this book:

1. *SWOT Assessment:* CEOs and senior management are used to conducting this assessment (strengths, weaknesses, opportunities, threats) as a way to begin strategic planning, business planning, annual planning, and change efforts.

2. *Action Research:* This practice is one of the basic foundations of OD and change consulting. Many consultants start the process by assessing where

the organization is today. They do a diagnosis and assessment, known as Action Research.

While these two approaches may at first seem like common sense, they are not Systems Thinking. Steven Covey's well-known quote, "Begin with the end in mind," embodies Systems Thinking.

That is why we first introduce Assessing the Enterprise at this point. *SWOT* and *Action Research* are still crucial to the change efforts, but they should not be the *first* steps.

In addition, the way these two approaches are often practiced is not comprehensive or systemic/holistic in nature. They are either a broad-brush SWOT or a specific set of action research steps focused on a specific change intervention. We therefore advocate a third alternative, an Enterprise-Wide Assessment.

This chapter introduces a new, best practices *Enterprise-Wide Assessment* framework to more thoroughly assess and guide your change journey and create an integrated whole. This framework is specifically designed to increase the probability of success. It is also specifically designed to eliminate each of the big three causes of failure originally presented in Chapter One.

1. An analytical, *piecemeal approach* involving multiple mindsets, holistic frameworks, consultants, and fads/silver bullets instead of a single mindset based on an organization as a living system

2. An *either/or mindset* mainly focusing on the *economic alignment of delivery* with primary focus on productivity, processes, and bottom-line economics instead of a combined approach with cultural attunement issues

3. A focus mainly on the *cultural attunement with people* with *primary focus on egalitarian, participative, people processes* instead of one combined approach with economic alignment issues

Some Mental Maps for Assessing Enterprises as Living Systems

This is not the first book to look at an *enterprise as a system* when trying to assess its current performance. There are a number of assessment frameworks or *mental maps* in the change field. In addition to the SWOT and action research alternatives, some of these assessment frameworks can be found in the Bibliography, including these well-known approaches:

- Jay Galbraith's *Star Model* (1993)
- David Nadler's *Congruence Model* (1977; Burke, 1987)
- Marv Weisbord's *Six-Box Model* (1978; Burke, 1987)
- McKinsey's *7-S Framework* (1982; Peters and Waterman, 1982)

It is not our intent to analyze each existing assessment model, although our research did identify thirteen different current organizational models. They can be found in Haines (2003). None uses a totally integrated systems perspective. Of the thirteen

- Only eight specified outputs,
- Only seven dealt with the environment,
- Only one had a Change Management *System*, and
- Only one had a feedback loop.

These limited mental maps help us understand why an estimated 75 percent of change journeys fail to achieve their desire outcomes. Because many executives and change consultants are not guided by one overall and systemic framework, no wonder many complex change efforts fail to include a comprehensive Enterprise-Wide Assessment.

In our view, failing to use a common framework to assess the enterprise and guide the EWC journey is *organizational malpractice.*

Organizational malpractice is analogous to a team of surgeons operating on one patient, all at one time, but without a common overall agreement of what the human system looks like and how it functions. To carry the analogy further, it would be compounded by a lack of sharing test results, findings, interventions, diagnoses, and treatment plans with each other.

> And it will fall out, as in a complication of diseases, that by applying a remedy to one sore, you will provoke another; and that which removes the one ill symptom produces others . . .
>
> *Sir Thomas Moore*

Intervening at the enterprise level without a critical overall mental map of an *enterprise as a system* isn't simply a question of who is "right" or "wrong"—the survival of the patient is often at stake. It is a question of *knowing the vital signs to look for* in a patient (organization). Following a comprehensive and informative mental map of an *enterprise as a living system* is clearly an ethical issue—as well as having obvious implications for achieving results.

> We have met the enemy and they are us.
>
> *Pogo*

Unqualified Enterprise-Wide Systems Doctors? It is a wonder any complex change efforts do succeed!

> If the band played a piece first with a piccolo, then with the brass horn, then with the clarinet, and then with the trumpet, there would be a hell of a lot of noise, but no music. To get harmony in music, each instrument must support the others. To get harmony in battle, each weapon must support the other. *Team play wins.*
>
> General George S. Patton, The Patton Papers *(Vol. 2)*

It is unfair to criticize executives and change consultants for not having clarity and simplicity of their organizations as systems. They are dealing every day with a complex enterprise in a dynamic environment.

However, an essential first step in coming to grips with this issue is recognizing and understanding that enterprises are *living systems,* a mixture of human and inanimate physical structures. They are not mechanistic; they are organic. They are not closed assembly lines, but open systems populated by groups and people, each of whom has a heart, mind, body, emotions, spirit, and goals.

Multiple Conflicting Mindsets or Mental Maps (Versus a Totally Integrated Enterprise-Wide Assessment)

> **THINK DIFFERENTLY**

An oil company CEO was employing three different consulting firms at one time—each with different and conflicting mental maps of how to assess the enterprise.

Our colleague was called in to assist with starting the needed Enterprise-Wide Change effort. At the same time, Consulting Firm number 2 was assisting with metrics by using "The Balanced Scorecard Strategy Map," a very different framework. Training Firm number 3 was helping to set up a "Corporate University" using a traditional, silo-based set of leadership training programs for management (one size fits all).

Obviously, the CEO saw the enterprise-wide planned change project as different from the metrics project, which was seen as different from the leadership training project. This is the normal view of most executives and organizations. However, the overlap and conflicts among the three external firms and their projects soon became apparent.

All three external firms had their own mental maps and assessment tools. Each was different, causing extra costs for the same work for the oil company. In addition, the time and use of different assessment tools created duplication, overlap, and frustration for the organization and employees. Further, the three projects created multiple messages, languages, and terminologies, as well as conflicting orientations to each aspect of the organizational change for which the projects were responsible.

Overall, this created confusion for the CEO, executives, and managers involved and affected by the multiple projects (remember, organizations are a web of relationships). The unintended negative consequences from the well-meaning three projects became so disruptive that they were all cancelled prematurely.

The regression in the company's pursuit of business excellence and its impact on the desired superior results were predictable.

Why did this happen? What were the root causes?

The oil company example is a common one. The different and conflicting mindsets or mental maps of the players of change become a problem in assessing and executing change strategies and new key initiatives.

To reiterate for emphasis and clarity: The first of the Big Three Failures in Enterprise-Wide Change is the result of multiple mindsets, organizational frameworks, fads, and silver bullets by both executives and change consultants. It results in a piecemeal/analytic organizational assessment approach to a *systems* problem rather than comprehensively assessing reality and then engaging the entire enterprise behind the changes as a totally integrated systems solution.

In Chapter One, we provided detailed examples of this piecemeal focus and discussed the Rubik's Cube effect: The numerous moving parts of an enterprise are beyond the ability of most of us to comprehend all the relationships and unintended consequence of our actions. *We can't see the forest for the trees.*

Instead of rising up in a helicopter to get a better perspective and a systems view of their problems and complex organizational workings, executives and change consultants often opt for a more concrete, specific, *quick fix* set of actions. It is like a horse with blinders on going down a road, not looking at the broader perspective. The narrow, different, and conflicting mindsets on what is important in an organization and how it really functions beyond the myth of the "organization chart" is too complex to understand. It is a puzzle like the Rubik's Cube that is almost impossible to solve.

Here is an exercise to illustrate the problem further (with thanks to our friend Jerry Kurtyka of El Paso):

> In a meeting with the change leadership team, ask them to think of a brown-and-white dog and then write down on a piece of paper a detailed and specific description of what it looks like.
>
> Now go around the room and ask each person to describe his or her dog (mental map). Answers will range from big to small, to different breeds, male or female, coloring, size of ears, and so on.
>
> If we each have different mental maps and images of something as straightforward as a dog, what are the chances that we have similar maps of an *organization as a system*?

⟳ THINK DIFFERENTLY

A complex major airport terminal and gate expansion was initiated in a large, well-known U.S. city. The airport authority hired an architectural firm to design the expansion plan.

The airport authority then put out a bid for the actual construction. They hired 186 contractors, subcontractors, and consultants to accomplish the $100M-plus expansion project.

While there was an overall blueprint for the project, anyone who has built a house knows that constant adjustments are made to the original plans. Constant interaction with all parties involved with the actual construction is required (owners, architects, general contractor, and subcontractors).

This particular authority did not have a Program Management Office (an overall general contractor), so you can imagine the results: numerous lawsuits, massive overruns, and an expansion plan that was seriously compromised from the original design.

The city will have to live with the results of these unintended consequences for many years.

What should we do about this problem? Just live with these kinds of situations, as we have always done?

One Mental Map of an Organization as a Living System

Here are six activities to prevent the failure that results from multiple conflicting mindsets. These activities will enable you to conduct a totally integrated best practices Enterprise-Wide Assessment:

Activity #1:   Hold a Change Leadership Team meeting to explicitly examine each other's multiple conflicting mindsets.

Activity #2:   Have the Change Leadership Team build a visual representation of their consensus on the description of an *Enterprise as a System*. Use the ABC's framework to do so.

Activity #3:   Share this visual and critique it with the collective management team. Finalize the system's framework.

Activity #4:   Build a questionnaire to reflect this system's framework and its details.

Activity #5:   Conduct a comprehensive current-state reality assessment of the performance of the organization based on your visual model. For example, you can conduct the assessment:

  • Online

- In a large group meeting as a more in-depth strengths-and-weaknesses assessment rather than the traditional SWOT
- By using subject-matter experts to conduct the assessment
- Through focus groups, or
- Use the assessment presented later in this chapter

Activity #6: Use the results of the Enterprise-Wide Assessment as you begin the EWC.

The systems problem is that a single, clear mental map of the organization's functioning and the relationships of its people, processes, and resources is absolutely essential to assess and execute EWC successfully. A shared mental map gives all the players of change both a language and a template to assess and guide their efforts.

One shared mental organizational map should enable executives to deal not only with changes in all processes within an organization but also with the collisions and collaboration of subsystems and hierarchies, like teams, departments, and lines of business. It allows us to diagnose problems, to design enterprise-wide interventions to deliver results, and to safely navigate the many hazards and unintended consequences in a complex enterprise.

And yet, a single mental map is almost always missing.

The problem is not that key players don't have a mental map—it is that *each* of them has a different mental map, and these maps are rarely shared, let alone reconciled.

Frequently, too much focus on cultural attunement (Failure Issue #3) reflects the mental map of change consultants, while focusing mainly on economic alignment (Failure Issue #2) reflects the mental map of the CEO, CFO, and line executives.

Here is where we have found Appreciative Inquiry (Cooperrider & Whitney, 1999) to be valuable. Executives and change consultants need intense discussions to come up with a single, explicit, systems-based mental map or model to assess and guide the EWC process.

In Systems Thinking terms, adopting the *ABCDE* Mental Map (Core Systems Concept #3) can simplify this process. Dialogue can then center on finding a simple way to describe the inner workings and relationships of the parts of the enterprise to each other and to desired positioning and culture. The inner workings correspond to Phase D of the Systems Thinking Model. The Strategic Thinking question it asks is, "How do we go from today (Phase C) to the future (Phase A) in a complete, holistic way?"

The answer is contained in the throughputs of the system—the inner workings and relationships of the enterprise (Phase D). The problem is how to describe the organization in a simple, understandable, yet comprehensive way so the description can be utilized as an assessment tool and guide throughout the EWC process.

Questions to Ponder

- What is your mental map of your organization as a system? Do others agree with you?

- What can you predict as the consequences of differing mental maps?

- Do you start your Enterprise-Wide Change process at Phase C or Phase A? Why? How does it work for you?

Some more questions to consider: How would you describe the way your enterprise functions? What are the key components that make up your mental map of an organization? Is it more than the organizational chart? If so, how would you describe it so you could use it to assess and guide your Enterprise-Wide Change effort?

To answer these questions, we often take senior management and change consultants as a team through the following steps:

DESCRIBING THE ENTERPRISE AS A LIVING SYSTEM

Step #1: What are the parts or elements of the ABCs of Phase D, The System (or, more accurately, the organization as a system)?

Step # 2: Brainstorm a list of all the organizational parts, terms, elements, phrases, and functions you can think of (try for thirty to start).

Here are three elements to get you going:

1. Finance	2. Promotions	3. Managers
4.	5.	6.
7.	8.	9.
10.	11.	12.
13.	14.	15.
16.	17.	18.
19.	20.	21.
22.	23.	24.
25.	26.	27.
28.	29.	30.

If you ask the Players of Change to complete this exercise, it's likely to reveal that *each* key player probably has a unique (and different) mental map of the enterprise. This is a good way to illustrate the difficulty executives and change consultants have when they approach the complexity of organizations from significantly different points of view.

Major System (Enterprise) Components

The question is how to describe the inner workings of Phase D, *the system*, in a simplified way, despite the thirty or so complex elements people have listed in the exercise. How would they "chunk" these words and terms into the *major enterprise components* so they have a common language to think, to act, and to achieve superior results? Most of us would naturally use the organizational chart as the "chunks." However, it is usually created by function and misses the horizontal integration needed to serve the customer and achieve business excellence and superior results year after year.

From a Systems Thinking perspective, a mental map of an enterprise as a living system begins with Phase A, the Star Positioning Model and the Quadruple Bottom Line, as the measurement of the desired outcomes/results you want to achieve (Phase B). The *ABCs* Enterprise-Wide Change Model might look like Figure 6.1, in *simplified* form:

Figure 6.1. The Enterprise as a Living System

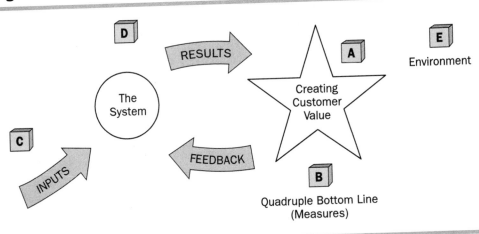

A New Enterprise-Wide Assessment Mental Map: A Business Excellence Architecture

In 1999, three organizations researched and worked in partnership for over two years to find a better way to describe an *enterprise as a system*. They were (1) Carla Carter & Associates of Phoenix, Arizona, using the Baldrige Quality Award Criteria for Performance Excellence; (2) TWOAI (The Coaches) of San Diego, California; and (3) the Centre for Strategic Management.

As a group, we researched and built a comprehensive Enterprise-Wide Assessment as a best practices organizational map as well as an associated Enterprise-Wide Assessment Tool. We also used a Baldrige questionnaire from the National Institute of Standards and Technology (www.quality.nist.gov), which you can download and use free of charge.

The short form of this assessment is at the end of this chapter, focusing on critical parts of the organization which need to fit, align, and be integrated to create customer value and superior results. These components also seem to be the natural way that executives think when they focus on change projects.

The Enterprise-Wide Assessment consists of eight modules designed to simplify your list of organization parts (from the previous exercise) into a simple yet comprehensive mental map. If these don't work for you, what is *your* model?

The eight modules—Building a Culture of Performance Excellence, Reinventing Strategic Planning, Leading Enterprise-Wide Change, Creating the People Edge, Achieving Leadership Excellence, Becoming Customer-Focused, Aligning Delivery, Creating Customer Value—are shown in Figure 6.2.

Review the A-B-C-D-E Enterprise-Wide Assessment framework that follows. Then review its eight internal modules on the next few pages to see if you can use this Mental Map in your change efforts. Focusing on the first seven modules as the internal workings of an *Enterprise as a System* is a way to become a better diagnostician and organizational doctor. They are the *vital signs* of a living effective organization to achieve Module #8—Customer Value and Superior Results.

Figure 6.2. The Enterprise-Wide Assessment

The Systems Thinking Approach^{SM}
to Creating Your Competitive Business Advantage

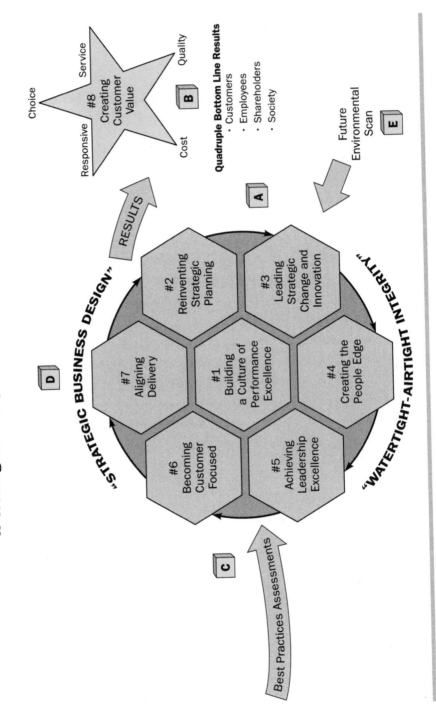

The key to an Enterprise-Wide Assessment is the *fit* and *linkage* among the inner workings of each module, not the "best answer/technique" per department. Techniques are not new; *fit is the innovation.*

Excellence is a matter of doing 10,000 little things right—and linking them together.

Module #1: Building a Culture of Performance Excellence

The foundation of this mental map includes Systems Thinking, innovation and creativity, fact-based decision making, and the organization's core values.

A culture of performance excellence is a crucial pillar of business excellence. Culture is defined as the collective behavior in the organization and is one of the four missing links described in Chapter Five.

Note: For further reading on *core values,* we recommend Hultman (2001). For further reading on *culture change,* we recommend Bellingham (2001).

Module #2: Reinventing Strategic Planning Based on Positioning

The essence of effective strategic thinking is resolving the issue of positioning and building measurable goals/key success measures. The resulting clarity of purpose must then become the core focus of the day-to-day EWC process: vision and positioning, metrics and strategies, business and annual plans, budgets, finance, and legal support, and a yearly strategic management cycle that includes all the above.

Note: For further reading on this subject, see Haines (2000).

Module #3: Leading Enterprise-Wide Change

Overall leadership and management of an Enterprise-Wide Change to create a more customer-focused organization is the essence of this module—and this book. The module includes a menu of change structures and infrastructure; the Rollercoaster of Change; staffing, budgeting, and resourcing change; communications, involvement, and teamwork; and change processes and projects.

> ## ➡ THINK DIFFERENTLY
>
> A few years ago a large Midwest automotive company division started an Enterprise-Wide Change project to build self-directed work teams as the basic building blocks of the organization, patterned after the then radical Saturn automotive plant in Spring Hill, Tennessee.
>
> However, even after putting all of the new union employees through a two-week-long training program, there was no follow-up program after the first year (after the CEO was promoted and transferred).
>
> Two years later, the organization called a consultant back in to "fix" the problems that continued to crop up. The cost to the company to get the project back on track was enormous—over $80,000 in one consulting check alone.
>
> Holding regular reviews and keeping up with the ongoing hard work of implementation would have been a lot less costly in money, emotions, and problems than hiring the consultants and paying their fees . . . again.

Note: For further reading on this change and innovation module alone, we recommend Dean Anderson and Linda Ackerman Anderson (2001) and Byrd and Brown (2002).

Module #4: Creating the People Edge

A key component of EWC is having *people* and *support elements* strategically *in tune* with each other, geared to achieving desired positioning. *Strategic people plans* are, unfortunately, missing from most organizations. We strongly believe that this is a corporate-wide issue for senior management (people stewardship is their responsibility), not just an HR functional issue. Organizations need a strategic *people* plan as much as they need a strategic marketing or financing plan.

Key components of this module include strategic people/HR plans, recruitment and retention, training and development, performance and rewards, and best people practices (detailed at the end of Chapter Nine).

We call this overall, strategic appreciation for human assets *The People Plan.* It typically includes attracting, hiring, motivating, developing, empowering, rewarding, and retaining all crucial staff.

Note: For further reading on this topic, see Bandt and Haines (2001).

Module #5: Achieving Leadership Excellence

Leadership is the foundation for everything else and is the number-one organization-wide core competency of successful organizations. Leadership development must be an initial and ongoing priority for the collective management team. This is especially true for the middle and senior executives of organizations, who would most directly need skills for success in EWC.

Critical aspects of this module are succession planning from the top down for senior management and key positions; a leadership development system for the entire organization (*cultural attunement*); 360-degree feedback, development, and individual development plans; business acumen (*economic alignment*); and six natural levels of leadership competencies (detailed at the end of Chapter Nine).

Note: For further reading on this topic, see Haines (2002).

Module #6: Becoming Customer-Focused

A customer focus includes being competitive at all five points on the star model (Figure 5.1) and also excelling in one of them. Wanting to be "customer-focused" is a basic truism for management. Everybody buys into the idea of customer focus. In reality, however, such a focus is often shockingly absent in the day-to-day operations of some enterprises.

Some of the key components of creating a customer focus include market analysis, strategic marketing plans, quality products and services, sales management, and customer service.

How Do You Know Whether an Enterprise Is Customer-Focused?

1. Ask for specifics. Does the enterprise have mechanisms to gather regular and measurable customer feedback?

2. Does it have a clear, explicit, and written strategy for recovering from errors and mistakes made with customers?

3. How often do the CEO and ALL members of the senior management team spend a full day visiting customers in the field?

In many enterprises, the answers can quickly help separate fiction from reality.

THINK DIFFERENTLY

One colleague has given over eighty CEO-level keynote talks to leaders of small-to-medium-sized businesses through The Executive Committee (TEC), an international organization of CEOs. He consistently finds that the answers to the three questions above are no, no, and rarely.

Note: For further reading, we recommend Ries and Trout (2001).

Module #7: Aligning Delivery

Some of the key elements of a successful delivery system are supply-chain management/distribution channels; process improvement, simplicity, and no waste; enterprise-wide technology; knowledge transfer; and organization redesign.

Success in creating customer value ultimately comes from strategically realigning the entire delivery system to support your positioning with the customer. Module #7 highlights key elements that require a strategic realignment toward that desired positioning.

 THINK DIFFERENTLY

One of our colleagues was asked to assist an East Coast manufacturer in developing an EWC process. During the initial meetings and discussions, it became clear that they were spending millions on another consulting firm for a major supply-chain management project. In meeting with this other firm, it became obvious they had their own mental map and framework that was not a systems approach, although the firm called it that.

As a result, the consultant declined to assist this manufacturer and instead recommended that they continue working just with this other firm. He also recommended that the company and its executives spend time in dialogue with the other consulting firm to develop a common understanding and mental map of their *organization as a system.*

Note: For further reading on supply-chain management, we recommend Ayers (1990).

Module #8: Superior Results: Creating Customer Value

Creating customer value through achievement of your positioning is a primary outcome. The other three Quadruple Bottom Line success measures are also important: Employee satisfaction, financial/shareholder satisfaction, and contribution to society. These were discussed earlier in Chapter Five.

Summary:
Enterprise-Wide Assessment and Vital Signs

Value results from a total effort rather than from one isolated step in
the process.

Alvin Toffler, Creating a New Civilization

This chapter was not about the eight modules. It was about an *organization as a living system* with interconnected, interdependent, and interacting parts. Separate change projects based on each of the eight modules, even when successful, still will not have the impact of an Enterprise-Wide Change effort from a totally integrated Systems Thinking Approach.

Creating customer value and superior results requires an approach that deals with the total efforts, processes, and people of the entire organization. This requires that every organizational element be efficiently aligned and effectively attuned with people as one system, focused on achieving the same positioning for customer value.

Some executives and change consultants may approach the eight modules as being nothing new, which misses the point. Understanding all the different issues, but trying to improve each in turn as a separate change project, is what many people do best. *But that is an analytic approach to a systems problem.* Unfortunately, in most piecemeal change projects, the unintended consequences come back to haunt us. Root causes become chronic issues.

The eight modules of Enterprise-Wide Assessment are a valuable assessment, guide, and resource for achieving business excellence and superior results. Failure to focus on and fully install strategies in any one of these modules generally results in poor *vital signs* and predictable failures in the areas shown in Table 6.1.

Table 6.1. Predictable Failures from a Poor Mental Map

Enterprise-Wide Assessment Modules	Predictable Failure Issues Created with Lack of Excellence in Module Performance
Module #1: Building a Culture of Performance Excellence	Bureaucracy and Mediocrity
Module #2: Reinventing Strategic Planning	Conflict Among Goals and Priorities
Module #3: Leading Enterprise-Wide Change	Stagnation of Business
Module #4: Creating the People Edge	Adversarial We-They Relationships
Module #5: Achieving Leadership Excellence	Incompetent Leadership
Module #6: Becoming Customer-Focused	Poor Service Quality
Module #7: Aligning Delivery	Fragmentation and Poor Delivery
Module #8: Creating Customer Value	Survival and Confusion

We frequently talk about unintended consequences and side effects as if they were a necessary reality. Not so. In reality, there are no unintended or side effects, just effects and consequences.

When we take action, there are various effects:

- The effects we thought of in advance, or were beneficial, we call these the main or intended effects.

- The effects we did not anticipate, the effects that harm the system, are the ones we claim to be side effects (or unintended consequences).

Side effects are not a feature of reality but a sign that our understanding of the system is narrow and flawed.

To avoid resistance and side effects and to find high leverage points requires us to expand the boundaries of our mental maps. We must become aware of and understand the implications of the *unintended* consequences created by the decisions we make. We must learn about the structure and dynamics of the increasingly complex systems in which we are embedded. Use the Enterprise-Wide Assessment to keep checking vital signs and ensure minimal side effects and unintended consequences.

What is your mental map of your enterprise as a system?

The systematic application of this model can expertly guide you along this journey of EWC to creating customer value. Start wherever you want and with whichever of the eight modules you wish. The key, as always in Systems Thinking, is to focus not only on parts, but also on the relationships, fit, and integration of the eight modules over time to achieve superior results.

Uses of the Enterprise-Wide Assessment

Ways to use the framework and Enterprise-Wide Assessment are many and include

- As a common tool to assess effectiveness in achieving *fit and integration* to both your marketplace positioning and your desired internal culture
- To structure the right questions to ask in making decisions about Enterprise-Wide Change
- To provide a common framework for thinking, communicating, and working together on EWC
- To heighten awareness, sensitivity, and understanding of how an organization works and on how the parts fit together in support of customers
- To create one roadmap through the organizational complexity for change leaders
- To eliminate mental map biases and mismatches across the management team
- To help narrow the scope and set priorities on areas needing improvement
- To diagnose root causes and solutions more effectively in organizations
- To clarify linkages where one part affects all others
- To help ensure that enterprise-level strategies and actions are based on a systems diagnosis

---

Questions to Ponder

- Do these eight modules make sense to you? Why or why not?
- Are there any missing modules? What are they?
- What other books would you recommend reading on each of the modules?

Developing and Implementing an Enterprise as a System Framework

Option #1   Visit the NIST website and download their free Baldrige Survey (www.quality.nist.gov).

Option #2   Build your own mental model and gain acceptance among senior management for any complex and strategic change effort. Remember, "People support what they help create."

Option #3   Use the short assessment form at the end of this chapter developed by the Centre and Carla Carter Associates for less complex organizations.

▶ COMPREHENSIVE CASE STUDY

East Coast Federal Credit Union Enterprise-Wide Change: Part 3

Activity #1. In this case, assessment is an ongoing process. The Short-Form Enterprise-Wide Assessment was conducted after reaching clarity of purpose (described in Chapter Five). Keeping this Enterprise as a System framework in senior management's minds was crucial in deliberations with the board.

It was, however, unrealistic to expect the board members (mostly retired executives) to fully understand the framework and realign their thinking. Their analytic bias was a real problem. They were not holistic thinkers as senior management was. Thus, the first type of failure—a piecemeal approach to EWC—was a constant struggle. The change, however, did slowly move in the right direction.

Regarding the potential for failure types 2 and 3, the CEO was mostly focused on *economic alignment* by necessity, as was the CFO. However, the COO, VP of operation, and VP of HR were focused on both *economic alignment and cultural attunement,* a refreshing perspective.

The board's main concern was for a group of customers in other states, not for the economics of the situation. This was an unusual reversal. Management had to constantly show the board that the customers in the other states would have the option to be better taken care of by a larger financial institution—one with more resources and better rates and convenience than ECFCU could provide, given their current financial challenges.

The employees in those states would be better off, too, a key variable for both management and the board. They would probably get higher salaries and benefits if their branches were sold to a larger financial institution.

Activity #2. Thus, constant informal business excellence assessments and reviews of the status of the Enterprise-Wide Change process, along with stay-in by the board, was crucial.

Activity #3. The CFO continually developed and updated simple, one-page economic documents. He used them to remind the board of the enormity of the situation. He also kept data in front of management and the board regarding the customers being poorly served in the branches in the other states where ECFCU's market share was minuscule. These documents proved to be extremely valuable in every board EWC meeting, as well as in all the management and PMO sessions.

To be continued . . . ◀

Chapter Six Recap

1. Those involved in leading an Enterprise-Wide Change effort must share the same mental map—and only one mental map. To make this happen, select *only one* consulting firm and adopt or revise their mental model.

2. The SWOT technique is a good diagnostic tool, but it is not the place to start a systems approach to Enterprise-Wide Change.

3. A comprehensive systems-based *enterprise as a system* mental model can be used to best deal with the complexity of strategic change.

4. The eight modules of an Enterprise-Wide Assessment can be used to clarify and simplify one's focus.

5. The eight modules are

   - Building a Culture of Performance Excellence

   - Reinventing Strategic Planning

- Leading Enterprise-Wide Change
- Creating the People Edge
- Achieving Leadership Excellence
- Becoming Customer-Focused
- Aligning Delivery
- Creating Customer Value

6. Whatever map you develop of your organization as a system, it is best served by using the Simplicity of Systems Thinking model as the core technology and ABCDE framework.

7. The simplified Enterprise-Wide Assessment template at the end of this chapter is a quick tool for a more in-depth assessment of an organization's strengths and weaknesses.

8. You can download the Baldrige Criteria for Performance Excellence directly from the National Institute of Standards and Technology at www.quality. nist.gov.

9. The six activities of an Enterprise-Wide Assessment process are

   Activity #1: Hold a Change Leadership Team meeting to build a mental map of the organization.

   Activity #2: Build a visual representation of this map of your organization as a system.

   Activity #3: Conduct a parallel involvement process with the collective management team to share, critique, and build consensus on it.

   Activity #4: Build a questionnaire to reflect the details of the system's framework.

   Activity #5: Conduct an Enterprise-Wide Assessment based on your visual model.

   Activity #6: Use the assessment results as you begin the formal "simplicity of execution" in the next chapter.

Enterprises are Living Systems—the natural way the world works. We need to learn the *synergy of systems solutions* versus the *failure of fragmented functions*. Although the dominant paradigm in our lives is *analytic thinking*, the natural order of life on Earth and in organizations is a *living systems* one.

ENTERPRISE-WIDE ASSESSMENT

Instructions:

1. Please list each module's strengths and weaknesses.
2. Then score each module. (Put an X - Low 1 to High 6.)
3. Connect the scores with a straight line.

Name of Organization _____

Date _____

| 1. Building a Culture of Performance Excellence | 2. Reinventing Strategic Planning | 3. Leading Enterprise-Wide Change | 4. Creating the People Plan | 5. Achieving Leadership Excellence | 6. Becoming Customer-Focused | 7. Aligning Delivery |

STRENGTHS

High 6 · · · · · (for each module)
5 · · · · · ·
4 · · · · · · ·

WEAKNESSES

3 · · · · · · ·
2 · · · · · · ·
1 · · · · · · ·
Low

7

Simplicity of Execution
Working *In* the Enterprise

D
Strategies
Actions

Chapter Purposes

- To cascade the Enterprise-Wide Change journey throughout the organization—go to work *in* the enterprise—through some key systems principles in the Simplicity of Execution

- To use the Systems Thinking Approach to develop shared and integrated core strategies, key initiatives, work plans, accountability, and rewards to engage the entire enterprise and all its employees

---

Enterprise-Wide Change Goal #2: Ensure Simplicity of Execution to Achieve Desired Results

---

The ABCs of Enterprise-Wide Change

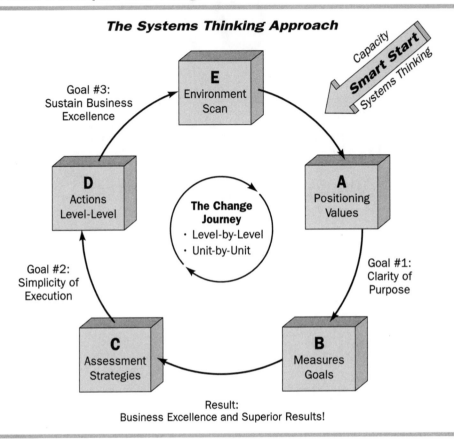

The Systems Thinking Approach

Goal #3:
Sustain Business
Excellence

E
Environment
Scan

Capacity
Smart Start
Systems Thinking

D
Actions
Level-Level

The Change Journey
· Level-by-Level
· Unit-by-Unit

A
Positioning
Values

Goal #2:
Simplicity of
Execution

Goal #1:
Clarity of
Purpose

C
Assessment
Strategies

B
Measures
Goals

Result:
Business Excellence and Superior Results!

Chapter Context

Simplicity. The trouble with so many of us is that we underestimate the
power of simplicity. We have a tendency to overcomplicate our lives and
forget what's important and what's not. We tend to focus on activities
instead of results.

Robert Stuberg

In the Systems Thinking concept and model described in Chapter Two, *Phase D* is the inner workings of the system or enterprise. This is where change gets messy, complex, and over-complicated. However, now we need to go to work *in* the enterprise, as opposed to the earlier work *on* the enterprise (clarity of purpose). There is no getting around this complexity. What helps is to find *simplicity on the far side of complexity*. What are some simple principles for the complex cascade of EWC? This chapter presents some of the answers to this question.

Second, so that you can understand Phase D: The enterprise's inner workings, this chapter shows how the Seven Levels of Living Systems can be applied to enterprises as the Seven Natural Rings of Reality. This second concept of Systems Thinking is repeated here for emphasis and will be used in the next two chapters. It is the concept of *systems within systems,* much like the earlier example of the Russian stacking dolls.

This means that you don't just implement change at a macro level. Executives and managers must lead the EWC execution at all levels in all departments, in all units, and in all locations. To reemphasize the point, see Figure 7.1.

Figure 7.1. The Seven Natural Rings of Reality

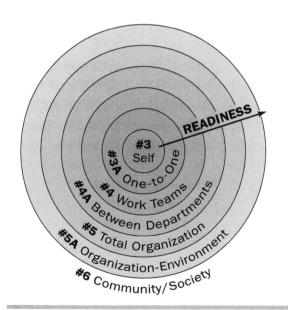

Environment Includes:
- Other people/groups
- Other organizations
- Customers/competitors
- Society/community
- Regions/earth

Increased Readiness:
- Complexity/chaos
- Readiness/willingness
- Skills/competencies growth

Note: Rings 3-4-5-6 are four of the "Seven Levels of Living Systems"

Rings 3A-4A-5A are "Collisions of Systems" with other systems

The Seven Natural Rings of Reality deal with the cascade of the clarity of purpose and Enterprise-Wide Change strategies from the total-enterprise ring to the business units (cross-functional) ring to the department and work team ring to each employee (self) ring.

Executing change by driving clarity of the strategies, the key initiatives, the work plans, and the accountability and rewards to all rings dramatically increases the probability of success in a total Enterprise-Wide Change journey.

Many TQM processes in the past failed for just that reason. TQM projects sometimes had a group of highly skilled quality experts trying to change the entire organization by themselves. It didn't work, as they did not take the size and scale of the entire enterprise and all of its people and complexity into account. They did not employ a totally integrated systems solution. The TQM projects that were successful, such as those at GE, did go to the enterprise-wide scale.

This type of failure is a classic *analytical* approach to a systems problem that requires a *systems* solution. Simplicity comes from clear tasks and goals with clear accountability and rewards working *in* the enterprise. This chapter explains how to create this.

In summary, *simplicity of execution* comes from having one to three simple frameworks to use as tools and signposts along the way so you can find your way through the complexity of the changing enterprise to its fundamental simplicity.

In this book, the macro framework we use is the A-B-C-D-E Systems Thinking framework (Systems Concept #3 in Chapter Three).

In this chapter, we are working on Phase D, the inner workings of the A-B-C-D-E System to reveal all its subsystems and levels. In order to visually understand this relationship, look at Figure 7.2.

Figure 7.2. The Seven Levels of Reality

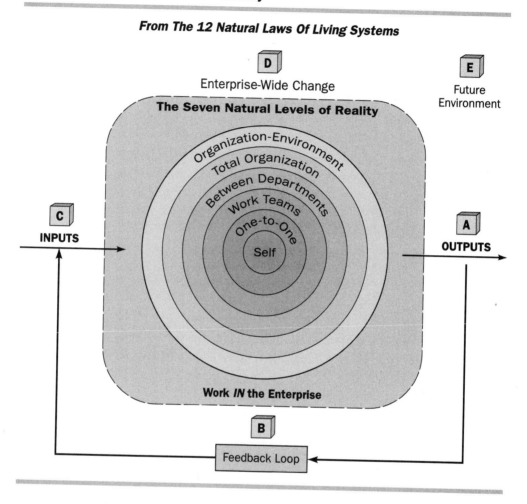

From The 12 Natural Laws Of Living Systems

The Seven Natural Levels of Reality

Organization-Environment

Total Organization

Between Departments

Work Teams

One-to-One

Self

D Enterprise-Wide Change

E Future Environment

C INPUTS

A OUTPUTS

Work *IN* the Enterprise

B Feedback Loop

Later, in Chapter Eight, we will use the third simple framework, the Roller-coaster of Change.

On the Path to Clarity and Simplicity

We have been on the path to simplicity from the beginning of this book.

We dealt with the foundations of Systems Thinking and Smart Start as the pre-work to Enterprise-Wide Change. We dealt with working *on* the enterprise to develop clarity of purpose (Goal #1) rather than prematurely setting in motion a reactionary, analytic, and simplistic set of change actions that achieve little but keep everyone busy.

Some readers may have been waiting all this time for *THE chapters on change*. In one sense, Chapters Seven, Eight, and Nine are those chapters. In another sense, such anticipation is a low-level remnant of analytic thinking in action—the tendency to think in parts (chapters), rather than in wholes (a book on Enterprise-Wide Change in its totality). Goal #2 is just the *formal* part of change.

This entire book is about change—and Enterprise-Wide Change began the moment that someone, usually the CEO, started thinking and talking about making some major changes throughout the organization.

Simplicity is the key to happiness in the modern world.

As we have said, execution of Enterprise-Wide Change must be simple by design, or it will not succeed. In complex organizations, *simplicity wins the game every time*. A critical key to simplicity includes having glue to hold the entire enterprise together. We have all heard about having a shared vision as the overall glue of the enterprise. We believe there are two other *glues* that give us a simple way to focus our attention in EWC:

- Shared core values are the *social and cultural glue*
- Shared strategies are the *business excellence glue*

Other keys to simplicity within enterprises include

- *The 80/20 Rule*—spend 20 percent of your time planning to leverage, 80 percent executing
- *The Rule of Three*—people are able to best remember things that are broken into sets of three
- *The Three Times Rule*—tell people something three times, before, during, and after you make a point
- *Elevator Speeches*—don't use anything you can't explain in thirty seconds
- *Focus, Focus, Focus*

- *One-Sheet Documents*—build short documents to simplify the communication of your clarity of purpose, Enterprise-Wide Change Game Plan, and yearly map of implementation/execution

Finally, continually ask throughout the change process these questions: If you could change anything about your Enterprise-Wide Change process and efforts, what would you do to make it

- Simpler?
- More meaningful?
- More flexible?
- More focused?
- Have a better overall approach?

> For every complex problem there is a simplistic (quick fix) answer
> and . . . it is always wrong.
>
> *H. L. Mencken*

Simplistic Knee-Jerk Implementation Techniques (Quick Fixes That Fail)

To solve a problem in an enterprise, have you ever tried any of these quick fixes?

- Formed a team or committee and held lots of meetings?
- Set up training programs?
- Improved communications through videos, intranet, memos?
- Improved the performance appraisal process?
- Empowered people?
- Relegated an important issue to a staff expert?
- Held a yearly retreat?
- Solved one issue at a time and ignored related problems?
- Cut costs across the board?
- Called a hiring freeze?

If these things happened in isolation, disconnected from any larger change effort, you had what Senge (1990) would call *Quick Fixes That Fail.*

THINK DIFFERENTLY

(Thanks to Admiral Dennis Blair, USN Retired): In the 1990s, when the Department of Defense was reduced in size after the Cold War, a civilian hiring freeze was instituted. The result was the average pay grades of civil servants increased by one full grade as they were "required" to do more with less. The payroll remained constant—a quick fix that failed.

Cascading the Changes: Strategies— Initiatives—Tasks—Accountability—Rewards

Most change consultants and executives already understand the importance of *core values,* which create the culture, the social glue and fabric of the organization, and the work environment for employees. Core values, whether spoken or unspoken, may leave the people in enterprises either satisfied, highly motivated, and committed to the desired changes or dissatisfied, unhappy, and disengaged mentally, spiritually, emotionally, and even physically.

Core values are the organization's *social glue.*

In this section we focus not on core values, but on core *strategies* as the business glue to cascade the EWC journey to all employees in all locations.

Conventional wisdom states that a *shared vision* is crucial to the success of any Enterprise-Wide Change effort. While we agree, our practical, ground-level work has found that *shared core strategies* are key to developing and cascading both alignment and attunement strategies (the Yin and Yang of Strategies).

Cascade #1: Shared Core EWC Strategies (Total-Organization Ring)

Shared core strategies as the business glue for the EWC serve as a primary *means* to the desired *ends*—unique positioning.

Core strategies are the primary ways in which an organization closes the *gap* between today (Phase C in the EWC Model) and its ultimate desired positioning (Phase A).

What is an EWC strategy?

- It is the foundation or basic approach to guide individual and EWC efforts toward the achievement of your organization's vision and positioning.

- It is also seen as the methods and groups of activities that can guide you in *bridging the gap* over the life of the EWC—from your current-state assessment to your ideal future vision.

- It defines the *how-to's* or major ways to reach the attainment of your positioning. Strategies are the primary *means* to the *ends*.

Strategies should also be few in number, generally two to seven (maximum). Fewer strategies allow for a more focused direction by the enterprise.

The criteria for EWC strategy selection requires that they

- Be integrated with each other—not separate silos
- Support the EWC vision and positioning
- Be linked to customers and product satisfaction (alignment of delivery)
- Be linked to people and culture (attunement with people's hearts and minds)
- Be expressed by a focused list—core strategies that are not comprehensive but few in number (less is more)
- Be clear, specific, and expressed by a one-to-three-word phrase for simplicity

One problem that must be rectified at the outset of this cascade is that, in many planned Enterprise-Wide Change efforts, core strategies are mostly the responsibility and purview of the CEO. The strategies are supposed to cross departmental boundaries in a horizontal, integrated fashion, but once they reach the departments, people and groups (subsystems) go about their business without internalizing the core strategies. The result is not unusual—the typical enterprise with functional silos, each with unique departmental goals that are somewhat unrelated to the true aims of the EWC.

The CEO wants enterprise-wide and integrated change, while departments continue to focus on more traditional functional operations.

When strategy and culture collide, which wins out? *Culture, of course!*

⟲ THINK DIFFERENTLY

A colleague was asked to help rectify and reenergize a TQM Enterprise-Wide Change with a technology manufacturer in the Western United States.

The project seemed to be the responsibility of a core group of committed people. The rest of the organization, however, continued to go about its daily business, uninvolved with the quality project. Naturally, this project was rejected by the existing culture and uninvolved participants, especially the uninvolved executives and department heads. They had other priorities and goals.

Complex systems are changed by small interventions—like shared strategies as department goals.

The *butterfly effect* is the theory that complex systems can be changed by small, sometimes unnoticed interventions. A butterfly flapping its wings in Nebraska, so the theory goes, sets in motion minute air waves that interact with other air waves, eventually colliding with millions of others in a complex cascade of cause and effect, until (it is speculated) a typhoon halfway around the globe can be traced directly back to that one little monarch.

While this may seem far-fetched, let's put it another way. *Minuscule events at the beginning of a chain of events can lead to massive effects at the end.* This is the point of finding leverage points in change.

Systems Thinking helps you see patterns in the world and spot the leverage points that, when acted on, can lead to lasting, beneficial changes. EWC requires a *set* of strategies that addresses the whole enterprise as a living system.

The purpose of having a set of focused change strategies is to keep you from being seduced by something that would be "nice to do."

The initial set of core strategies is usually chosen by the CEO and the executives. Once these have been identified, it becomes the change consultant's obligation to look at them from a higher view and challenge the executives to think harder about whether they may be missing some other core strategies that seem insignificant now, but could have major impact down the road.

In the authors' experience, usually one issue—economic alignment (Failure #2) or cultural attunement (Failure #3)—receives inadequate attention at the outset, due to *ingrained patterns* of analytic thinking and a *flawed model* of an organization as a system.

⟫ THINK DIFFERENTLY

A colleague worked an EWC process with a medium-sized financial services firm that "got it" when it came to these leverage points for change. The client tailored the EWC themselves and has achieved business excellence over the past three years despite a recessionary economy. They have won local awards as an employee-friendly company (cultural attunement) and marketplace visibility for their purple ATMs and highly profitable results (economic alignment). Further, they have a stellar public reputation for serving underserved markets (cultural attunement and contribution to society).

To structure shared core strategies that can function as the *business glue,* we recommend the following sequence of activities:

Activity #1:   The CEO and senior management team meet as the Enterprise-Wide Change Leadership Team. They develop the initial set of core change strategies.

Activity #2:   Since these core change strategies may hit most employees "where they live and work," use a large group parallel involvement process to gather feedback. This is an excellent way to develop shared key initiatives under the shared core strategies. To preserve senior management prerogative, we recommend that this be a participatory process only to develop an *initial* draft of three to five key initiatives under each strategy.

Activity #3:   Next, there can be a final review and "cleanup" of the draft initiatives by senior management, since they are the people who ultimately will be held responsible for the change execution.

People support what they help create applies first and foremost to senior management. (See the format for the shared core strategies and key initiatives after the Chapter Recap.)

Cascade #2: Department Change Plans (Work-Teams Ring)

In most of the organizations we have worked with over the past decade, each department set individual goals based on functional responsibilities. In every one of these organizations, silo departmental goal setting was eliminated in the first year of the Enterprise-Wide Change journey.

Instead, the core strategies of the Enterprise-Wide Change effort become a set of *shared core strategies* that *every department and business unit adopts*. In other words, all departments *adopt the same set of strategies* as their department goals for the next year, with three to four key initiatives under each core strategy as the guide to the specifics of their work plans.

The only real question left to answer for each department is, "What *specific role* will we play in supporting the shared core strategies and key initiatives?" Not *whether* they will support them, but *how*. Each unit looks at each core strategy and determines which key initiatives they will lead, which ones they must support, and which ones do not involve them.

The net result is that, in every case, cross-functional teamwork goes up, and conflict goes down. This is because potential conflict is no longer about *what to do* but about the lower-order question of *work plans* to achieve the desired results.

This is an example of the kind of synergy you can accomplish through the Systems Thinking Approach. One simple change in the structure of departmental goal-setting procedures increases system integration and interdependency, with far-reaching results. It may have been possible to achieve similar results through a disjointed group of individual change initiatives, but it's not likely—no more likely than randomly twisting a jumbled Rubik's Cube will result in a solved puzzle.

To accomplish this step in the cascade of change, we recommend the following two activities:

Activity #4:   The different business units, divisions, and major departments adopt the core strategies and key initiatives as their department goals for the next year. Unit/department heads (along with their teams) develop detailed *work plans* to support these strategies and initiatives. This is one place we recommend using a standard format. It gets everyone reading from the same sheet of music regarding the EWC.

The Work Plan Format after the Chapter Recap has a column titled "Who Else to Involve." Since enterprises are a web of relationships, this involvement is key to a Systems Thinking Approach. Knowing whom to involve in any specific web of relationships for each key initiative is crucial to breaking down silos.

Activity #5:   After unit work plans have been developed, they should be shared with the same group of people who participated in Activity #2, Enterprise-Wide Department Change Plans. The goal of this activity is to build all the interpersonal linkages required to successfully execute the work plans.

Cascade #3: Large-Group EWC Cross-Functional Reviews (Between-Departments Ring)

The difference in this last activity is that it is accomplished through a large-group departmental review meeting, in which three or four unit executives lead a smaller cross-section subgroup (one-third of the total attendees) in a *give-and-take review and critique* of the unit's work plan. Each unit executive presents his or her work plan three times in succession, as each subgroup rotates to hear different presenters in a sequence of presentations. (See Figure 7.3.) This process creates greater interaction and more energy, commitment, understanding, buy-in, and teamwork to execute the Enterprise-Wide Change Plan.

Figure 7.3. Large-Group Ballroom Setting

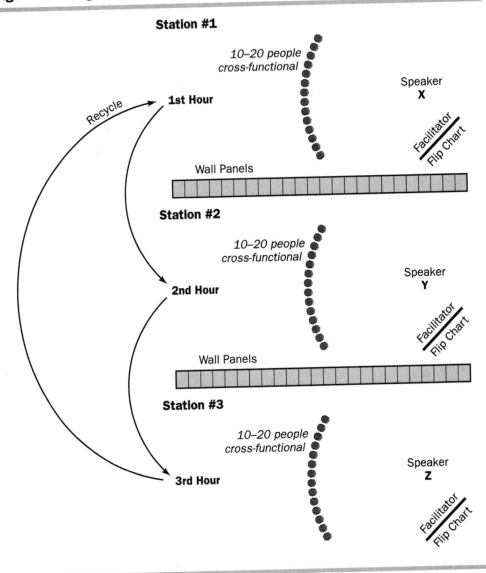

This large-group EWC review meeting has four purposes, to

1. Ensure that each unit executive and his or her team is *on board* with the shared core strategies and key initiatives of the Enterprise-Wide Change.

2. Enhance commitment of all executives and their teams by presenting to their peers and the rest of the employees three times in a public forum—something rarely done.

3. Build understanding and consensus among all employees involved to both (1) improve teamwork and (2) lower conflict during the execution phases of the Enterprise-Wide Change.

4. Build in functional accountability across the entire enterprise. This is no small matter in many enterprises—again, a Systems Thinking Approach to a system-wide problem.

 THINK DIFFERENTLY

A colleague trained his client on this large-group review meeting process so they could conduct it themselves. This multi-million-dollar financial services firm on the West Coast used the large-group review meeting process as a vital part of their EWC process.

The CEO invited another CEO to view the day-long process because the guest CEO was looking for a way to change her culture. She was so impressed with the energy and focus of this large-group process that she hired the consultant sight unseen—the shortest sales effort in his consulting career. The guest CEO's firm is now embarked on their own EWC process with a primary focus on dramatically improving their positioning around customer service.

Cascade #4: EWC Execution Vehicles (Innovative Process and Project Teams/Between-Departments Ring)

Activity #6: At this point, the Enterprise-Wide Change Leadership Team meets again with the Program Management Office and sets up key vehicles for successful execution of this multi-year journey: This activity yields process and project teams to lead execution of the key initiatives *across functions*.

The problem of execution is one that a cloth weaver would understand. Strength and durability in fabric come with the weaving of the warp and weft together in a matrix-like structure. By the same token, a beach chair's webbing is strong enough to hold a 300-pound person only if it has the same matrix-like structure.

See Figure 7.4 to better understand the vertical and horizontal integration and differentiation dilemma first presented long ago in the management literature by Dalton, Lawrence, and Lorsch (1970) in *Organizational Structure and Design*. For readers not familiar with their work, this is a highly recommended book. It helps to fully understand that inherent in every enterprise as a system there are both horizontal integration and functional/silo differentiation problems.

Figure 7.4. The Web of Functional Silos and Core Strategies

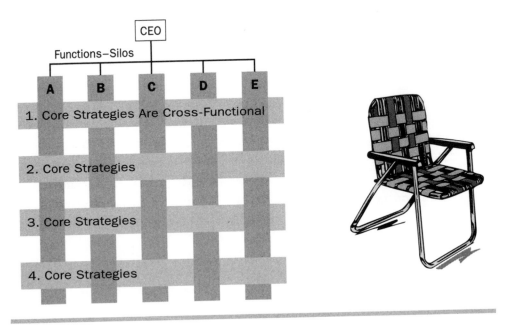

Core Strategies Are Like the Webbing in a Beach Chair
"The Glue That Holds It All Together"

Despite a recent focus on *execution,* the change consulting profession has long had the basic team and facilitation tools it needs to work with clients to ensure that things get done. Such tools include team chartering, responsibility matrices, and the art and science of process and project management.

The following is not intended to be a primer on process and project management, but just a few key points unique and important to Enterprise-Wide Change from a Systems Thinking perspective.

Once a decision has been made to establish a process or project team, the group needs a purpose (begin with the end in mind) and charter. The first task of any innovative process/project team is to *understand, assess, organize,* and *tailor* the process/project to the desired outcomes. The project team must define what results it wants to create. It's at this stage that the project team is chartered and sponsored.

The purposes will drive who should be members of the project team and what skill sets are required. The question of who will lead and sponsor the project or process is a key one. Is it the functional department executive with accountability for this project team task area, or is it another member of the top executive team? There are pros and cons for each that should be discussed prior to attempting consensus on which to choose.

Next, the team should be identified as either a *decision-making* team (that is, it makes the final decision as to the project) or a *recommending* team. If it is a recommending team, then its outputs are only *recommendations* to the Enterprise-Wide Change Leadership Team. Last, where possible, and in keeping with the fact that *people support what they help create,* asking for qualified volunteers to fill out the team is always preferable. Be clear on expectations up-front.

◗ THINK DIFFERENTLY

A pharmaceutical industry client in Eastern Canada asked for assistance in evaluating a non-prescription seasonal product launch that had been plagued with problems. The initial request from the product brand manager was for a meeting to capture the learnings, to help with the planning for the upcoming seasonal product launch. It quickly became clear to us that we were running into a collision of systems.

If our colleague had accepted the assignment operating at the product brand manager level, she certainly could have provided the requested service to the client. But it would have been the wrong service.

By taking a helicopter view of the product launch process, the consultant quickly discovered that there were other levels of systems (outside of the product manager's realm) that needed to be included in this review. They discovered that, although the organization had recently completed two organizational acquisitions, it had not yet streamlined its product launch process—resulting in overlaps and complexities in agency relationships and competition between brands from the two companies that had just been acquired.

To truly address the problems of the product launch, the consultant had to ensure that the sponsor for the project was senior enough to make decisions in his own area (marketing) and to effectively influence the decisions of the other senior stakeholders (in global manufacturing, supply chain, sales, quality assurance, warehousing, and distribution) in the matrix-based organization.

We have been using the word *innovative* when referring to these process and project teams for a reason. Any team that is not innovating and using proven best practices from Systems Thinking will not necessarily find the future-oriented solutions needed for EWC success.

The distinction between creativity and innovation is critical to understanding and ensuring the success of EWC. Andrew Papageorge is the creator of *The Go-Innovate! System of Innovation* (www.goinnovate.com). In his view, creativity is the starting point—the creation of new and useful ideas. But creativity alone won't do the trick. Enterprises need to ensure that they also have the content, process, structures, competencies, and resources in place to ensure that the new idea is translated into a tangible innovation that generates wealth.

Papageorge also says a new idea does not always have to be an original idea—it only has to be new to your particular situation. In a similar vein, he defines wealth in the context of what is valued by the individual, team, and enterprise sponsoring the innovation.

A simple A-B-C-D-E project management tool that can be used by each project team to assess its readiness and capacity for supporting creativity and innovation is in the chapter recap.

Our A-B-C-D-E Simplicity of Systems Thinking framework has been applied throughout this book as a macro Systems Thinking model. It is also an excellent framework for all teams, but especially for innovative process and project teams, as found in Haines (2003). Figure 7.5 is an example of the ABCs applied to project teams:

Figure 7.5. The ABCs of High-Performance Project/Process Teams

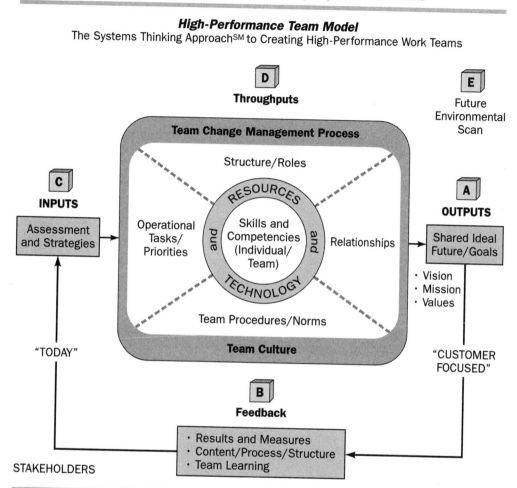

High-Performance Team Model
The Systems Thinking Approach℠ to Creating High-Performance Work Teams

Table 7.1 provides a partial list (that keeps growing) of different ways to use the ABCs. We seem to be restricted only by the limits of our imagination when looking for ways in which the ABCs can be applied to all aspects of EWC.

Table 7.1. Some Uses of the A-B-C-D-E Simplicity-of-Thinking Framework

Ten ABCs Applications	One Key Purpose
1. Team effectiveness	To comprehensively focus on all aspects of teams to dramatically enhance their outcomesand effectiveness
2. Leadership development system	To enhance leadership roles and competencies as a competitive business edge
3. Strategic HR management	To create the "people edge"
4. Creating the learning organization	To use systems thinking framework and concepts, including environmental scanning, clarity of outcomes, and regular feedback
5. Innovation as a specific cultural change	To meet the need for flexibility, adaptability, empowerment, and agility as key success values and variables
6. Reorganizations and redesigns of organizations	To ensure watertight integrity and business excellence
7. Cultural change	To base organizational core values in balance with alignment and attunement
8. Becoming more customer- or market-focused	To improve the enterprise's positioning
9. Large-scale process improvement changes	To improve processes through TQM, Six Sigma, and reengineering efforts
10. Strategic planning	To develop a strategic planning process for an entire organization followed by an Enterprise-Wide Change journey

 THINK DIFFERENTLY

Just forming groups of people does not create effective teams. It takes systematic work on the part of the team.

As part of a contract to provide team development and coaching support for a large project at a successful architectural firm, a colleague used the ABCs model of the Systems Thinking Approach as the basis for the team development sessions. In addition, the consultant also wanted the executives to see the value of adopting Systems Thinking as a natural way for them to react to the pressure situations in the project.

During a session in which they were having a conversation about crises, a team member had an emergency that needed to be handled. Without thinking, the executive jumped up and headed for the phone on a side table in the meeting room and was ready to react to the crisis.

The executive was asked to stop and reflect on what was happening. After a moment she said, "I'm doing it again, aren't I?" The consultant asked what her desired outcome was. He also asked what the desired outcome was from the distraught employee who had interrupted the session. These questions helped the executive recognize that by responding immediately to the request for help, she was in fact reinforcing the very behavior she was hoping that her employee would change.

Cascade #5: Performance Management and Rewards (Both One-to-One and Self Rings)

Activity #7: Remember the Systems Thinking concept of finding the *leverage points in change*? Complex systems are changed by small interventions. No book on EWC would be complete without mention of the leverage of *rewards systems* in two important ways.

- The obvious one is to tie all pay programs such as merit increases, bonuses, and incentives to the goals of EWC at all the different systems levels of results required, including individual performance, team/department or unit results, and the enterprise as a whole.

- The other powerful leverage point is *frequent recognition programs*. Be careful, however, of an employee-of-the-year program, which is another analytical approach that will yield negative, unintended side effects.

THINK DIFFERENTLY

The most powerful reward is a personal handwritten thank-you card to someone you saw do something right to move the EWC ahead. The first President Bush was famous for this throughout his career. He continued it while he was President of the United States with the foreign leaders he met. And the result? When the 1991 Persian Gulf War to retake Kuwait from Iraq required an invasion, he had allies from all the governments of the world.

Note: For further reading, we recommend Nelson (1994).

Questions to Ponder

- What other ways can you ensure simplicity wins the day in execution?

- What is your thirty-second elevator speech about the need for shared core strategies?

- What can your organization do to improve its vital need for innovation?

- What is your reaction to the sequence of activities presented here?

Work *In* the Enterprise

Cascade the EWC Journey throughout the organization:

Cascade #1: Shared Core EWC Strategies (Total-Organization Ring)

Cascade #2: Department Change Plans (Work-Teams Ring)

Cascade #3: Large-Group EWC Cross-Functional Reviews (Between-Departments Ring)

Cascade #4: EWC Execution Vehicles—Innovative Process and Project Teams (Between-Departments Ring)

Cascade #5: Performance Management and Rewards (Both One-to-One and Self Rings)

> The parts must fit. Success is not the result of one action, but many actions, each bringing us closer to our goal.
>
> *Leadership for Life Academy*

The Top Ten Fragmented Parts of an Enterprise

1. Fragmented Information Systems

2. Fragmented Training and Development Efforts

3. Fragmented Departments Goal Setting

4. Fragmented Unit Plans

5. Fragmented Measurements of Success

6. Fragmented Priorities and Mindsets

7. Fragmented Performance Appraisals

8. Fragmented Reward System

9. Fragmented Projects and Consultants

10. Fragmented Leadership Development Efforts

▶ COMPREHENSIVE CASE STUDY
East Coast Federal Credit Union Enterprise-Wide Change: Part 4

Activity #1. After the board/management retreat in October, we met with management in November. Management confirmed their commitment and resolve to *Take Charge of Change,* their "rallying cry." Detailed strategies and action plans were developed and individual accountability assigned. They were now clear about how to successfully complete their *consensus list/action plan* of ten key decisions (a major change list) to transform the Credit Union. Innovative Project Teams were formed to focus on each one. Preparation for the December board EWC meeting also ensued.

Activity #2. We assisted management in conducting a one-day large-group session with key employees, including developing a draft set of core values. Senior management finalized these afterward. The board subsequently approved the core values at the December board meeting. There was no opposition—an unexpected consensus.

Activity #3. In discussions with the board chair, the CEO received a clear picture of backsliding by the board members. Entropy by the board was setting in as expected. Senior management and the Program Management Office held another one-day retreat in early December to prepare for the board meeting. Management clarified their thinking and the purposes, strategy, and agenda for the upcoming board meeting, keeping the high road in mind at all times.

Activity #4. The December board meeting had six agenda items and purposes that were actually accomplished.

The first objective was to revisit their dire financial situation. This included a list of numerous specific poor board rubber-stamp approvals of prior CEO decisions in the past seven years (NCUA had already noted these), decisions which had led to their perilous situation. It was a very difficult facilitation process, to say the least.

The second and third agenda items presented them with a stark set of options and decisions (*choice points*), as there were seven possible actions. Six of the choices would lead to a death spiral within two years. The board chose the only viable option available—focusing on the future marketplace near their headquarters.

These two *tough* agenda items did succeed in setting the stage for approvals of the other four agenda items that followed:

- The next year's annual plans, priorities, and budgets to carry out the goals of the EWC

- The *criteria* to be used in deciding the fate of the branches in the other states—where some board members lived—including one new branch the board had spent millions to build four years before (now worth only 40 percent of its initial value)

- The *process* for deciding the future fate of the three branches by the following June

- A new credit union name that reflected both their heritage and the location in which they were going to focus and position themselves for long-term success

  Note: A name change was in the Ten Consensus Decisions List noted above. However, the board never felt it would happen, despite the absolute necessity to reposition the credit union, now lacking its previous sponsor. The COO came up with a new name, *America the Beautiful Credit Union* (fictitious name). It was so brilliant that the patriotic board members immediately embraced it.

  To be continued . . . ◄

Chapter Seven Recap

1. Simplistic, knee-jerk, or isolated actions are just that—quick fixes that fail.

2. Core strategies are the business glue of an Enterprise-Wide Change.

3. In the Systems Thinking Approach, both alignment and attunement strategies must be taken into consideration.

4. Integration and differentiation are the age-old problems in organizations undergoing EWC.

5. There are five levels of the cascade of the business *glue* in EWC:

   Cascade #1: Shared Core EWC Strategies (Total-Organization Ring)

   Cascade #2: Department Change Plans (Work-Teams Ring)

   Cascade #3: Large-Group EWC Cross-Functional Reviews (Between-Departments Ring)

   Cascade #4: EWC Execution Vehicles—Innovative Process and Project Teams (Between-Departments Ring)

   Cascade #5: Performance Management and Rewards (Both One-to-One and Self Rings)

6. Innovative Process and Project Teams are the primary vehicles for execution of EWC.

7. Project Teams can use the A-B-C-D-Es of Simplicity of the Systems Thinking Framework to keep their work clear and simple.

8. Other uses of the ABC Model in EWC might include

   - Team effectiveness
   - Leadership development system
   - Strategic Human Resource management
   - Creating the learning organization
   - Innovation as a specific cultural change

- Reorganizations and re-designs of organizations
- Cultural change overall of any type
- Becoming more customer or market focused
- Large-scale process improvement changes
- Strategic planning and/or Three-year business planning

9. The activities for the simplicity of execution include

Activity #1: The Change Leadership Team develops the draft of the EWC core strategies and key initiatives

Activity #2: A parallel involvement process reviews, critiques, and extends this set of core strategies

Activity #3: A final review and clean-up of the draft is completed

Activity #4: Business units and departments develop *work plans* to support the strategies and key initiatives

Activity #5: A parallel involvement process is held to critique these work plans

Activity #6: Innovative process and project teams are set up as the key execution vehicles

Activity #7: All reward systems—compensation and recognition programs—are tied to the desired EWC results

ANNUAL PLANS: YEARLY "CHEAT SHEET" AND TO-DO LIST

What are the top 3–4 priority initiatives for each Core Strategy which need to be accomplished?

Core Strategies and Top Priority Initiatives	Who's Responsible?	When Done?
Core Strategy #1 1. 2. 3. 4.		
Core Strategy #2 1. 2. 3. 4.		
Core Strategy #3 1. 2. 3. 4.		
Core Strategy #4 1. 2. 3. 4.		
Core Strategy #5 1. 2. 3. 4.		
Core Strategy #6 1. 2. 3. 4.		
Core Strategy #7 1. 2. 3. 4.		

Department: _____

Date: _____
Fiscal Year: _____

ANNUAL WORK PLAN FORMAT
(Also for functional/division work plans)

_____ : Strategy/Goals: _____

Yearly Priority #	Action Items (Actions/Objectives/How?)	Support/Resources Needed	Who Is Responsible?	Who Else to Involve?	When Done?	How to Measure? (Optional)	Status

STRATEGIC THINKING: ABCs TEMPLATE
"The Simplicity of Systems Thinking"

_____ (Name of the System – Issue – Problem – Project – Change Effort)

E **Future Environmental Scan:**
What will be changing in your future environment that will affect you?

• • • • • •

D **System Throughput/Processes:**
How do we get there (close the gap from [C] → [A])?

↑ **CORE STRATEGIES: TOP PRIORITY ACTIONS:** ↑

• • • • •

C **Current State Assessments:**
Where are we now (SWOT)?

Inputs ←

Strengths

• • • • • • • •

Weaknesses

• • • • • • • • •

A

Outputs →

Desired Outcomes—
#1 Systems Question:
Where do we want to be?

• • • • •

↓

B **Feedback Loop/Measurements:**
How will we know when we get there?

• • • • •

Opportunities

• • • • • • • •

Threats

• • • • • •

(8)

Wave After Wave
of Changes

D
Strategies
Actions

Chapter Purposes

- To explore the six natural and normal stages of change outlined in the Roller-coaster of Change model

- To learn how and where change occurs, wave after wave—both individually and enterprise-wide

- To learn how to classify and encompass all traditional change and OD interventions as part of the Systems Thinking Approach to Enterprise-Wide Change

Thinking is easy. Acting is difficult. To put one's thoughts into action is the most difficult thing in the world.

Goethe

The ABCs of Enterprise-Wide Change

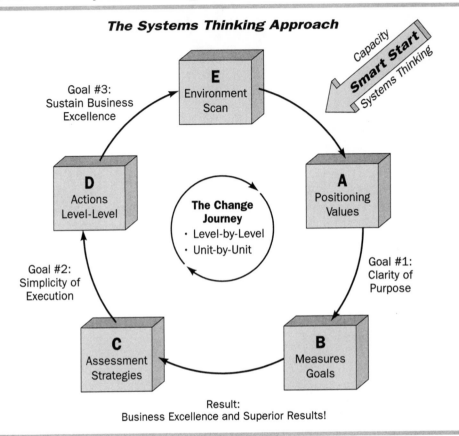

The Systems Thinking Approach

Goal #3:
Sustain Business
Excellence

E
Environment
Scan

Capacity
Smart Start
Systems Thinking

D
Actions
Level-Level

The Change
Journey
· Level-by-Level
· Unit-by-Unit

A
Positioning
Values

Goal #1:
Clarity of
Purpose

Goal #2:
Simplicity of
Execution

C
Assessment
Strategies

B
Measures
Goals

Result:
Business Excellence and Superior Results!

D
Strategies
Actions

Chapter Context
The Cascade of Change Continues

Phase D in the Systems Thinking concept (Chapter Three) represents the enterprise as a living system.

Chapter Seven began the cascade of change within the enterprise using the business glue of core EWC strategies. They were cascaded down and throughout the organization to ensure clarity of enterprise-wide goals, key enterprise-wide initiatives, personal accountability, performance, and rewards. The concept of the Seven

Levels of Living Systems was translated and applied as the Seven Natural Rings of Reality in Chapter Seven, and we will continue the discussion here.

We now reintroduce the last core concept of Systems Thinking from Chapter Three, the Rollercoaster of Change. It applies to every change situation that exists and is repeated here for clarity and emphasis (see Figure 8.1).

Figure 8.1. The Rollercoaster of Change

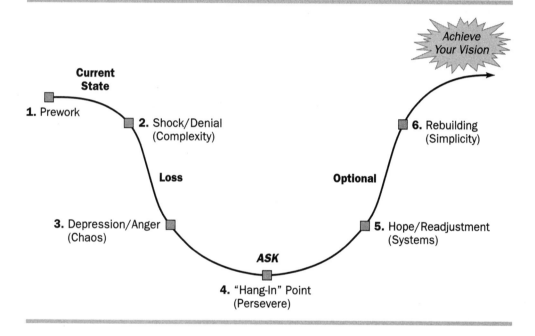

In this chapter, we will apply the Rollercoaster of Change to two basic living systems levels in every enterprise: (1) individuals and employees and (2) the total enterprise.

Enterprise-Wide Change must be focused on these two levels throughout if the cascade of change is to succeed. The level of departments, units, and project teams is also critical and was covered in Chapter Seven as Cascade #4—EWC Execution Vehicles.

To see how Systems Thinking integrates with (1) our macro A-B-C-D-E Systems Model and with Phase D, inner workings of an enterprise, and (2) with the Rollercoaster of Change, examine Figure 8.2.

Figure 8.2. The Inner Workings of the System

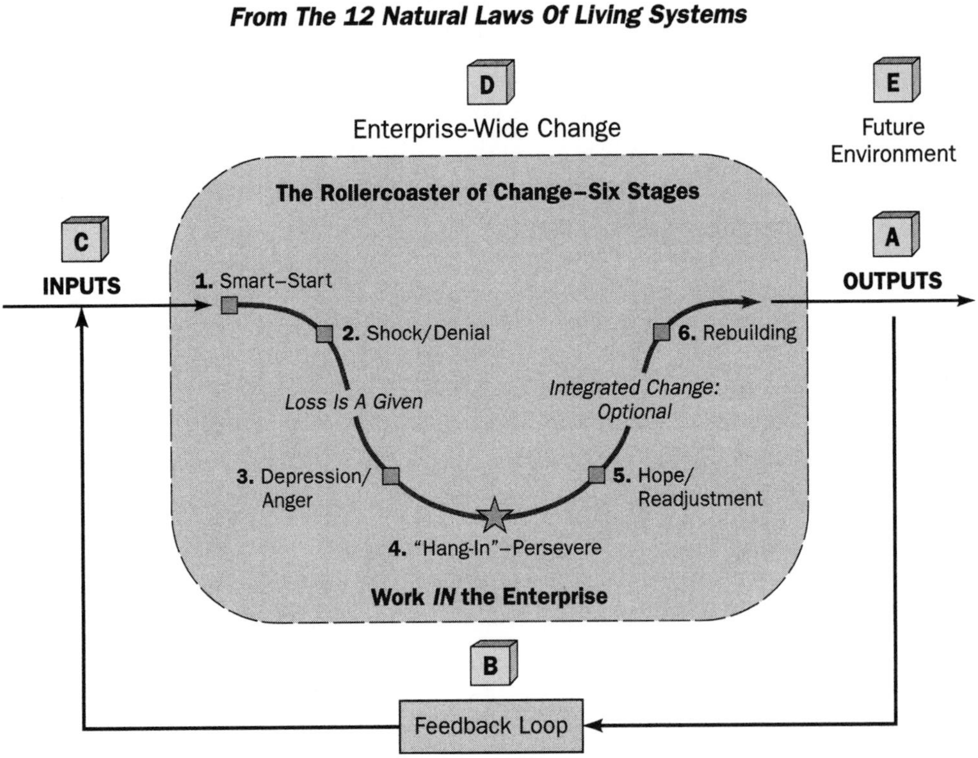

From The 12 Natural Laws Of Living Systems

Simplicity: Do you see it? You see . . . everything is simple but . . . you just have to see it.

> *Josefa Brandenberg, Tour Guide,*
> *Regensburg, Germany, December 2003*

Individual Change: The Rollercoaster of Change

Led by the formation of the Enterprise-Wide Change Leadership Team, the Program Management Office, and Innovative Project Teams, you are ready for the *formal* execution of the Enterprise-Wide Change journey. A key question is how to keep this process simple.

The Rollercoaster of Change illustrates the natural and normal way people react to change. It doesn't matter whether the system is an individual, an interpersonal relationship, an intact team, a cross-functional team, or a total organization; it is still a living, organic system. In his seminal work on the transition aspect of change, Bridges (1991) discusses this concept extensively.

The Rollercoaster is perhaps the most important concept change consultants can use to understand the process of EWC. The Rollercoaster can be applied to *every* change initiative within an overall Enterprise-Wide Change effort.

In an EWC journey, a major concern is the right-hand side of the Rollercoaster, which requires the involvement and participation of many people. Enlisting participation contributes to the new, shared vision and desired outcomes, both for the people involved and for the organization as a whole. The right-hand side of the Rollercoaster allows people to discover for themselves *what's in it for me* (WIIFM).

Any kind of new learning that helps people feel they are growing also helps to get an enterprise through the Rollercoaster. Unfortunately, change leaders can experience five different pathways with the Rollercoaster, not all of them yielding the superior results desired.

> It takes eighteen months to two years of steady disciplined effort to feel comfortable with new behavior.
>
> *Harles Cone*

Why does it take so long?

Successful individual change requires changes in people's knowledge, skills, and attitudes resulting in three waves of change.

Wave #1:   Knowledge = Acquired new intellectual understanding

Wave #2:   Skills = Developed through active involvement, participation, and practice

Wave #3:   Attitude = Supported emotionally by peers and supervisors

Rollercoaster Questions

Question #1:   *It is not whether or not we will go through* shock and depression . . . but rather, *when* will it occur?

Question #2:   *How deep will the trough be?* The depth of psychological change will take away from the energy for performance in a person's or a team's life.

Question #3:   *How long will it take to get over to the right-hand side, rebuilding?* It is *not* a given that the Rollercoaster has to involve a major dip during a change process. The depth and the length of the change frequently depend on leadership's ability to manage themselves and others through this curve so that the curve itself is as shallow as possible.

Question #4:   Will we *get up to the right-hand side of the curve and rebuild at all?* The left-hand side of the Rollercoaster is a given, but as Figure 8.1 illustrates, reaching a high point on the right-hand side is not. Reaching the "top" of the right-hand side requires doing many things right and having proactive strategies to guide the organization through change.

Question #5:   *Will we rebuild to the highest level of new achievement—one that makes the entire change process and pain worthwhile?* Viewing the situation from the current state, you should carefully examine whether the outcome or final rebuilding stage is at a higher level, the same level, or some lower level than where you were before. The only reason to undergo change at all is to end up with an improvement that is worth your tolerating the pain and the dysfunctional behavior during the chaos, complexity, and emotions of the Rollercoaster's dip.

Question #6:   *How many different Rollercoasters might we have to experience at any one time?* This is a particularly troubling question in the 21st Century. From a Systems Thinking perspective, no organization ever experiences only one Rollercoaster at a time. Since people's personal and professional lives are intertwined, they experience a confluence of many different changes at the same time. The conflicting emotions that we have about change are often the result of multiple concurrent changes.

Question #7:   *Will we hang in and persevere through the change?* The hang-in point is where many EWC processes fail. The key is to recognize that this is a Rollercoaster, understand what the hang-in point feels like as it is occurring, and persist despite depression and/or anger. The perils of attempting to *stop* an EWC midway through are many, as you can see. An interrupted change leaves you in a lower position than you were in to begin with—even more reason to persevere through that "hang in" point.

The only alternative to persistence is failure. Nothing in the world can take the place of persistence. Talent will not; nothing is more common than unsuccessful men with talent. Genius will not; unrewarded genius is almost a proverb. Education alone will not; the world is full of educated idiots. Persistence and determination alone are omnipotent.

Calvin Coolidge

Question #8:   *How can we deal with normal resistance?* The reality is that depression, anger, pessimism, cynicism, other negative emotions, and the accompanying resistance are normal. Leadership can either assist it by applying the methods described earlier or make it far worse by saying things like "You shouldn't be upset" or "If you don't change, I'm going to fire you." Dealing with resistance is better done through participation, empathy, and open communication than through command-and-control pushing, which is often the first instinct of inexperienced (and sometimes incompetent) managers.

Question #9:   *How can we create a critical mass in support of the change?* There are always some early adopters, but large groups—the silent majority—take a wait-and-see attitude about EWC. And often a few people are strong resisters. Failure in change can occur when leadership focuses on the small group of resisters, rather than trying to work with early adopters and the silent majority to create a critical mass in positive support of the change. Change leaders can go a long way by involving people early in the process and showing them *exactly* what's in it for them (WIIFM). The people who have recently been brought on board can become informal leaders of the critical mass and eventually assist the resisters in adapting to the change. Then the change becomes one that cannot be stopped.

All Change Is a Loss Experience

Perceived loss creates a feeling of depression for people. They lose preferred modes of attaining and giving affection and handling aggression. Dependency needs *familiar routines* that have evolved and are usually taken for granted.

Loss is a difficult experience to handle, particularly if the loss is psychologically important. All loss must be mourned and one's feelings must be expressed if a restitution process is to operate effectively.

Most organization change flounders because the experience of loss is not taken into account. To undertake successful organizational change, leaders must anticipate and provide the means of working through that loss (adapted from Levinson, 1976).

> The basic truth of management—if not of life—is that nearly everything looks like a failure in the middle . . . persistent, consistent execution is unglamorous, time-consuming, and boring. Overvaluing strategy (by which many companies mean Big Ideas and Big Decisions) and undervaluing execution lead not only to implementation shortfalls but also to misinterpreting the reasons for success or failure.
>
> *Rosabeth Moss-Kanter*

Enterprise-Wide Change and the Rollercoaster of Change

When viewing the Rollercoaster of Change, keep in mind that Enterprise-Wide Change is unique, complex, and a confusing Rubik's Cube of activities, many with unintended consequences. As a result there are five different pathways the change can take, shown in Figure 8.3 and Table 8.1.

Figure 8.3. Five Possible Pathways of the Rollercoaster

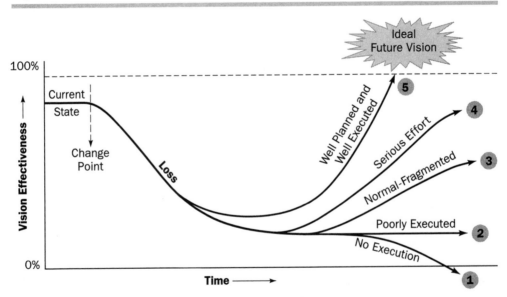

Table 8.1. The Five Possible Pathways

Pathway	Possible Cause	Possible Result
Pathway 1	**Incompetence;** no execution	Going out of business
Pathway 2	**Technical compliance;** poor execution	Dogged pursuit of mediocrity
Pathway 3	**Basic management;** "normal," fragmented execution	Present and accounted for
Pathway 4	**Leadership;** serious efforts in execution	A visible serious effort
Pathway 5	**Visionary leadership;** well planned and executed	Developing an art form

Which pathway is your enterprise pursuing or likely to pursue? Be honest.

Throughout the complexities and the chaos of the Rollercoaster, people, teams, and organizations must continually

- Reinforce and articulate the new vision and positioning and why change is important
- Provide rewards, reinforcement, and recognition for others as they proceed through the Rollercoaster toward the new positioning

Only in the final stage of the Rollercoaster (rebuilding) can people be empowered to work effectively in their jobs and teams. That is because the rebuilding stage is the only stage of *high performance* in the entire Rollercoaster of Change—the only stage in which every person and subsystem has the ability and tools to reach full potential.

When viewed from the enterprise-wide perspective that the Change Leadership Team and Program Management Office must take, the Rollercoaster of Change has six stages as it traverses the multi-year effort required, as seen in Figure 8.4.

Figure 8.4. Six Stages of the Rollercoaster of Change

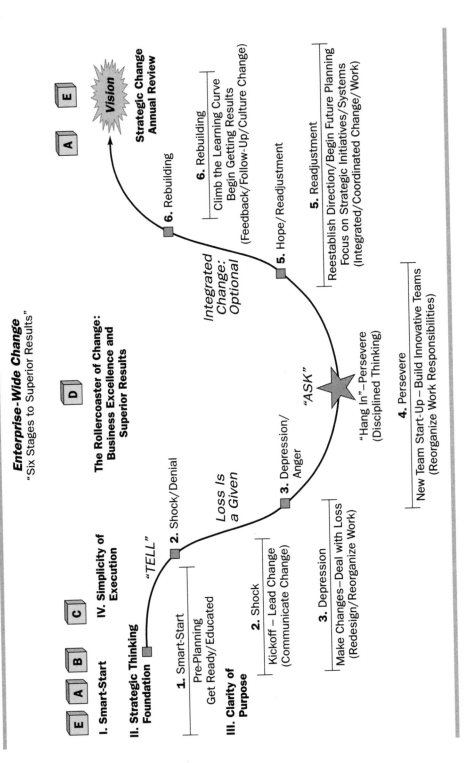

In summary there are six more stages of the Rollercoaster journey through Phase D to reach your vision.

Stage 1: Smart Start. This is the pre-planning stage we covered earlier (educate—assess—organize—and tailor).

Stage 2: Shock and Denial. This is the overt, formal rollout of the Enterprise-Wide Change. Here the change is announced and communicated to employees. Communications must adhere to the principles of clarity and simplicity, and the message must be repeated at least three times, preferably more. This is where resistance begins to be visible.

Stage 3: Anger and Depression. This is the predictable stage in which depression, anger, and a sense of loss occur. It cannot be avoided. This is where the actual changes start having an impact. Redesign and reorganizing, changing of jobs, changing the reward system, and other physical manifestations of the change start happening. Major change consultant work and facilitation are needed here. This is not a stage to be feared, but to be celebrated, because it means the change is actually happening. The *denial* from Stage 2 is over.

Stage 4: Hang In and Persevere. New team start-up and the reorganization of the work responsibilities begin. This is where new relationships with new supervisors, peers, and subordinates need to be established, and this is where many changes fail. Often executives pretend that these new groups are actually (*poof!*) effective teams ready to do good work. Alas, no. In the Rollercoaster of Change, *things always get worse before they get better.* Major change consultant work and facilitation are also needed here, and one huge caveat for the entire Change Leadership Team is to make sure that adequate staff and resources are on hand. Otherwise, failure is almost inevitable.

This is usually a good time for Change Leadership Team/PMO meetings for mid-course corrections as different milestones are met. Regular checkups, feedback, and adjustments on the EWC journey are essential for success.

Stage 5: Hope and Readjustment. Now the readjustment begins. The learning curve must be climbed. The choice of which of the five pathways will be taken depends on the seriousness of the leadership team at this stage. An initial, serious focus on re-establishing the goals and future direction of the new teams and units is crucial. Smart Start and planned change efforts should be the norm here. Repeated and frequent clarification of goals and roles is paramount.

Stage 6: Rebuilding and Results. In the rebuilding stage, a completely refocused new business begins to emerge. It is only here that effective teamwork, high performance, and business excellence can begin. The question is not whether to rebuild, but at *which of the five levels of excellence will the enterprise rebuild*? Will superior results occur?

 THINK DIFFERENTLY

In 2003, Gateway Computers of San Diego, California, decided to conduct a major refocusing of its business away from its money-losing computer manufacturing business. The company decided to move into consumer electronics as if this was a new market with few competitors. Wall Street analysts have serious questions about whether Gateway's Enterprise-Wide Change has any chance of success. A merger has since ensued.

At a minimum, a new focus such as this will cause a major Rollercoaster of Change: Things will get worse before they get better.

Gateway's lack of positioning in the marketplace is a reality. They are newcomers to a highly competitive market with major competitors.

Making the new products for the first time at a high level of quality is not assured. The company has become non-competitive in computers, and a quick switch like this might be *the Quick Fix that fails.*

Questions to Ponder
- Are you clear on the details of how the Rollercoaster operates?
- Can you apply the Rollercoaster to a change you are experiencing in your personal life?
- Is there any change you can think of where this Rollercoaster would not apply?

The Cascade of Change: Wave After Wave

Life's a dance. You learn as you go.

Country and Western refrain, sung by John Michael Montgomery,
written by Allen Shamblin/Steve Seskin

Successful EWC is made much more difficult due to the resistance inherent in the Rollercoaster of Change. It requires a great deal of flexibility and dancing to the music as it unfolds. This includes some type of cultural change. The good news is that employees *want* to be happy, engaged, and satisfied with the culture and environment. If they are not, customers see and feel the difference.

Although *organizational change* is a common term in the OD field and one we have used in this book, it is, technically, a misnomer. Organizations are high-level living systems and change only when their subsystems (people, units, departments, and groups) change *their* behaviors. As we discussed when we explored the Rollercoaster of Change, people change at different rates and depths due to a variety of internal and external factors. When a significant number of people within an enterprise change their behaviors in the same direction, *organizational change* is the result. This does not just happen by osmosis.

The Destructive Change Myth: Salute and Execute

Everyone

    is for it

        feels they understand it

            thinks execution is only a matter of following natural inclinations

                feels that problems are caused by other people

Instead of *salute and execute*, think about ocean waves and how they crash onto the shore, wave after wave, one after the other, changing each other in the process. In a very real sense, this is also how change occurs across an entire enterprise—wave after wave, level after level. This phenomenon is a demonstration of the interrelated dynamics of the Seven Levels (waves) of Living Systems and its Seven Natural Rings of Reality at work. They make this EWC process even more difficult.

The Cascade of Enterprise-Wide Change

The first three waves of change are intra-personal—within an individual—acquiring the knowledge (*Wave #1*), attitudes (*Wave #2*), and skills (*Wave #3*) to adjust to fit the EWC. However, that is just the beginning of the waves of change.

Keep in mind that organizations are systems . . . within systems . . . within systems. How does change really occur? Here are some different waves to think about when dealing with the waves of change:

- Individually (Knowledge—Attitudes—Skills) (*Waves #1, #2, #3*)
- Level-by-Level Wave (*Wave #4*)

  Top executives

  Middle managers

  Skilled professionals

  All other employees
- Unit-by-Unit Wave

  Small units/sections

  Functional work teams

  Cross-functional teams

  Project/process teams

- Department-by-Department Wave

  Operations

  Human Resources

  Information Systems

  Legal

  Finance

  Marketing

  Sales

  Engineering

- Different Subculture Waves

  Operating business units

  Ethnic/cultural/linguistic

  Field locations

  Social/professional

  Male/female

- Adversarial Cultures Waves

  Line versus staff departments

  Manufacturing versus marketing

  Headquarters versus field

  Division versus division

  Union versus management

This cascade of change (*Wave #4*) must specifically impact and enlist all the above waves, including all strategic business units, lines of business, operating and geographical divisions, and teams. It must also include all major company-wide support departments such as finance, HR, marketing, and IT.

This is a commonly missed step in EWC and a serious omission. Regardless of the specific vision of the EWC, you must effectively cascade the process to all these units, levels, and waves.

Wave #5: The most challenging level of change in an organization is to change the business processes and overall culture required to support the desired outcomes (see Figure 8.5).

Figure 8.5. Waves of Change in an Organization

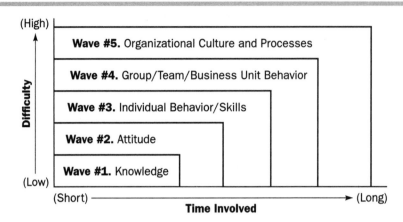

When you take into account the complex interactions and relationships among all of an enterprise's subcultures, professional orientations, and physical locations, and then complicate the picture with diversity of language, culture, social, and economic orientations, it is actually a wonder that *any* Enterprise-Wide Change is successful.

Because an organization is a system with many subsystems (all of which are interconnected and affect one another) and since Systems Thinking requires awareness of the web of interrelationships between the parts, what can change consultants actually do to effectively help leadership *change all these subsystems*?

There is truth in the maxim "The devil is in the details." The *inner workings* of the organization as a living system, like the Rubik's Cube, are impossible to enumerate when you try to break them down one-by-one. There are over a trillion possible moves on a Rubik's Cube, and there are probably the same number of relationships within a living, open system like an enterprise.

The only way to successfully deal with these waves and waves of the Rollercoaster of Change is to find the *simplicity on the far side of complexity*. The Change Leadership Team and change consultants can improve the chances of guiding a positive change if they attend to the key points below. There is no lock-step process in Enterprise-Wide Change:

- Enterprise-Wide Change is a constantly unfolding discovery, creation, and re-creation process that cascades through and across the organization. The

Change Leadership Team will have to continually review and update its EWC Game Plan. This is being flexible and responsive to a changing internal and external environment.

- Expect that emergent strategies and new key initiatives will come up on a regular basis.

- The Systems Thinking approach to living systems tells us that each *wave* of subsystem change must be planned, discussed, led, and implemented in relationship to other subsystems. The Change Leadership Team must work with those responsible for all these subsystems every step of the way. There is no easy answer—just the guiding concepts and principles of Systems Thinking, including Rollercoaster of Change.

- Each of these subsystems (and the people in them) goes through the predictable six stages of the Rollercoaster of Change at different depths and rates—thus requiring different actions. Three different levels are the broadbrush view of change: executives, managers, and workers.

- The Program Management Office should lead these activities on a day-to-day basis to keep Failure #1 (Multiple Conflicting Mental Maps) from rearing its ugly head.

- The Systems Thinking Approach can and should be *bolstered by traditional OD interventions,* but these must always be linked to the larger purpose—Enterprise-Wide Change.

> When the drumbeat changes, the dance changes.
>
> *Hausa people*

 THINK DIFFERENTLY

A large savings and loan on the East Coast was in danger of failing, having lost many millions over the past five years. As a result, a new CEO and a three-person turnaround team were hired.

There was no time for a full EWC process as wave after wave of change was required in short order. Thus, the CEO and turnaround team came up with a vision of solid profitability within one year. In addition, they used a Systems Thinking, enterprise-wide methodology that borrowed heavily from the beliefs presented in this chapter.

They created a large thirty-person Change Leadership Team of all the top and middle management. A Program Management Office, jointly staffed by an internal executive and an external systems consultant, facilitated it. All key subsystems (departments and lines of business) were represented.

This team met weekly and worked from a massive 100-item list of major changes recommended by the grassroots employees in a Parallel Involvement Process. In an innovative approach, the CEO declared this list to be an accurate representation of needed changes. Each week, five to ten of the items were assigned to members of the Change Leadership Team to investigate and come back the next week with a specific proposed key initiative to resolve the issue.

Of course, what was really happening was a fast evaluation of each executive's ability to think, problem solve, and get *on board* with the urgency of the turnaround and EWC. Many traditional OD interventions ensued. Change consultants were ready and in place to resource the EWC, and the PMO led the overall effort.

The result was over a $100M pre-tax profit in the first full year of the EWC. Many of the existing executives had to be replaced as they failed the evaluation. Employee morale went up, as they already knew of the poor executive performance that had led to the massive losses.

In successful Enterprise-Wide Change journeys such as the above, a need exists for lots of mini-change projects within the overall PMO concept. These are usually traditional, mainstream OD and change interventions. The good news about Systems Thinking is that it does not lend itself to false either-or questions like the following:

"Should we use a Systems Thinking Approach to Enterprise-Wide Change— or—use a more traditional change and OD intervention?" The answer, happily, is an unequivocal "Yes, both!"

In order to integrate these two basic approaches to EWC, we will show how the traditional, mainstream OD and change interventions fit within the cascade and waves of change. The skill to use these interventions is essential to Enterprise-Wide Change. We have already discussed many of these in the Think Differently stories, as well as in the specific activities we have recommended throughout this book. We show this integration of EWC and traditional change interventions by using the Seven Natural Rings of Reality again, as it is a simple way to think about the cascade and different waves of change.

Seven Natural Rings of Reality: Classifying Mainstream OD Change Interventions

The Seven Natural Rings of Reality hold a key to holistic and long-lasting change, as the model provides a simple framework to understand the changes cascading through all the levels of an organization.

The seven rings also illustrate again why organization-wide change is so difficult to achieve. It requires not only changes at the three levels of individual, team, and organization, but also at each of the three intersections between the levels, as well as considering external and community factors.

Traditional mainstream OD interventions are extremely useful within an EWC journey that uses a Systems Thinking framework. So long as change consultants and executives keep in mind that relationships between the levels are just as important as the levels themselves, these interventions use proven and reliable tactics for achieving change at the various levels and subsystems needing changes. The Seven Natural Rings of Reality framework can help change consultants quickly select which interventions are appropriate based on the level(s) of desired change. In any application of the seven rings, keep in mind that the complexity and difficulty of execution increase as we move from the inner ring (individual) toward the outer ring (community/society). Table 8.2 maps the rings against various intervention goals.

Table 8.2. Traditional OD Goals and the Rings

Ring	Goals	OD and Change Intervention Topics
Ring #3: Self-Mastery	Improve personal competency and effectiveness (Trustworthiness issues within oneself)	Presentation Skills Communication Skills Core Competencies Distance Learning Leadership Development Executive Development Management Development Training Programs in General Core Values Knowledge/Skill-Based Pay
Ring #3A: One-to-One Interpersonal Relationships	Improve interpersonal and working relationships with others (Trust issues between individuals)	Performance Improvement Performance Evaluation Personal Styles Coaching Mentoring Counseling Performance Management Employee Selection Recognition/Thank-You Cards 360-Degree Feedback/Peer Reviews Incentive Compensation Programs EEO/Harassment/Diversity Retention of Employees Situational Leadership™ Job Rotation/Cross-Training Individual Development Plans Human Interaction Labs T-Groups Conflict Management
Ring #4: Work Teams/Groups	Improve the effectiveness of the work team (Empowerment and role/relationship issues)	Problem Solving Decision Making High-Performance Technology Conflict Management Group Development Team Building Empowerment Processes/Involvement Group/Team-Based Compensation

Table 8.2. Traditional OD Goals and the Rings, Cont'd

Ring	Goals	OD and Change Intervention Topics
Ring #4A: Inter-Group/ Cross-Functional Groups	Improve the working relationships and business processes between departments (Horizontal collaboration/ integration issues)	Project Management Quality Circles Task Forces Problem-Solving Teams Productivity Improvement Process Improvement Total Quality Management Business Process Reengineering Conflict Management Advocacy and Inquiry/Dialogue Appreciative Inquiry Self-Directed Work Teams Workout/Blowout Bureaucracy Causal Loop Learning/Archetypes Cost Accounting
Ring #5: Total Organization	Improve the organization's structures and processes to achieve business results (Alignment and attunement issues)	Cultural Change/Transformation Values Development Installing a Strategic Management System Strategic Change Management/ Implementation Customer Service Key Success Measures/Metrics Force Field Analysis The Balanced Scorecard Human Resource Planning HR Strategic Planning The Learning Organization Transition Management Whole Systems Approach Whole-Scale Change Real-Time Strategic Change Knowledge Management Workforce Management Experiential Learning Cycle Accelerated Learning Power and Influence/Org. Workshop Open Space Technology Gestalt Organizations

Table 8.2. Traditional OD Goals and the Rings, Cont'd

Ring	Goals	OD and Change Intervention Topics
		Systems Engineering
		Systems Dynamics
		Self-Organizing Systems
		Complex Adaptive Systems
		Chaos Theory
		Profit Sharing/Gain Sharing
		Merger Integration Teams/Search Conferences
		Strategic Communications
		Organization/Strategic Business Design
		Strategic Marketing and Sales
		Operational Planning
Ring #5A: Organization Environment	Improve the organization's sense of direction, response to its customers, and proactive management of its environment (Adaptation to environmental issues)	Strategic Planning
		Strategic Thinking
		Business Unit Planning
		Vision and Mission Development
		Scenario Planning/Contingency Planning
		Value-Chain Management
		Corporate University
		Systems Thinking
		Creativity/Innovation as a System
		Critical Thinking
		Needs/Stakeholder Analysis
		Six Sigma
		Future Environmental Scanning
		Survey Feedback
		Action Research
		Baldrige Criteria for Performance Excellence
		ESOPs (Employee Stock Ownership Programs)
		Benchmarking
Ring #6: Environment (Community/ Society)	Societal/community improvement	Societal Change Initiatives
		Community Activism
		Political Involvement
		Special-Interest Groups
		Community Development

Note that the interventions are not listed in any priority. If you are dealing with change at a high level (such as Ring #4, Work Teams), you are automatically also dealing with all the rings lower than #4—The Self and the One-to-One levels as well.

This is not intended to be an exhaustive list of change intervention topics, and we make no claim that we have included every one.

These OD and change interventions can be more effective, in many cases, by utilizing the Simplicity of Systems Thinking (ABC Model) as well. Remember that the ABCs are a new orientation to life, including all aspects of an EWC process.

Over the years the Simplicity of Systems Thinking (ABC Model) has been successfully used in a variety of different ways on all parts of EWC processes. Just as you would adjust the zoom of a camera lens to fit the subject to be photographed, you also adjust the focus level and simplicity of the basic ABC Simplicity of Systems Thinking Model to fit the degree of complexity of the subject matter and wave of change at hand.

Whenever mainstream OD and change interventions are being used, some key analytical thinking errors creep in that clients and consultants alike can unwittingly fall prey to. No matter how much the authors try, these are daily Systems Thinking errors we continue to make.

Top Ten Day-to-Day Errors Using Analytical Thinking

1. Failure to know your unintended negative consequences (analytic approach to a systems problem)

2. Focusing on symptoms rather than root causes (root causes are delayed in time and space)

3. Using either-or thinking ("yes, both" versus "yes, but")

4. Seeking one best way/one outcome only ("win-lose" versus "win-win")

5. Lacking booster shots and follow-ups (reverse the entropy)

6. Missing the web of relationships—who else to analyze/key stakeholders (people support what they help create)

7. Grabbing Quick Fixes that fail: "action-reaction" (simplistic knee-jerk reactions to fix your immediate pain)

8. Implementing silo projects and actions

9. Doing it *to* them, not *with* them (adults learn best by doing—struggling)

10. Lacking ongoing feedback and regular environmental scanning (skeptics are my best friends)

And the Big Two Bonus Errors

11. Failing to clarify your goals and purposes first (begin with the end in mind)

12. Failing to keep it simple (KISS: simplicity wins the game every time)

This list illustrates the *failure of fragmented functions* versus the *synergy of systems solutions*.

Questions to Ponder

- Do the Seven Natural Rings of Reality make sense to you as a fact of living systems? Why or why not?

- Do you agree with the goals of each level or ring of reality? Why or why not?

- Can you think of an OD/change intervention that does not fit somewhere in these rings?

- If you disagree with a placement, is there another level in which you would place the intervention instead?

- What else would you add to the list of change intervention topics?

The Seven Natural Rings of Reality is one way to map and clarify the different ways that the Rollercoaster of Change plays out in every single mainstream organization development and change intervention.

Mapping the Internal Working of a Living System

The A-B-C-D-E Simplicity of Systems Thinking is the macro-model in this book. However, within Phase D, the inner workings of a living system (enterprise), there is one final integration of the four main concepts of Systems Thinking, the integration of the Rollercoaster of Change and the Seven Natural Rings of Reality shown in the matrix of Table 8.3.

The Seven Natural Rings of Reality Matrix and the Impact of the Rollercoaster of Change

Simplifying the Many Uses of the Rollercoaster of Change

The matrix in Table 8.3 shows different applications of the Rollercoaster at the different Rings of Reality—many of which are familiar to change consultants. This table shows how the change process and Rollercoaster of Change operate in a similar fashion at all rings, levels, and waves of change.

Enterprise-Wide Change includes Rollercoaster dynamics at the enterprise level and also has concrete effects at the individual, interpersonal, team, and cross-functional levels. "Organizations change only when people change" is a basic truism. At the same time, organizations must implement collective behavioral and process changes to deal with constant and dynamic changes.

It's no wonder that EWC is so difficult. Effective Enterprise-Wide Change requires every person, every team, in every department, in every relationship, and in every project and process, to undergo some kind of behavioral change—each at its own natural pace.

Table 8.3. The Rollercoaster and the Seven Rings Matrix

Uses	Stage #2: Shock	Stage #3: Depression	Stage #4: Hang-In	Stage #5: Hope	Stage #6: Rebuilding
Ring #3: SELF-CHANGE: Understanding People/Change (Death and Dying)	Shock/Denial	Depression, Anger/Blame	Immobilization	Acceptance, Hope/Acknowledge/Readjust	Rebuilding, Constructive Work
Ring #3A: INTERPERSONAL CHANGES (adapted from Schutz) Relationships	Inclusion Desire, Contact/Purpose	Control Issues, Chaos or Compatibility	Growth Desire, Continuous Relationships	Openness, Contract/Norms	High Performance, Collaboration/Work
Ring #4: TEAMS (adapted from Tuckman)	Forming	Storming	"Hang-in"	Norming	Performing
Ring #4A: INTERGROUP CHANGE: Learning Stages (People/Teams/Organizations)	Activity, Experience	*What?* Process the Activity/Feelings/Trends	Transition to Learning Action	*So What?* What have we learned?	*Now What?* Apply the Learning (Application)
Ring #5: ORGANIZATIONAL CHANGE: Strategic Management System (Including Strategic Change)	Where are we today? (Current State Assessment)	Holding On	Letting Go	Fit of Parts, Align	Where do we want to be? (Vision, Values, and Measures)
Ring #5A: ORGANIZATION/ENVIRONMENT: Partnerships/Alliances	Scouting, Entry/Contact	Buyer's Remorse	Openness and Conflict	Clarify Goals, Values, Norms, and Trust	High Performing, Alliance
Ring # 6: COMMUNITY/SOCIETY: Social Involvement	Resistance, Dismay and Skepticism	Political Unrest and Pushback	Factions Formed for/Against	Critical Mass, Support Grows	Enthusiasm Builds for the New Order

◗ THINK DIFFERENTLY

Ring #4A of the Rollercoaster is about intergroup change. Developing process/project teams and creating learning organizations where knowledge is shared across departments/boundaries is not easy. The Experiential Learning Cycle, as well as accelerated learning, have, at their core, the fact that *adults learn best by doing.* Effective training and development build on this.

It is not enough to just acquire knowledge. It requires emotional stimulation, practice, learning from the experiences, and applying the learnings.

Learning results in changing a person. Learners go through the Rollercoaster of Change as well. Change agents must ask three key questions to finish the cycle: *What? So What? Now What?*

One of the authors at one point in his career was hired to be the president of University Associates Training and Consulting. He was brought in to turn the business around. He found that the EWC process could not begin and that he had no credibility until he became lead trainer and was able to apply the Experiential Learning Cycle in training programs. He had not fully understood the cycle until then and it was a seminal learning experience in his own career and life.

Simplicity: The Rollercoaster of Change

The Rollercoaster is a vital tool for change consultants to learn and apply at all different levels within an organization. The Rollercoaster reflects the natural and normal cycle of change. It should be recognized, shared, and appreciated as such by all members of the organization.

Exactly how change occurs is different and unique at each of the levels of living systems: at the self level, the interpersonal level, the department level, the cross-functional team level, and the organization-wide level. They all must be attended to, a complex undertaking. Enterprise-Wide Change can seem highly complex, but through *the simplicity of the Rollercoaster* consultants can spread the word.

Use the Rollercoaster concept to create simplicity on the far side of complexity. It is natural, normal, and highly predictable.

Implications for the Enterprise-Wide Change Journey

When the Rollercoaster of Change begins on its downward trajectory, cascading through all levels and subsystems and seeming out of control, how can change consultants and leaders stay focused on the simplicity to be found in the model day-to-day?

We recommend the following activities:

Activity #1:   Regular meetings of the Enterprise-Wide Change Leadership Team

Activity #2:   Tracking and regular reporting of results and key success measures, core strategies, and key initiatives

Activity #3:   Creating a full-time Program Management Office to oversee and implement the process

Activity #4:   Conducting an impact exercise to search for any unintended consequences within each of the key initiatives

It is not enough that EWC requires core strategies, key initiatives, and work plans that are implemented through vertical department plans and horizontal innovative project/process teams. These process/project teams also must consider the impact of their initiatives, the unintended consequences, by conducting an Enterprise-Wide Assessment, as described in Chapter Six.

In Summary

Throughout EWC, you obviously cannot know everything in advance. The plan you have at the beginning must be continually updated as the journey progresses. The EWC Game Plan is by nature a *living, breathing document*, subject to change as a result of dynamic discoveries, unintended consequences, starts and stops, and the inevitable unpredictable complications that will occur.

Furthermore, the time and attention of executive leadership usually will be focused on the day-to-day tasks and stresses, rather than on the change effort. Human nature being what it is, which do most of us choose?

Servicing Today's Business—or—Creating the Future Business

It takes almost superhuman discipline to rise above the stress and pressure of servicing today's business. Today's *urgent* matters usually drive attention away from the future's *important* matters. The urgent usually trumps the important in time-management terms.

While the day-to-day organization chart defines jobs in terms of servicing today's business, change is a completely different matter. Asking the current organization to change itself is folly—it cannot. That is where the Change Menu, the Change Leadership Team, the Program Management Office, and the systems consultant become indispensable. They remove the heavy responsibility of piloting Enterprise-Wide Change from the people who must turn most of their attention to the day-to-day pressures of servicing today's business.

 ## THINK DIFFERENTLY

A well-run, medium-sized financial services firm in California embarked on a long-term EWC process. The CEO gave a talk at a local association meeting (source requested anonymity) where she discussed the phases of her firm's EWC journey.

Phase I was consultant-driven and resulted in only superficial implementation.

Phase II turned into a homegrown, department-driven EWC that became operational in nature with functional (analytical) thinking dominating.

Phase III was facilitator-driven using a Systems Thinking Approach. It was much harder work, as they had to struggle with the answers and Game Plan themselves.

However, Phase III also saw them reach their major key success measure of doubling in size in three years to achieve greater economies of scale. The Experiential Learning Cycle was in operation. The benefits of the Systems Thinking Approach included a more sophisticated, disciplined, and open collective management team. There were many spillover benefits for all elements of the EWC process, with many integrated project improvements.

Questions to Ponder

- What are the two most important relationships not working well in your organization—that are negatively affecting your Enterprise-Wide Change results?

- Where do you see a void when you look for *root causes* in your Enterprise-Wide Change process?

- Where do you see a void when you look for *unintended consequences* in your Enterprise-Wide Change process?

The Ultimate Wisdom: The only alternative to perseverance is failure.

► COMPREHENSIVE CASE STUDY
East Coast Federal Credit Union Enterprise-Wide Change: Part 5

Ongoing Activities. At this point in the Enterprise-Wide Change process, the new year brought continued losses due to the IT International data system contract and CarLoan, Inc., contracts, as well as high operating costs. Project teams worked diligently on all these issues. Predictions for the latter half of the year included losses in most months.

Even as this book is being written, these two outsourcing contracts create a continued financial burden:

- Renegotiation of the IT International agreement is ongoing and a new contract is expected in the first half of next year.
- The CarLoan losses are scheduled to be amortized by the end of 2004. There is a fraud investigation and a long-term insurance claim to be negotiated, all positive developments.

However, some drastic economic change was still called for by June 30.

Activity #1. The Program Management Office (CEO and systems consultant) continued regular contact and coaching by telephone and in person. By February it was clear a one-agenda one-day meeting of the senior management and project team was needed on the branch sale project, and it was scheduled for early March. At that meeting, the status of the project was reviewed and adjusted and preparation was begun for the late March board session.

Activity #2. The board/management session was held. Once again the board was updated on the EWC plan and the continued reality of the situation. The earlier options were reviewed again, as were the criteria and progress for decision making on the fate of the branches. A commitment to a June timetable for THE BIG DECISION was made.

Ongoing Activities. By now, there was project team progress to report to the board regarding the new name. Progress included beginning to expand their main marketplace presence, a move to a critically needed new headquarters building (with a branch) in the center of their focused marketplace, the hiring of a new director of marketing to help establish the new brand identity, and the growing confidence of the regulators. All ten of the *consensus actions* were completed or were being actively pursued. A revised to-do list was submitted and approved.

The June board session was scheduled so that decision making on the expected branch project could occur on schedule. The explicit, yet quiet, goal of management was that the branches could be sold to a larger credit union for $X million by that time.

That sale of money-losing branches and the infusion of $X capital would put them on a solid Phase III EWC. They would be a new company, with a new name and financial strength, essentially starting anew in their main chosen marketplace and state.

Activity #3. The CEO took the lead in sending out an RFP to a few chosen credit unions and found two who were quite interested in the branches. Discussions ensued.

Activity #4. By the time of the appointed June board meeting, a deal had been struck by the CEO to sell the branches for almost the ideal amount that was their goal. The board approved the sale, as they really had no choice. It was a win for the customer (member), a win for the affected employees, and a win for the new credit union. Now they could actually work to acquire a presence in their chosen marketplaces.

Finally, it was a significant win for ECFCU, as it immediately got rid of money-losing branches, streamlined costs, and provided them the capital to amortize the newly built branch's excess construction costs over its value. It also gave them the capital needed to begin planning for new branches and aggressive marketplace advertising and awareness of their new brand name. They achieved in parallel with all these activities a Code #2 in the NCUA ratings as a normal and successful credit union. Their capital ratio moved into the desired range, and they have the capital to withstand the IT International and CarLoan, Inc., financial problems.

To be continued . . . ◀

Chapter Eight Recap

1. How does change occur? Level by level and unit by unit, creating serious problems in getting the desired Enterprise-Wide Change throughout the enterprise.

2. The four main activities that ride these waves successfully are

   - *Activity #1*: Regular meetings of the Enterprise-Wide Change Leadership Team

   - *Activity #2:* Tracking and regular reporting of results and key success measures, core strategies, and key initiatives

   - *Activity #3:* Overseeing and implementing the EWC process by a full-time Program Management Office

   - *Activity 4:* Conducting an EWC impact exercise on each of the key initiatives that support the shared core strategies (the content of the desired change)

3. The successful way to guide an EWC in a positive direction includes these key points:

   - Emergent strategies and initiatives will come up on a regular basis.

   - The Change Leadership Team will have to constantly review and update its EWC Game Plan as it cascades across the organization.

   - The Change Leadership Team and PMO must work with those responsible for each subsystem every step of the way.

   - Each of these subsystems (and the people in them) goes through the predictable six stages of the Rollercoaster of Change at different depths and rates—thus requiring different actions.

   - The PMO should lead these activities on a day-to-day basis.

   - The Systems Thinking Approach can and should be bolstered by *traditional* OD interventions, but these must always be linked to the larger clarity of purposes.

4. Changing the culture as part of an Enterprise-Wide Change is extremely difficult due to the diverse nature of different subcultures in any complex enterprise.

5. Enterprise-Wide Change is a constant rediscovery, reexamination, and re-creation process with unforeseen actions required to deal with the waves and waves of change.

6. Two major issues are always present in Enterprise-Wide Change:

   - The alignment of the delivery processes to satisfy the customer (economic alignment)

   - The attunement with people's hearts and minds in support of the customer (cultural attunement)

7. The number-one absolute for successful strategic change is a well-functioning Change Leadership Team and a Project Management Office.

8. All traditional change and OD interventions are still important as parts of an overall Enterprise-Wide Change process, rather than silo projects by themselves.

9. Use the Seven Natural Rings of Reality to choose which change and OD interventions are appropriate for what purposes/desired outcomes, and remember that individual and team levels of change are crucial.

10. The Rollercoaster of Change is natural and normal—and a vital process and framework you need to know about changing living systems.

11. The Rollercoaster can be applied to all learning and change applications, such as coaching, group dynamics, and Situational Leadership.

12. *Forming, storming, norming,* and *performing* are group dynamics terms for the core stages of the Rollercoaster.

13. *What? So what? Now what?* are the three key questions of the Rollercoaster in the adult learning cycle terms. *Adults learn best by doing.*

14. Anger and depression are natural and normal in any change process. Don't deny them. Listen, empathize, and then explain *why* the change is necessary (in that order).

15. The only alternative to persistence is failure. *Hanging in* is the key to successful complex and chaotic change.

16. WIIFM (What's in it for me?) is key in change. Ask it often.

17. The six stages of the Rollercoaster of Change that everyone goes through—and that must be *planned for*—include

- *Smart Start:* Educate, Assess, Organize, Tailor (including Systems Thinking)
- *Shock:* Communication and Kick-off of the Enterprise-Wide Change effort
- *Depression/Anger:* Changes start happening and resistance is normal
- *Hang In/Persevere:* Take on new responsibilities/form new teams, don't give up
- *Hope/Readjustment:* Climb the learning curve (planning)
- *Rebuilding:* The place of high performance and results

The law of nature is change (chaos), while the dream of man is order.

Henry Adams

9

Sustain
Business Excellence
To Achieve Superior Results
Year After Year

D
Strategies
Actions

Chapter Purposes

- To learn how to sustain superior results of Enterprise-Wide Change on a multi-year basis through the mid-course EWC reviews at least annually

- To ensure you build a capacity for Enterprise-Wide Change into your organization so you can build and sustain your efforts phase after phase, stage after stage, and year after year (Figure 9.1)

Enterprise-Wide Change Goal #3: Build and Sustain Business Excellence

---

Figure 9.1. The Continuous Improvement Helix

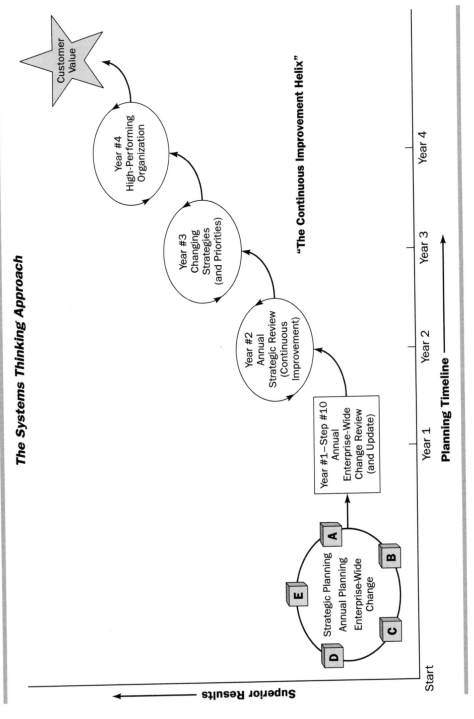

The Systems Thinking Approach

Customer Value

Year #4
High-Performing Organization

Year #3
Changing Strategies
(and Priorities)

Year #2
Annual
Strategic Review
(Continuous Improvement)

Year #1–Step #10
Annual
Enterprise-Wide
Change Review
(and Update)

"The Continuous Improvement Helix"

Strategic Planning
Annual Planning
Enterprise-Wide
Change

A
B
C
D
E

Superior Results

Start

Year 1   Year 2   Year 3   Year 4

Planning Timeline

Effective Enterprise-Wide Change takes two or more years, even with con-
centrated and continual efforts.

The Mid-Course Enterprise-Wide Change Review: Fighting Entropy in Enterprise-Wide Change

---

Booster Shots. In life and golf, follow-through makes the difference.

The final part of the ABC cycle and a key to persevering in Enterprise-Wide Change is the need for regular mid-course reviews. At a minimum, conduct an Enterprise-Wide Change Review and Update annually. Each EWC journey has a natural life-cycle with major milestones and phases of the change itself. Regular checkups are key.

Lack of follow-through on EWC efforts is not unusual. In fact, it follows from a natural law of living systems—entropy, one of the twelve characteristics of Systems Thinking. Simply put, entropy is the natural tendency of all systems to degrade, or *run down,* until they reach a uniformly inert state (death).

In all organizations, the natural force that drags down forward motion is entropy. A set of forces is needed to initially lead the entire enterprise *into* forward and integrated motion, along with ongoing feedback and regular booster shots to maintain the momentum.

A good example of entropy is a fireworks display. Each rocket begins with great initial velocity upward; a huge explosion at the apex of its trajectory results in spec-tacular colors; and then the remnants slowly disappear into a cloud of dust that floats back to earth, having spent its energy.

Thus, all change initiatives, like fireworks, carry within them the seeds of their own destruction. The feeble decline of the Enterprise-Wide Change that was an-nounced with such great fanfare only a year earlier is stunningly common. Once the change requires continuing hard work, follow-up, and institutionalization in a *second* year, it tends to be ignored, while the newest, latest, greatest silver bullet, initiative, or fad gains the favor of executives.

The solution to the problem of entropy in EWC is not rocket science. We have regular checkups for our cars, our teeth, our families, and our friends. Why not for

EWC? The solutions to the problems have been articulated in the sections of this book on the Iceberg Theory of Change, the Rollercoaster of Change, and the menu of structures that build in up-front discipline and commitment. However, even the yearly map of implementation and the ongoing operation of the PMO and Change Leadership Team are not enough. Booster shots are needed again and again. Perseverance is usually the deciding factor in whether the EWC and all its six stages will span one to two years, three years, or even five years.

The six activities in Table 9.1 can be planned at the beginning of an EWC journey to try to avoid the effects of entropy and build in the perseverance needed through mid-course/annual EWC reviews and updates.

Table 9.1. Mid-Course EWC Review Activities

Activity #1   Hold a two-day offsite meeting with the Enterprise-Wide Change Leadership Team and PMO—a maximum of fifteen people

- Review changes completed so far and discuss upcoming further planned change

- Use ABCs of Enterprise-Wide Change Model as a framework

- **Phase E:** Conduct a new environmental scanning process

- **Phase A:** Rebuild commitment to clarity of purpose, vision, values, and positioning

- **Phase B:** Review status of key measures of success (Quadruple Bottom Line)

- **Phase C:** Conduct an honest current-state Enterprise-Wide Assessment on actual results versus your vision/positioning, focusing on core strategies and key initiatives

- Assess your capacity for continued EWC success (see format at end of the chapter)

- **Phase D:** Build and develop further commitment to a revised EWC Game Plan with updated core strategies (both alignment and attunement) and updated key initiatives

Activity #2   Create another Parallel Involvement Process to involve the entire organization in helping to review and critique the Game Plan and new key initiatives again

Table 9.1. Mid-Course EWC Review Activities, Cont'd

Activity #3   Conduct a second offsite meeting with senior management to review and finalize the revised Game Plan as well as to assess the status of your commitment and capacity to sustain the EWC successfully (see the section that follows)

Activity #4   Develop new unit/division/department work plans based on shared core strategies and enterprise-wide key initiatives

Activity #5   Conduct another large-group department review day to ensure continued commitment, common direction, and consensus about the EWC

Activity #6   Continue meetings throughout the year by the Enterprise-Wide Change Leadership Team and the ongoing PMO operations according to a new yearly map of execution

A note on these activities: Be sure any strategic plan, business plan, or annual operations plan is explicitly linked with your Enterprise-Wide Change Game Plan so you don't have two plans—otherwise an analytical, silo view could result. It's best to have one overall strategic and EWC plan—all tied to your budgeting cycle—since your major, radical desired changes are usually strategic in nature.

Entropy is natural and normal, and is to be expected. Without mid-course change reviews, no complex or multi-year EWC efforts we have seen have achieved superior results.

On the other hand, when regular mid-course follow-up review sessions *are* conducted, we can almost guarantee that the desired changes will occur.

What you focus on gets done. What you ignore sends a message to others that it is not important and/or you were never serious about the change.

⟫ THINK DIFFERENTLY

In working on Enterprise-Wide Change in a large automotive company division in the Midwest, a consultant completed phases E-A-B-C (Clarity of Purpose) quite well. However, the company had a corporate-directed implementation plan and assumed responsibility for that phase themselves with no regular EWC review and update planned.

Fifteen months later, the division called the consultants back in to help clean up the mess that had been made by the corporate-directed, one-size-fits-all implementation. It didn't fit this situation, especially with the deterioration of union-management relations and wildcat strikes.

Enterprise-Wide Change, almost without exception, fails when each module is worked separately, with different consultants and different frameworks. Whenever we bring up this point among our external consultant colleagues, they nod their heads in vigorous recognition.

Reasons to conduct an EWC Review include:

- To conduct a candid assessment of the degree of acceptance and integration of your EWC within the organization
- To revisit your Ideal Future Vision and test its validity
- To identify why those aspects of your Game Plan have been successful or have not been successfully executed and why
- To review the achievement of your key success measures/positioning
- To assess the legitimacy and continued relevance of your core EWC strategies
- To modify the next phase of your EWC Game Plan:
  - Carry over outstanding key initiatives from Year One
  - Bring forward and reschedule ideas from Years Two and Three, based on your progress to date
- To get an indication as to your success in establishing the rhythm of your Systems Thinking Approach to EWC
- To recognize, acknowledge, and thank EWC supporters
- To take the opportunity for a booster shot as you renew and recharge employee motivation

Sustaining Excellence: After one year of any major Enterprise-Wide Change effort, there is a massive tendency for the energy to dissipate. The wonderful Game Plan starts running down and often is ignored. Achieving major, large-scale or complex change is thus very difficult, with a low probability of success (see Figure 9.2). Complete the short exercise in Table 9.2 to check your own journey.

Table 9.2. Exercise

What is your Enterprise-Wide Change journey pathway? (check one)

- ☐ 1. Incompetence with no execution
- ☐ 2. Unplanned or poorly controlled, executed, and followed up
- ☐ 3. Normal, fragmented analytic and piecemeal approach
- ☐ 4. Make a serious effort for one year
- ☐ 5. Well-planned and well-executed over multiple years

Figure 9.2. The Rollercoaster of Change

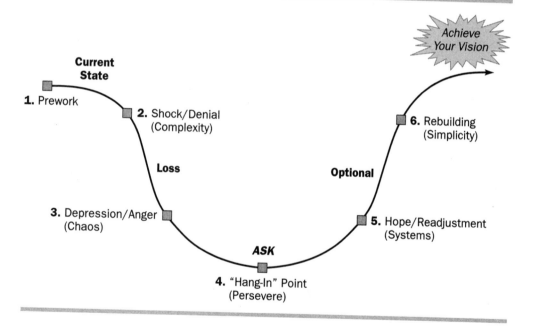

Reverse the Entropy! Give booster shots/rockets—like the space shuttle's. It is the only way to get into orbit.

Questions to Ponder

- Does your organization have a Change Leadership Team and PMO—led by top executives—to guide the annual review and update of your EWC?

- Do you have a skilled PMO and internal support staff to facilitate your change process and annual update?

- Have you created a map for the next year showing a specific implementation plan, and have you allocated the proper resources for it?

- Are you continually tracking progress on your key success measures?

- Is your organization firmly committed to an annual Enterprise-Wide Change Review?

Annual Review of Organizational Capacity

The change from the current state to the future state has traditionally been underestimated, understaffed, and inadequately addressed.

Bill Veltrop

The Iceberg Theory of Change (Figure 9.3) is definitely not a true *theory*, but a model, a *practical guide* to EWC as you look at its components. The five components below the surface (Processes, Structure, Culture/Commitment, Competencies, and Resources) represent areas of the enterprise's capacity that must be present to undertake, build, and sustain the results you want to achieve. Without them your probability of failure is 75 percent in EWC, as you must persevere through the natural cascade of change on a level-by-level and unit-by-unit basis. The Capacity Assessment at the end of this chapter must be part of the annual EWC review.

Figure 9.3. The Iceberg Theory of Change

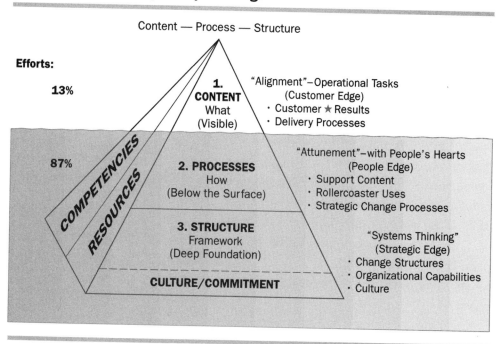

Capacity is the ability to grasp something new, absorb it, hold onto, and retain it over time (like a vessel that carries water). It is the sustained ability to do something effectively over time.

This vessel can be seen in two ways: It could be seen as a *wishing well* that is empty or only partly full of water. On the other hand, it could be seen as an *operating well* that is full to the brim with an underground spring filling it and with the *capacity* to provide water over the long-term.

Five Organizational Capacity Components

The five components shown in the iceberg model in Figure 9.3 of this *operating well* are

1. Demonstrated commitment by the collective leadership team to the long-term cultural change required for the EWC process to succeed (*foundation* of the iceberg). It includes both buy-in and staying power over the long term.

2. Effective organizational change processes to facilitate a successful EWC process.

3. Effective organizational change infrastructures in place to guide the EWC.

4. High-level individual *competencies* to lead the EWC effort effectively.

5. Adequate *resources* devoted exclusively to EWC.

Let's examine these one at a time, building on what we have said previously.

#1 Organizational Capacity: Demonstrated Commitment to Cultural Change

It should be pretty obvious by now that the demonstrated *understanding and long-term commitment* by the CEO, senior management, and the board of directors is the foundation for success. However, building a critical mass of employees in support of the EWC is also critical. This is required to effect culture change.

It can take a long time to build the critical mass needed for large-scale Enterprise-Wide Change. Check-ups, follow-ups, and booster shots are the keys to sustained success. Otherwise the leaders never get the *silent majority and skeptics* on board (see Figure 9.4).

Once the change has started, several approaches can be used to build buy-in and maintain stay-in over the long term. This is key to success, as the top 20 percent of the change implementers (scouts and pioneers) usually have buy-in and stay-in naturally, yet the cynics never will.

Figure 9.4. The Bell Curve of Buy-In and Stay-In

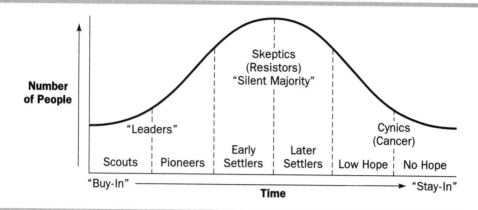

Ways to Develop Buy-In and Stay-In

- Modify the drafts of the Game Plan: Listen, share, and gain feedback from those affected.

- Continue to hold meetings with key stakeholders throughout execution.

- Develop trust in leadership by keeping the Change Leadership Team open to dialogue and two-way communication.

- Involve skeptics and listen to them every day.

- Encourage constructive questions and challenges.

- Create updates after each Enterprise-Wide Change Leadership Team meeting and ask for feedback.

- Use process and project teams as change leaders and change consultants for each major initiative.

- Review reward systems and the performance appraisal form to reinforce the new core values and core strategies of the Enterprise-Wide Change effort.

- Have each person answer the question, "What's in It for Me?" (WIIFM)—keep looking at the political and cultural issues with the desired changes.

#2 Organizational Capacity: Effective Organizational Change Processes

We have covered a number of change processes already in this book, including the Parallel Involvement Process and the Rollercoaster of Change Process and its waves of change.

In addition, the EWC requires support and reinforcement through the organization's recognition and rewards policies and practices.

Another effective change process is providing *strategic communications* on an ongoing basis about the EWC using the single-sheet-of-paper idea explored earlier. Management providing the organization with open, face-to-face and honest communication and sharing and exchanging information on a timely basis is crucial to offsetting the rumor mill.

Last, the process of transferring knowledge and learning across and down the organization is crucial to build the workforce competencies to succeed in the desired future vision.

Note: For more information on the learning organization, read Peter Senge's *The Fifth Discipline.*

#3 Organizational Capacity: Effective Organizational Change Infrastructures

We have also covered the key infrastructures that must be set in place in order to organize and guide the overall EWC process. These include the Change Leadership Team, Program Management Office, Yearly Map of Implementation, Innovative Process/Project Teams, and a Positive Work Culture (the very bottom of the iceberg and quite resistant to change). Unleashing the potential of the workforce in support of the change through creating a positive climate and work culture is very important.

#4 Organizational Capacity: High-Level Individual Competencies

The competencies of the collective management team to lead, manage, and effectively execute the EWC are paramount. While we touched on it earlier, it is important to repeat the point clearly. These competencies include

- *Systems Thinking applications,* including the four concepts presented as well as all the tools, tips, and techniques throughout this book.

- The need for *creativity and innovation,* especially for the process/project teams, the key implementation vehicles.

- Consistency in *daily best people practices* by the collective management team is crucial to develop and maintain the positive work climate and culture required for success. See the extensive research and work in this area that is listed in the Chapter Recap.

- It may be obvious, but it is also crucial to have a high level of *business acumen* regarding your customers, markets, competitors, industry, company, finances, products and services, technology, and delivery channels. (See the complete list of best practices at the end of this chapter.)

- And last, and most important, *leadership excellence* by your collective management team is the number-one core competency for success in every organization.

#5 Organizational Capacity: Adequate Resources

Finally, in today's tough economic times, there must be a commitment to devote the proper resources exclusively to the EWC effort. This includes not only the traditional list of *people, money,* and *materials* (physical facilities, equipment, hardware), but also the *time* (our scarcest and only non-renewable resource), *information, access,* and *processing of information* (not just on a need-to-know basis, but transparently for those who want to know).

Summary of Organizational Capacity

The five Enterprise-Wide Change capacities and commitments just discussed are often overlooked during the daily stress of work and change. "We'll get to them later" is a frequent refrain. Later never comes, and the organization's capacity and talent pool remains or becomes shallow. The consequences for EWC and organizational results overall are obvious if this is not part of the annual review.

To rate your current status on all five organizational capacities, see the assessment at the end of this chapter.

These five capacities may need to be enhanced either prior to or in parallel with the change process and journey itself. They are key leverage points for EWC success. Think of them as the organization's "carrying capacity":

- What's the size and magnitude of the EWC?

- How much employee energy needs to be directed to the EWC itself (working *on* the business)?

- How does this constrain the organization's ongoing service delivery (working *in* the business)?

- How many other changes are also going on (comprehensive change under-takings)?
- How can you be wise and *hold off* on some initiatives—to enable the work-force to regroup, reenergize, and refocus before throwing another change at them?
- What's the organization's collective change tolerance level or stress level?

A Note on Capacity: For those interested in learning more about the funda-mental capacity of human systems to change based on their personal val-ues, the late Dr. Clare W. Graves' concept of Spiral Dynamics makes for fascinating reading. See www.spiraldynamics.org, the National Values Cen-ter led by Christopher Cowan and Natasha Todorovic. They cover the three different layers of human values that help or prevent EWC strategies from happening: *surface values, hidden values,* and *deep values.*

Cowan and Todorovic say that these values create "Eight States of Orga-nizations" with different objectives, approaches to work, and levels of effec-tiveness: animalistic, tribal, egocentric, absolute obedience, self-fulfillment, relative/common good, systemic, and holistic organizations.

Questions to Ponder
- Are there other capacities that you feel should be added for your organization?
- Do you agree with the five capacities discussed above? Why or why not?

▶ COMPREHENSIVE CASE STUDY
East Coast Federal Credit Union Enterprise-Wide Change: Part 6

A recap of the survival and transformation so far:

Phase I, Survival, had been achieved over the past eighteen months by the changes senior management was able to accomplish in its Enter-prise-Wide Change process.

Phase II, Transformation to a new credit union, was assured with the sale of the branches and the capital infusion.

Phase III, Future profitable growth, was now a possibility on the immediate horizon.

Activity #1. It was now time for ECFCU to build their next-phase game plan for Enterprise-Wide Change. Senior management met in September on a two-day offsite with the consultants and conducted their annual EWC review (and update). In this retreat they updated their environmental scan, reconfirmed their vision, and revised their positioning statement to focus on their desired responsiveness as a competitive advantage in their main marketplace. They now had an opportunity to be the most convenient and responsive credit union in their local marketplace.

They built a balanced set of Key Success Measures, including traditional financial measurements, yet added goals for customer and employee satisfaction. They also conducted a current state assessment, using the business excellence architecture, to get a more detailed look internally at their strengths and weaknesses.

They developed a revised set of five core change strategies and key initiatives (and another major change list) to guide their future profitable growth. These included

- Technology modernization
- Aggressive marketing
- Financial soundness
- Facilities upgrading, relocation, and growth
- Employee relations

Activity #2. Their newest vision is to enter Phase IV, "Long-Term Marketplace Competitiveness," within three years. In October they gained board approval and support for *Phases III and IV.*

Activity #3. They must also rebuild and grow their employee talent base to serve their customers, the next daunting change challenge they face (core strategy #5 above). Finally, they are focusing on employees and *cultural attunement* as a key strategy.

Activity #4. They now know they have just begun the first of many waves of change. The branches' sale has become public and a set of parallel involvement processes was successfully conducted. Affected customers were also communicated with and responded to on a personal basis, as much as possible.

Activity #5. In addition, they conducted a Capacity Assessment that revealed the following strengths and weaknesses regarding EWC, shown in Table 9.3.

Table 9.3. East Coast Federal Credit Union Capacity Assessment

Capacity Area	Status of Building the EWC Capacity
1. Demonstrated Long-Term Commitment	**High** for the CEO and senior management **Low** for the board of directors, as a number are quite unhappy with the changes
2. Effective Change Processes	**Medium** for the involvement process and EWC processes to date **Low** where some major upgrades for the future involvement of the entire organization are needed
3. Effective Change Infrastructures	**High** for the Change Leadership Team, Program Management Office, and Yearly Map of Implementation **Low** for more innovative process teams and the need for a more positive work culture
4. High-Level Individual Competencies	**Medium** regarding leadership excellence, business acumen, and Systems Thinking for senior management **Low** regarding needed waves of competencies cascading throughout the credit union
5. Adequate EWC Resources	**Medium** regarding the resources to devote to the EWC and needed competitive moves, a major transformation from the past survival crises

Phase IV, Long-Term Marketplace Competitiveness.

More work is still needed, as indicated earlier. Perseverance through Phases III and IV of the Enterprise-Wide Change process is a must. ◄

Chapter Nine Recap

1. The annual Enterprise-Wide Change Review and Update is a key to building and sustaining superior results over the long term.

2. Entropy is a natural phenomenon that can be counted on (100 percent) to emerge during a long-term EWC. Awareness of this tendency will help to combat its effects.

3. Booster shots and other predictable organizational interventions are key tools for effective strategic and complex change over the long term.

4. The number-one corporate-wide core competency is achieving leadership excellence for the collective managerial and supervisory positions.

5. The five required components of the organizational capacity to undergo EWC successfully are

   - Demonstrated commitment by the collective leadership team to the long-term cultural change EWC requires

   - Effective organizational change processes to facilitate a successful EWC

   - Effective organizational change infrastructures in place to guide the EWC

   - High-level individual competencies to lead the EWC effort effectively

   - Adequate resources devoted exclusively to EWC

Words or Deeds: Brave Words Versus Bold Actions. Which is it?

ORGANIZATIONAL CAPACITY TO UNDERGO ENTERPRISE-WIDE CHANGE SUCCESSFULLY

Instructions: Rate your current collective organizational capacity to build and sustain EWC on a multi-year basis (rate the leadership and management team as well as all employees).

Scoring: (H—M—L)	Comments:
I. Demonstrated Long-Term Commitment: by the collective leadership team to cultural change 1 ____ CEO 2 ____ Senior Management 3 ____ Board of Directors 4 ____ Collective Management Team 5 ____ All Employees	1 2 3 4 5
II. Effective Organizational Change Processes: to facilitate a successful EWC process 6 ____ Parallel Involvement Process 7 ____ Rollercoaster of Change Process/Waves 8 ____ Knowledge Transfer/Learning Processes 9 ____ HR Best People Policies and Practices 10 ____ Strategic Communications Processes	6 7 8 9 10
III. Effective Organizational Change Infrastructures: in place to guide the EWC process 11 ____ Change Leadership Team 12 ____ Program Management Office/Change Team 13 ____ Yearly Map of Implementation 14 ____ Innovative Process/Project Teams 15 ____ Positive Work Culture	11 12 13 14 15
IV. High-Level Individual Competencies: to lead the EWC effort effectively 16 ____ Leadership Excellence 17 ____ Business Acumen 18 ____ Daily People Management Practices 19 ____ Systems Thinking Application 20 ____ Creativity and Innovation Applications	16 17 18 19 20
V. Adequate EWC Resources: devoted exclusively to EWC 21 ____ People 22 ____ Time 23 ____ Money 24 ____ Information, Access, and Processing 25 ____ Physical Equipment, Facilities, Hardware	21 22 23 24 25

Enterprise-Wide People Edge Best Practices

People resources are probably the last great investment cost that is relatively unmanaged and unreported/measured.

Many organizations engaged in EWC want to transform their people and culture (*the People Edge*) into becoming their competitive advantage in the marketplace. To do so usually means rethinking your entire set of enterprise-wide practices and policies regarding employees.

Why Is the People Edge Important to You?

It is the *Blinding Flash of the Obvious.* Everything in an organization is inert; it takes people to run systems and make things happen. The People Edge is difficult to create and sustain, making it the one competitive edge that can really differentiate you in today's *commodity* world. It is also just plain good business practice to do this.

The approach to the People Edge we have used with clients is patterned on the same six levels/rings described in Chapter Eight. It provides a benchmark against which to assess an organization's people practices. Under each of these levels/rings, we researched and organized thirty "People Edge Best Practices" (Bandt & Haines, 2001). As always, of course, *there is no silver bullet.* These practices are listed in Table 9.4 and the rings are explained in Table 9.5.

Table 9.4. People Edge Best Practices

Level/Ring	Best Practices
#1. Acquiring the Desired Workforce (The Individual)	1. Individual capability requirements 2. Alternative workforce arrangements 3. Workforce, succession, and retention planning 4. Career development 5. Recruiting methods to hire the desired employees
#2. Engaging the Workforce (Interpersonal)	6. Performance management systems 7. Compensation systems 8. Recognition systems 9. Flexible benefit programs 10. Dealing with poor performance
#3. Organizing High-Performance Teams (Team)	11. Developing teams 12. Developing small-unit team leaders 13. Empowering work teams 14. Participative management skills 15. Rewarding and reinforcing teamwork
#4. Creating a Learning Organization (Interdepartmental)	16. Spreading learning and intellectual capital 17. Institutionalizing Systems Thinking 18. Measuring human resources 19. Valuing debriefing events/projects/processes 20. Encouraging creative thinking
#5. Facilitating Cultural Change (Organization)	21. Redesigning organization culture 22. Developing the collective management skills 23. Aligning and streamlining all HR processes 24. Organizing change structures 25. Developing strategic change experts
#6. Collaborating with Stakeholders (Organization-Environment)	26. Operating in a global environment 27. Maintaining strategic alliances 28. Positive people environment 29. Focusing on customers 30. Balancing value contribution

Table 9.5. Achieving Leadership Excellence in the Six Rings

Level/Ring	Competency and Skills
I. Enhancing Self-Mastery: Goal Is a Balanced Life	1. Personal Goal Setting 2. Balancing Body-Mind-Spirit 3. Acting with Conscious Intent 4. Ethics and Character Development 5. Accurate Self-Awareness
Level I: Motivational Force	**Possesses Self-Awareness**
II. Building Interpersonal Relationships: Goal Is Trust	6. Caring 7. Effectively Communicating 8. Mentoring and Coaching 9. Managing Conflict 10. Creativity and Innovation
Level II: Motivational Force	**Builds and Maintains Reputation for Integrity**
III. Facilitating Empowered Teams: Goal Is Mission Attainment	11. Practicing Participative Management 12. Facilitating Groups 13. Delegating and Empowering 14. Training Others 15. Building Effective Teams
Level III: Motivational Force	**Recognizes Interdependence with Others**
IV. Collaborating Across Functions: Goal Is Customer Focused	16. Installing Cross-Functional Teamwork 17. Integrating Business Processes 18. Institutionalizing Systems Thinking 19. Valuing and Serving Others 20. Managing People Processes
Level IV: Motivational Force	**Values Providing Service to Others**
V. Integrating Organizational Outcomes: Goal Is to Add Value to the Customer	21. Organizing Effectively 22. Mastering Strategic Communications 23. Cascade of Planning 24. Leading Cultural Change 25. Organizing and Designing
Level V: Motivational Force	**Understands and Agrees with the Organization's Vision and Values**

Table 9.5. Achieving Leadership Excellence in the Six Rings, Cont'd

Level/Ring	Competency and Skills
Level VI. Creating Strategic Positioning: Goal Is to Be Globally Competitive	26. Scanning the Global Environment 27. Reinventing Strategic Planning 28. Networking and Managing Alliances 29. Positioning in the Marketplace 30. International Effectiveness
Level VI: Motivational Force	**Believes in Mutual Influence and Synergistic Efforts**

The research and client feedback that supports these last two listings—People Edge Best Practices and Achieving Leadership Excellence—can be found at www.SystemsThinkingPress.com.

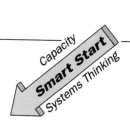

Part C

How to Begin
Enterprise-Wide Change

PART C IS A CRUCIAL SECTION of this book, because now you will learn how to begin using the concepts you have read so far. Not all enterprises are large, complex, or in need of a comprehensive, multi-year Enterprise-Wide Change effort. Not all enterprises need to transform themselves in a radical, cultural, or large-scale strategic and fundamental way. However, all organizations must deal with the environment in which we live in the 21st Century.

This book is designed with a circular Systems Thinking approach (and modular chapters). Thus, every CEO and his or her enterprise, no matter how small or large, can use some portions or some chapters to guide change in a more holistic way.

The two key concepts here are as follows:

First, begin with a bite-sized approach. Don't tackle more than you need right now. Maybe you will go through a two-to-four-year evolution to a new desired vision rather than transform the enterprise all at once. Maybe the changes are business unit-, division-, or department-wide not enterprise-wide. The principles, techniques, and tools are the same: *It is the size and scale that make a difference.*

Second, over time ask yourself, your change leadership team, your program management office, and change consultants the five strategic A-B-C-D-E questions in the proper sequence. They are repeated on the next page for emphasis, as we end this book where we began—with the Systems Thinking Approach. The model can be applied to understanding and changing any living system in a holistic, totally integrated, systems manner. It can be used for a person's life, team, department, business unit, geographic region, or total enterprise. It is useful for any change project or process you wish to make.

> Science. The whole of Science is nothing more than a refinement of everyday thinking.
>
> *Albert Einstein*

Just define the system or entity to be changed before you begin.

STRATEGIC THINKING: ABCs TEMPLATE
"The Simplicity of Systems Thinking"

_____ (Name of the System – Issue – Problem – Project – Change Effort)

C

Current State Assessments:
Where are we now (SWOT)?

Inputs

Strengths

Weaknesses

Opportunities

Threats

D

System Throughput/Processes:
How do we get there (close the gap from **C** → **A** *)?*

→ **CORE STRATEGIES: TOP PRIORITY ACTIONS:**

B

Feedback Loop/Measurements:
How will we know when we get there?

E

Future Environmental Scan:
What will be changing in your future environment that will affect you?

Outputs →

A

**Desired Outcomes—
#1 Systems Question:**
Where do we want to be?

Enterprise-Wide Change. Copyright © 2005 by John Wiley & Sons, Inc. Reproduced by permission of Pfeiffer, an Imprint of Wiley. www.pfeiffer.com

10

Working on the Enterprise
The Bite-Sized Approach

Chapter Purpose

- To explore some different, bite-sized options on *how to begin* working *on* the organization to build the enterprise's capacity to successfully execute Enterprise-Wide Change

---

The journey of a thousand miles begins with a single helicopter ride.

The future is shaped by those who see possibilities before they become obvious.

New Strait Times, *October 11, 2003*

How to Begin: Tailored to Your Needs

Enterprise-Wide Change is a unique challenge, requiring a unique set of structures, processes, and capabilities—and the perseverance to build and sustain business excellence and superior results, year after year. There are many different types of Enterprise-Wide Change. They all require a Systems Thinking approach and a *helicopter view* to deal with the systems problems, systemic issues, and myriad of unintended consequences and relationships of the complex Rubik's Cubes that enterprises have become.

If your need for Enterprise-Wide Change is immediate and intense, this book should serve as a practical and specific guide to success.

On the other hand, if your organization's time has not quite come for an intense and dynamic Enterprise-Wide Change effort, there are a number of options for how you can begin moving in that direction now. Every organization's time will come when the crucial need is present for an Enterprise-Wide Change effort. The dynamic, global, and instantaneous nature of the 21st Century has seen to that. Remember Jack Welch's words: "If you are doing things now the way you were five years ago, you are doing something wrong."

In either case, the place to start is a *Tailored to Your Needs* exercise on your specific EWC goals and processes. Such an exercise is included at the end of this chapter.

Engineer Success Up-Front

Once you have tailored the process to your needs, there are a number of options on how to begin progress (*engineer success up-front*) toward your desired future and marketplace positioning.

The bottom line on how to begin might include establishing the following options:

1. Install the Executive Team as the Change Leadership Team with the necessary sub-structures.

2. Set up and train an "internal support cadre" with the knowledge and skills to accomplish your new initiatives and desired outcomes.

3. Establish a program management office with joint leaders—a credible internal executive and a credible outside consultant.

4. Train your collective management team to acquire the knowledge and skills to accomplish your desired outcomes.

5. Conduct the needed organizational/marketplace business excellence architecture assessments versus proven best practices to ensure that you have a solid base of reality from which to begin.

6. Develop an overall one-to-three-year Enterprise-Wide Change "game plan."

7. Design a rollout, communications, development, and sustained involvement process for *buy-in* and *stay-in* to the desired outcomes.

8. Develop a yearly comprehensive map of execution for the next twelve months.

9. Develop a budget and resources to support your game plan along with some ROI targets.

10. Redesign performance, incentive, and recognition programs to support these efforts.

Regardless of which option(s) you choose, initial steps should include

- Establishing an enterprise-wide sense of urgency.
- Generating short-term *wins* that show progress.
- Hiring, recognizing, rewarding, and promoting people who are fully committed to the EWC vision.

Twelve Absolutes for Success

Regardless of your specific short-term needs, once you get serious about proceeding with Enterprise-Wide Change, there are a number of *absolutes* required for becoming one of the 25 percent long-term EWC success stories. These include the following:

1. Have a clear vision and positioning with shared values of your ideal future.

2. Develop focused and shared core strategies as the *glue* for setting and reviewing action plans for all departments with a single *tri-fold* to communicate the EWC game plan.

3. Set up Quadruple Bottom Line measures and a tracking system to ensure clarity of purpose and focus on the scoreboard for success. Cascade it down with clear accountability for results at all levels—unit by unit/department by department.

4. Focus on the vital few leverage points of business excellence, based on an enterprise-wide mental map and assessment of an organization as a system.

5. Document the top EWC priorities on a single sheet of paper to help everyone to focus on what is important.

6. Conduct large-group EWC review and critique meetings to ensure that everyone is in sync with everyone else.

7. Institutionalize the Parallel Involvement Process with all key stakeholders as the new participative way you plan, change, and run your business day-to-day. Create a critical mass for EWC that *goes ballistic* and becomes self-sustaining.

8. Develop and gain public commitments to *personal leadership plans* to achieve leadership excellence and build a leadership development system for all management personnel.

9. Redo your HR management practices to support the positioning and values, especially your performance management and rewards systems.

10. Establish an Enterprise-Wide Change Leadership Team led by the CEO and facilitated by an external change consultant using a single-page Yearly Comprehensive Map of Implementation that meets on a monthly basis to lead all major changes.

11. Establish a Program Management Office, along with innovative project/ process teams of cross-functional leaders for each key initiative, to implement, track, and monitor each key initiative. Set up an internal support cadre to sustain the program management office.

12. Conduct the annual EWC review and update in the manner of an independent financial audit to ensure the constant updating of your EWC Game Plan.

Remember, the Science of Living Systems is the natural way that the world works, and successful participants must learn and use its rules. There are fifty years of solid research behind its simple concepts, principles, questions, and tools presented in this book.

How you think is how you act is how you are, and that determines the results you achieve.

Table 10.1. How You Think

	Analytic Thinking	Systems Thinking
1. How you think	piecemeal, separate	holistic, relational
2. Is how you act	narrow choices, parts focused	broader, different answers, root causes
3. Are the results you achieve	missed alternatives, deals with symptoms, partial solutions	better solutions, longer-lasting, fewer side effects

The Results

Systems Thinking has seven primary, far-reaching benefits in Enterprise-Wide Change.

The Benefits of Systems Thinking

1. A framework and way to make sense out of life's complexities, since all living things *are* systems.

2. A way to learn new things more easily. Its basic rules are simple and consistent—they stay the same from system to system and organization to organization.

3. A better way to integrate new ideas within the systems context.

4. A clearer way to see and understand what is going on in any organization and its environment. Complex problems become easier to understand, as do the interrelationships of parts and multiple cause-and-effect cycles.

5. A new and better way to create strategies, to problem solve, and to make superior decisions while finding leverage points for change, keeping the outcomes (positioning) and goals in mind at all times.

6. A better way to stay focused on outcomes is by using the key Systems Thinking question: . . . *What are the desired outcomes?* Use this question to begin the discussion about any issue, change, and complex problem you have.

7. Systems Thinking provides a better language and a more complete and holistic way of thinking. Its principles are a camera's wide-angle lens. It gives us a better view on our "radar scope"—a more effective way of thinking, communicating, acting, and achieving superior results.

End with the Beginning in Mind

Many of us can envision ourselves up in a helicopter 5,000 feet above the ground getting a systems view of an enterprise. Now try to envision yourself as an astronaut 260 miles above Earth, floating in space. Only then can we conduct an environmental scan on the largest living system in our world, Earth—the starting point for Enterprise-Wide Change.

When we talk of *working ON the system* first, we mean having this holistic view of our global economic and Internet village. The importance of global environmental scanning (Phase E) cannot be overstated in Enterprise-Wide Change. It is THE context for building our clarity of purpose (Phase A): our shared ideal future vision, core values, and marketplace positioning.

Once we have *worked ON the enterprise as a system*, then we *can work IN the system,* making a "Smart Start" in our Enterprise-Wide Change journey. This requires an intense commitment to simplicity of execution, despite having to deal with the normal complexity inherent in wave after wave of change.

For those 25 percent of enterprises finding simplicity on the far side of complexity and achieving EWC success, their superior results can include dramatically better

- Customer Satisfaction
- Employee Satisfaction
- Shareholder/Owner Satisfaction
- Contribution to Society and Community

The world (Figure 10.1) is in your hands—grab it and run . . . with a System Thinking Approach.

Figure 10.1. The Globe

The Winning Formula

Preparation, discipline, talent, and persistence (with a Systems Thinking framework) is the winning formula for Enterprise-Wide Change.

He who hesitates is not only lost, but miles from the next exit.

TAILORED-TO-YOUR-NEEDS EXERCISE

Based on your understanding of the Systems Thinking Approach to Enterprise-Wide Change, list the importance of the new initiatives listed below for achieving business excellence and superior results for your organization.

> **H = High:** Start within the next six months
> **M = Moderate:** Start within the next twelve months
> **L = Low:** Start within the next one to three years
> **N/A = Not applicable:** No further work needed

Required New Initiatives for Enterprise-Wide Change

_____ 1. Define and implement a full Enterprise-Wide Change Vision and Game Plan (clarity of purpose and simplicity of execution).

_____ 2. Develop strategic thinkers among our collective management on a daily basis.

_____ 3. Develop strategic thinkers among all employees on a daily basis.

_____ 4. Develop a common model (paradigm/framework/mental map) to use for our organization as a system.

_____ 5. Conduct an Enterprise-Wide Business Excellence Assessment (building on the Baldrige best practices).

_____ 6. Conduct a one-agenda strategic thinking day on a critical issue. List topic: _____.

_____ 7. New Systems Thinking language becomes a key part of our culture.

_____ 8. Identify and install an enterprise-wide resource planning technology system.

_____ 9. Prepare for a rapid and aggressive growth and expansion of revenues and profits, including possible global expansion.

_____ 10. Develop and implement people as a competitive edge through a three-year business plan for line units, divisions, LOBs, and SBUs.

_____ 11. Develop and implement people as a competitive edge through a three-year people plan for the enterprise (strategic HR plan).

TAILORED-TO-YOUR-NEEDS EXERCISE, Cont'd

_____ 12. Develop and implement a customer-focused organization through a three-year strategic marketing and sales plan.

_____ 13. Clarify our unique positioning in the marketplace versus the competition in the eyes of the customer to create customer value.

_____ 14. Create a system of achieving leadership excellence for the collective management team.

_____ 15. Create a system of succession planning for key jobs/roles (include executives).

_____ 16. Create a culture change to a positive work environment and a high-performance organization.

_____ 17. Create innovation as a core value and set of skills throughout the organization.

_____ 18. Create a knowledge management system and a "learning organization."

_____ 19. Develop and implement a radically different strategic plan using the ABCs of a strategic thinking approach.

_____ 20. Develop your own unique strategic management system and yearly cycle.

_____ 21. Enhance business excellence (effectiveness and efficiency) and alignment of delivery on a day-to-day operational level—simplicity of execution and elimination of waste.

_____ 22. Reorganize and restructure our supply-chain to create more simplicity, flexibility, and responsiveness to changes in the marketplace.

_____ 23. Turn around an unprofitable or low-performing business.

_____ 24. Develop a lower cost structure; improve process and efficiencies as our competitive edge.

_____ 25. Pursue a merger or acquisition to grow our marketplace positioning.

_____ 26. Identify and develop a new joint venture, strategic alliance, and/or outsourcing.

Websites

Organization	Website
Ackoff Center for Advancement of Systems Approaches	www.acasa.upenn.edu
American Management Association	www.amanet.org
Baldrige National Quality Program at the National Institute of Standards and Technology	www.quality.nist.gov
Berkana Institute	www.berkana.org
Buckminster Fuller Institute	www.bfi.org
Capra, Fritjof	www.fritjofcapra.net
Carter, Carla, and Associates	http://changeexcellence.com
Center for Ecoliteracy	www.ecoliteracy.org
Centre for Strategic Management	www.csmintl.com
Collins, Jim, author of *Good to Great*	www.jimcollins.com

Dannemiller Tyson Associates	www.dannemillertyson.com
Fred Emery Institute	www.fredemery.com.au
Future Search	www.futuresearch.net
GoInnovate!	www.goinnovate.com
Hultman, Ken, Motivational System Mapping™ Facilitator	www.kenhultman.com
International Council on Systems Engineering (INCOSE)	www.incose.org
International Organization Development Association (IODA)	www.ioda.cl
International Society for Systems Science	www.isss.org
Jossey-Bass	www.josseybass.com
National Institute of Standards and Technology	www.quality.nist.gov
New England Complex Systems Institute	www.necsi.org
Pegasus Communications, Inc.	www.pegasuscom.com
Pfeiffer	www.pfeiffer.com
Plexus Institute	www.plexusinstitute.com
Santa Fe Institute	www.santafe.edu
Society for Organizational Learning (SoL)	http://sol-ne.org
Spiral Dynamics, the work of Dr. Clare W. Graves on Value Systems	www.spiraldynamics.com
System Dynamics Society	www.systemdynamics.org
Systems Thinking Press, worldwide portal of systems thinking applications with over 200 links	www.systemsthinkingpress.com
von Bertalanffy, Karl Ludwig	www.bertalanffy.org
W. Edwards Deming Institute	www.deming.org
Whole Systems	www.worldtrans.org/whole.html
World Future Society	www.wfs.org

Bibliography

Ackoff, R. (1970). *A concept of corporate planning.* New York: John Wiley & Sons, Inc.

Ackoff, R. (1974). *Redesigning the future: A systems approach to societal problems.* New York: John Wiley & Sons, Inc.

Ackoff, R. (1991). *Ackoff's fables: Irreverent reflections on business and bureaucracy.* New York: John Wiley & Sons, Inc.

Ackoff, R. (1999). *Ackoff's best: Classical writings on management.* Chichester, England: John Wiley & Sons, Inc.

Adams, C., Adams, W. A., & Bowker, B. (1999). *The whole systems approach: Involving everyone in the company to transform and run your business.* Provo, UT: Executive Excellence Publishing.

Alban, B., & Bunker, B. (1997). *Large group interventions: Engaging the whole system for rapid change.* San Francisco, CA: Jossey-Bass.

Anderson, D., & Ackerman Anderson, L. (2001). *Beyond change management: Advanced strategies for today's transformational leaders.* San Francisco, CA: Jossey-Bass.

Argyris, C., & Schon, D. (1978). *Organizational learning: A theory of action perspective.* Reading, MA: Addison-Wesley.

Ayers, J. B. (1990). *Improving your competitive positioning: A project management approach.* Dearborn, MI: Society of Manufacturing Engineers.

Bak, P. (1996). *How nature works: The science of self-organized criticality.* New York: Copernicus.

Baldwin, J. (1996). *Bucky works: Buckminster Fuller's ideas for today.* New York: John Wiley & Sons.

Banathy, B. A. (1991). *Systems design of education: A journey to create the future.* Englewood Cliffs, NJ: Educational Technology Publications, Inc.

Bandt, A., & Haines, S. G. (2001). *Successful strategic human resource planning.* San Diego, CA: Systems Thinking Press.

Barker, J. A. (1992). *The future edge: Discovering the new paradigms of success.* New York: William Morrow.

Beckhard, R. (1969). *Organization development: Strategies and models.* Reading, MA: Addison-Wesley.

Beckhard, R., & Harris, R. (1987). *Organization transitions: Managing complex change* (2nd ed.). Reading, MA: Addison-Wesley.

Beckhard, R., & Pritchard, W. (1992). *Changing the essence: The art of creating and leading fundamental change in organizations.* San Francisco, CA: Jossey-Bass.

Beer, M., & Nohria, N. (Eds.). (2000). *Breaking the code of change.* Boston, MA: Harvard Business School Press.

Bellingham, R. (2001). *The manager's pocket guide to corporate culture change.* Amherst, MA: HRD Press.

Bossidy, L., Charan, R., & Burck, C. (2002). *Execution: The discipline of getting things done.* New York: Crown Business.

Boulding, K. (1964). *The meaning of the 20th Century.* Englewood Cliffs, NJ: Prentice-Hall.

Bradford, R. W., & Duncan, J. P. (2000). *Simplified strategic planning: A no-nonsense guide for busy people who want results fast!* Worcester, MA: Chandler House Press.

Bridges, W. (1991). *Managing transitions: Making the most of change.* Reading, MA: Addison-Wesley.

Brown, L. R. (2001). *Eco-economy: Building an economy for the earth.* New York: W. W. Norton.

Buckingham, M., & Coffman, C. (1999). *First break all the rules: What the world's greatest managers do differently.* New York: Simon & Schuster.

Burke, W. Warner (1987). *Organization development: A normative view.* Reading, MA: Addison-Wesley.

Byrd, J., & Brown, P. L. (2002). *The innovation equation: Building creativity and risk taking in your organization.* San Francisco, CA: Jossey-Bass.

Capra, F. (1976). *The tao of physics.* New York: Bantam Books.

Capra, F. (1996). *The web of life.* New York: Anchor Books.

Capra, F. (2002). *The hidden connections: A science for sustainable living.* New York: Anchor Books.

Capra, F. (2004, February). *Life and leadership: A systems approach.* Available www.fritjofcapra.net/summary.html.

Centre for Strategic Management. (2002). *Comprehensive reference library volume I: Reinventing strategic planning for the 21st century.* San Diego, CA: Systems Thinking Press.

Checkland, P. (1999). *Systems thinking, systems practice: A 30-year retrospective.* New York: John Wiley & Sons.

Churchman, C. W. (1968). *The systems approach.* New York: Dell.

Collins, J. (2001). *Good to great: Why some companies make the leap . . . and others don't.* New York: HarperCollins.

Collins, J. C., & Porras, J. I. (1997). *Built to last: Successful habits of visionary companies.* New York: HarperCollins.

Conner, D. R. (1992). *Managing at the speed of change.* New York: Villard Books.

Conner, D. R. (1998). *Leading at the edge of chaos.* New York: John Wiley & Sons.

Cooperrider, D. L., & Whitney, D. (1999). *Collaborating for change: Appreciative inquiry.* San Francisco, CA: Berrett-Koehler.

Cummings, T. G., & Srivastva, S. (1977). *Management of work: A sociotechnical systems approach.* San Diego, CA: University Associates.

Dalton, G. W., Lawrence, P. R., & Lorsch, J. W. (Eds.). (1970). *Organizational structure and design.* Homewood, IL: Richard D. Irwin and Dorsey Press.

Dannemiller, K., & Associates. (2000). *Whole-scale change.* San Francisco, CA: Berrett-Koehler.

Davidson, M. (1983). *Uncommon sense: The life and times of Ludwig von Bertalanffy.* Los Angeles, CA: J. P. Tarcher.

de Bono, E. (1999). *Simplicity.* New York: Penguin Books.

DeGeus, A. (1997). *The Living Company.* Cambridge, MA: Harvard Business School Press.

Degraff, J., & Lawrence, K. (2002). *Creativity at work: Developing the right practices to make innovation happen.* San Francisco, CA: Jossey-Bass.

Drucker, P. (1995). *Managing in a time of great change.* New York: Dutton.

Dryden, G., & Voss, J. (1999). *The learning revolution: To change the way the world learns.* Torrance, CA: The Learning Web.

Eoyang, G. H. (1997). *Coping with chaos: Seven simple tools.* Circle Pines, MN: Lagumo.

Flood, R. L., & Jackson, M. C. (1996). *Critical systems thinking: Directed readings.* New York: John Wiley & Sons.

Forrester, J. W. (1971). *Principles of systems.* Norwalk, CT: Productivity Press.

Galbraith, J. R. (1993). *Organizing for the future: The new logic for managing complex organizations.* San Francisco, CA: Jossey-Bass.

Gelatt, H. G., Gelatt, H. B., & Crisp, M. (1991). *Creative decision making: Using positive uncertainty.* Menlo Park, CA: Crisp.

Gell-Mann, M. (1995). *The quark and the jaguar.* New York: W. H. Freeman.

Gharajedaghi, J. (1999). *Systems thinking: Managing chaos and complexity—A platform for designing business architecture.* Woburn, MA: Butterworth-Heinemann.

Gleick, J. (1987). *Chaos: Making a new science.* New York: Viking.

Haines, S. G. (1998). *The Manager's Pocket Guide to Systems Thinking and Learning.* Amherst, MA: HRD Press.

Haines, S. G. (2000). *The complete guide to systems thinking and learning.* Amherst, MA: HRD Press.

Haines, S. G. (2000). *Successful career and life planning.* Menlo Park, CA: Crisp.

Haines, S. G. (2000). *The systems thinking approach to strategic planning and management.* Boca Raton, FL: St. Lucie Press.

Haines, S. G. (2001). *Employee handbook #2: The simplicity of systems thinking.* San Diego, CA: Systems Thinking Press.

Haines, S. G. (2002). *Employee handbook #1: The top 10 everyday tools for daily problem solving.* San Diego: Systems Thinking Press.

Haines, S. (Ed.) (2002). *50 one-minute tips for leaders.* San Diego, CA: Systems Thinking Press.

Haines, S. G. (Ed.). (2003). *Comprehensive reference library on strategic management: Volumes I–XI.* San Diego, CA: Systems Thinking Press.

Hamel, G., & Prahalad, C. K. (1994). *Competing for the future.* Boston, MA: Harvard Business School Press.

Hammer, M., & Champy, J. (1993). *Reengineering the corporation: A manifesto for business revolution.* New York: HarperCollins.

Hammond, D. (2003). *The science of synthesis: Exploring the social implications of general systems theory.* Boulder, CO: University of Colorado Press.

Hanna, D. P. (2001). *Leadership for the ages: Delivering today's results, building tomorrow's legacy.* Provo, UT: Executive Excellence Publishing.

Harrington, H. J., Conner, D. R., & Horney, N. F. (2000). *Project change management: Applying change management to improvement projects.* New York: McGraw-Hill.

Hiam, A. (1998). *The manager's pocket guide to creativity.* Amherst, MA: HRD Press.

Hock, D. (1999). *Birth of the Chaordic Age.* San Francisco, CA: Berrett-Koehler.

Holman, P., & Devane, T. (Eds.). (1999). *The change handbook: Group methods for shaping the future.* San Francisco, CA: Berrett-Koehler.

Hultman, K. (2001). *Balancing individual and organizational values: Walking the tightrope to success.* San Francisco, CA: Jossey-Bass.

Jackson, M. C. (2003). *Systems thinking: Creative holism for managers.* West Sussex, England: John Wiley & Sons.

Jantsch, E. (1980). *The self-organizing universe.* Oxford, England: Elsevier Science.

Jensen, W. D. (2000). *Simplicity: The new competitive advantage in a world of more, better, faster.* New York: Perseus.

Kaplan, R. S., & Norton, D. P. (1996). *The balanced scorecard.* Boston, MA: Harvard Business School Press.

Kauffman, S. (1995). *At home in the universe.* New York: Oxford University Press.

Kim, D. (1994). *Systems thinking tools: A user's reference guide.* Cambridge, MA: Pegasus.

Klir, G. (1969). *An approach to general systems theory.* New York: Van Nostrand.

Kübler-Ross, E. (1969). *On death and dying: What the dying have to teach doctors, nurses, clergy, and their own families.* New York: Scribner.

Kuhn, T. (1970). *The structure of scientific revolutions* (2nd ed.). Chicago, IL: University of Chicago Press.

Laszlo, E. (1972). *The relevance of general systems theory.* New York: George Braziller.

Laszlo, E. (1996). *The systems view of the world.* Cresskill, NJ: Hampton Press.

Lawrence, P. R., & Nohria, N. (2002). *Driven: How human nature shapes our choices.* San Francisco, CA: Jossey-Bass.

Levinson, H. (1976). *Psychological man.* Cambridge, MA: The Levinson Institute, Inc.

Magruder Watkins, J., & Mohr, B. J. (2001). *Appreciative inquiry: Change at the speed of imagination.* San Francisco, CA: Jossey-Bass.

Mesarovic, M. (Ed.). (1967). *Views on general systems theory.* New York: John Wiley & Sons.

Miller, J. G. (1995). *Living systems.* Boulder, CO: University Press of Colorado.

Mintzberg, H. (1994). *The rise and fall of strategic planning.* New York: The Free Press.

Mintzberg, H., Ahlstrand, B., & Lampel, J. (1998). *Strategy safari: A guided tour through the wilds of strategic management.* New York: The Free Press.

Nelson, B. (1994). *1001 ways to reward employees.* New York: Workman Publishing.

O'Connor, J., & McDermott, I. (1997). *The art of systems thinking: Essential skills for creativity and problem solving.* Hammersmith, London, England: Thorsons.

Olson, E. E., & Eoyang, G. H. (2001). *Facilitating organization change: Lessons from complexity science.* San Francisco, CA: Jossey-Bass.

Oshry, B. (1995). *Seeing systems: Unlocking the mysteries of organizational life.* San Francisco, CA: Berrett-Koehler.

Oshry, B. (1999). *Leading systems: Lessons from the power lab.* San Francisco, CA: Berrett-Koehler.

Peters, T., & Waterman, R. H., Jr. (1982). *In search of excellence: Lessons from America's best-run companies.* New York: Harper and Row.

Peters, T. (1994). *Liberation management: Necessary disorganization for the nanosecond nineties.* New York: Fawcett Books.

Petzinger, T., Jr. (1999). *The new pioneers: The men and women who are transforming the workplace and marketplace.* New York: Simon & Schuster.

Pink, D. (2002). *Free agent nation: The future of working for yourself.* New York: Warner Books.

Prigogine, I., & Stengers, I. (1984). *Order out of chaos.* New York: Bantam Books.

Quade, K., & Brown, R. M. (2001). *The conscious consultant: Mastering change from the inside out.* San Francisco, CA: Jossey-Bass.

Ries, A., & Trout, J. (2001). *Positioning: The battle for your mind* (20th Anniv. Ed.). New York: McGraw-Hill.

Rubik, E. (1997, April 4). In M. Bellis, *Rubik and the cube: The history of Rubik's cube and inventor Enro Rubik.* Available www.rubikscube.com/media_print.html

Sanders, T. I. (1998). *Strategic thinking and the new science: Planning in the midst of chaos, complexity, and change.* New York: The Free Press.

Schein, E. (1969). *Process consultation: Its role in organization development.* Reading, MA: Addison-Wesley.

Scholtes, P. R. (1988). *The team handbook.* Madison, WI: Joiner & Associates.

Senge, P. M. (1990). *The fifth discipline: The art and practice of the learning organization.* New York: Doubleday/Currency.

Senge, P. M., Roberts, C., Ross, R. B., Smith, B. J., & Kleiner, A. (1994). *The fifth discipline field book: Strategies and tools for building a learning organization.* New York: Doubleday/Currency.

Shapiro, E. C. (1995). *Fad surfing in the boardroom: Managing in the age of instant answers.* Reading, MA: Addison-Wesley.

Shrode, W. A., & Voich, D., Jr. (1974). *Organization and management: Basic systems concepts.* Homewood, IL: Irwin.

Stacey, R., Griffin, D., & Shaw, P. (2000). *Complexity and management: Fad or radical challenge to systems thinking.* London, England: Routledge.

Sterman, J. D. (2000). *Business dynamics: Systems thinking and modeling for a complex world.* New York: McGraw-Hill.

Treacy, M., & Wiersema, F. (1997). *The discipline of market leaders: Choose your customers, narrow your focus, dominate your market.* Cambridge, MA: Perseus Publishing.

Trist, E., & Emery, F. (1973). *Toward a social ecology.* New York: Plenum.

Ulrich, D., Ashkenas, R. N., & Prahalad, C. K. (1995). *The boundaryless organization.* San Francisco, CA: Jossey-Bass.

Ulrich, D., Zenger, J., & Smallwood, N. (1999). *Results-based leadership.* Cambridge, MA: Harvard Business School Press.

Vickers, G. (Ed.). (1972). *A classification of systems.* Washington, DC: Yearbook of the Society for General Systems Research/Academy of Management Research.

Von Bertalanffy, L. (1967). *Robots, men and minds: Psychology in the modem world.* New York: George Braziller.

Von Bertalanffy, L. (1998). *General systems theory: Foundations, development, and applications* (rev. ed.). New York: George Braziller.

Waldrop, M. M. (1992). *Complexity: The emerging science at the edge of order and chaos.* New York: Touchstone.

Weinberg, G. M. (2001). *An introduction to general systems thinking* (25th Anniv. Ed.). New York: Dorset House.

Weisbord, M. (1992*). Discovering common ground.* San Francisco, CA: Jossey-Bass.

Wheatley, M. J. (1992). *Leadership and the new science.* San Francisco, CA: Berrett-Koehler.

Wheatley, M. J., & Kellner-Rogers, M. (1996). *A simpler way.* San Francisco, CA: Berrett-Koehler.

About the Series

THERE ARE WATERSHED MOMENTS in history that change everything after them. The attack on Pearl Harbor was one of those. The bombing of Hiroshima was another. The terrorist attack on the World Trade Center in New York City was our most recent. All resulted in significant change that transformed many lives and organizations.

Practicing Organization Development: The Change Agent Series for Groups and Organizations was launched to help those who must cope with or create change. The series is designed to share what is working or not working, to provoke critical thinking about change, and to offer creative ways to deal with change, rather than the destructive ones noted above.

The Current State of Change Management and Organization Development

Almost as soon as the ink was dry on the first wave of books published in this series, we heard that its focus was too narrow. We heard that the need for theory and practice extended beyond OD into change management. More than one respected authority urged us to reconsider our focus, moving beyond OD to include books on change management generally.

Organization development is not the only way that change can be engineered or coped with in organizational settings. We always knew that, of course. And we remain grounded in the view that change management, however it is carried out, should be based on such values as respect for the individual, participation and involvement in change by those affected by it, and interest in the improvement of organizational settings on many levels—including productivity improvement, but also improvement in achieving work/life balance and in a values-based approach to management and to change.

A Brief History of the Genesis of the Series

A few years ago, and as a direct result of the success of *Practicing Organization Development: A Guide for Practitioners* by Rothwell, Sullivan, and McLean, the publisher—feeling that OD was experiencing a rebirth of interest in the United States and in other nations—wanted to launch a new OD series. The goal of this new series was not to replace, or even compete directly with, the well-established Addison-Wesley OD Series (edited by Edgar Schein). Instead, as the editors saw it, the series would provide a means by which the most promising authors in OD whose voices had not previously been heard could share their ideas. The publisher enlisted the support of Bill Rothwell, Roland Sullivan, and Kristine Quade to turn the dream of a series into a reality.

This series was long in the making and has been steadily evolving since its inception. The original vision was an ambitious one—and involved no less than reinventing OD and re-energizing interest in the research and practice surrounding it. Sponsoring books was one means to that end. Another is the series website (www.pfeiffer.com/go/od). Far more than just a place to advertise the series, it serves as a real-time learning community for OD practitioners.

What Distinguishes the Books in this Series

The books in this series are meant to be challenging, cutting-edge, and state-of-the-art in their approach to OD and change management. The goal of the series is to provide an outlet for proven authorities in OD and change management who have not put their ideas into print or for up-and-coming writers in OD and change management who have new, sometimes unorthodox, approaches that are stimulating and exciting. Some books in this series describe inspirational concepts that can lead to actionable change and purvey ideas so new that they are not fully developed.

Unique to this series is the cutting-edge emphasis, the immediate applicability, and the ease of transferability of the concepts. The aim of this series is nothing less than to reinvent, re-energize, and reinvigorate OD and change management. In each book, we have also recommended that the author(s) provide:

- A research base of some kind, meaning new information derived from practice and/or systematic investigation, and

- Practical tools, worksheets, case studies, and other ready-to-go approaches that help the authors drag "theory" to "practice" to make these new, cutting-edge approaches more concrete.

Subject Matter That Will (and Will Not) Be Covered

The books in this series are varied in their approach, but they are united by their focus. All share an emphasis on organization development (OD) and change management (CM). Hence, books in this series are about participative change efforts. They are not about such other popular topics as leadership, management development, consulting, or group dynamics—unless those topics are treated in new, cutting-edge ways and are geared to OD and change management practitioners.

This Book

What does it mean to change an enterprise, and how can systems thinking help in that process? This book about the management of change addresses this important two-part question in a straightforward fashion. It deals with a complex, and sometimes frustratingly difficult, topic in a must-see way for today's organizational leaders. As the authors note, the book provides readers with four important outcomes: (1) build frameworks for facilitating enterprise-wide change, (2) conduct holistic organizational diagnosis and design, (3) provide superior decision-making abilities, and (4) achieve and sustain a unique marketplace positioning. The book is structured in three parts and ten chapters. Part A focuses on an introduction to systems thinking and superior results. It comprises three chapters that provide definitions, dramatize the changes occurring in recent years, and provide a framework for systems thinking. Part B presents a practical application to enterprise-wide change. Its six chapters examine enterprise-wide change in a holistic fashion. Part C tells how to begin enterprise-wide change. It concludes the book with one chapter that positions readers to apply the principles of the book to changing an enterprise. This book is an important addition to the *Practicing Organization Development Series* because it examines current thinking about the applications of systems theory to change.

William J. Rothwell
University Park, PA

Roland Sullivan
Deephaven, MN

Kristine Quade
Minnetonka, MN

Statement
of the Board

❶T IS OUR PLEASURE TO PARTICIPATE in and influence the start-up of *Practicing Organization Development: The Change Agent Series for Groups and Organizations.* The purpose of the series is to stimulate the profession and influence how organization change is defined and practiced. This statement is intended to set the context for the series by addressing three important questions: (1) What are the key issues facing organization change and development in the 21st Century? (2) Where does—or should—OD fit in the field of organization change and development? and (3) What is the purpose of this series?

What Are the Key Issues Facing Organization Change and Development in the 21st Century?

One of the questions is the extent to which leaders can control forces or can only be reactive. Will globalization and external forces be so powerful that they will prevent organizations from being able to "stay ahead of the change curve"? And what will be the role of technology, especially information technology, in the change process? To what extent can it be a carrier of change (as well as a source of change)?

What will the relationship be between imposed change and collaborative change? Will the increased education of the workforce demand the latter, or will the requirement of having to make fundamental changes demand leadership that sets goals that participants would not willingly set on their own? And what is the relationship between these two forms of change?

Who will be the change agent? Is this a separate profession, or will that increasingly be the responsibility of the organization's leaders? If the latter, how does that change the role of the change professional?

What will be the role of values for change in the 21st Century? Will the key values be performance—efficiency and effectiveness? And what role will the humanistic values of more traditional OD play? Or will the growth of knowledge (and human competence) as an organization's core competence make this a moot point in that performance can only occur if one takes account of humanistic values?

What is the relationship between other fields and the area of change? Can any change process that is not closely linked with strategy be truly effective? Can change agents focus only on process, or do they need to be knowledgeable and actively involved in the organization's products/services and understand the market niche in which the organization operates?

Where Does—or Should—OD Fit in the Field of Organization Change and Development?

We offer the following definition of OD to stimulate debate:

> Organization development is a system-wide and values-based collaborative process of applying behavioral science knowledge to the adaptive development, improvement, and reinforcement of such organizational features as the strategies, structures, processes, people, and cultures that lead to organization effectiveness.

The definition suggests that OD can be understood in terms of its several foci:

First, *OD is a system-wide process.* It works with whole systems. In the past, the bias has been toward working at the individual and group levels. More recently, the focus has shifted to organizations and multi-organization systems. We support that trend in general, but honor and acknowledge the fact that the traditional focus on smaller systems is both legitimate and necessary.

Second, *OD is values-based.* Traditionally, OD has attempted to distinguish itself from other forms of planned change and applied behavioral science by promoting a set of humanistic values and by emphasizing the importance of personal growth as a key to its practice. Today, that focus is blurred and there is much debate about the value base underlying the practice of OD. We support a more formal and direct conversation about what these values are and how the field is related to them.

Third, *OD is collaborative.* Our first value commitment as OD practitioners is to bring about an inclusive, diverse workforce with a focus of integrating differences into a world-wide culture mentality.

Fourth, *OD is based on behavioral science knowledge.* Organization development should incorporate and apply knowledge from sociology, psychology, anthropology, technology, and economics toward the end of making systems more effective. We support the continued emphasis in OD on behavioral science knowledge and believe that OD practitioners should be widely read and comfortable with several of the disciplines.

Fifth, *OD is concerned with the adaptive development, improvement, and reinforcement of strategies, structures, processes, people, culture, and other features of organizational life.* This statement describes not only the organizational elements that are the target of change but also the process by which effectiveness is increased. That is, OD works in a variety of areas, and it is focused on improving those areas. We believe that such a statement of process and content strongly implies that a key feature of OD is the transference of knowledge and skill to the system so that it is more able to handle and manage change in the future.

Sixth and finally, *OD is about improving organization effectiveness.* It is not just about making people happy; it is also concerned with meeting financial goals, improving productivity, and addressing stakeholder satisfaction. We believe that OD's future is closely tied to the incorporation of this value in its purpose and the demonstration of this objective in its practice.

This definition raises a host of questions:

- Are OD and organization change and development one and the same, or are they different?

- Has OD become just a collection of tools, methods, and techniques? Has it lost its values?

- Does it talk "systems," but ignore them in practice?

- Are consultants facilitators of change or activists of change?

- To what extent should consulting be driven by consultant value versus holding only the value of increasing the client's effectiveness?

- How can OD practitioners help formulate strategy, shape the strategy development process, contribute to the content of strategy, and drive how strategy will be implemented?

- How can OD focus on the drivers of change external to individuals, such as the external environment, business strategy, organization change, and culture change, as well as on the drivers of change internal to individuals, such as individual interpretations of culture, behavior, style, and mindset?

- How much should OD be part of the competencies of all leaders? How much should it be the sole domain of professionally trained, career-oriented OD practitioners?

What Is the Purpose of This Series?

This series is intended to provide current thinking about organization change and development as a field and to provide practical approaches based on sound theory and research. It is targeted for full-time external or internal change practitioners; top executives in charge of enterprise-wide change; and managers, HR practitioners, training and development professionals, and others who have responsibility for change in organizational and trans-organizational settings. At the same time, these books will be directed toward cutting-edge thinking and state-of-the-art approaches. In some cases, the ideas, approaches, or techniques described are still evolving, so the books are intended to open up dialogue.

We know that the books in this series will provide a leading forum for thought-provoking dialogue within the field.

About the Board Members

David Bradford is senior lecturer in organizational behavior at the Graduate School of Business, Stanford University, Palo Alto, California. He is co-author (with Allan R. Cohen) of *Managing for Excellence, Influence Without Authority,* and *POWER UP: Transforming Organizations Through Shared Leadership.*

W. Warner Burke is professor of psychology and education in the department of organization and leadership at Teachers College at Columbia University in New York. He also serves as a senior advisor to PricewaterhouseCoopers. His most recent publication is *Business Profiles of Climate Shifts: Profiles of Change Makers,* with William Trahant and Richard Koonce.

Edith Whitfield Seashore is an organization consultant and co-founder (with Morley Segal) of AUNTL Masters Program in Organization Development. She is co-author of *What Did You Say?* and *The Art of Giving and Receiving Feedback* and co-editor of *The Promise of Diversity.*

Robert Tannenbaum was emeritus professor of development of human systems, Graduate School of Management, University of California, Los Angeles, and recipient of the Lifetime Achievement Award by the National OD Network. He published numerous books, including *Human Systems Development* (with Newton Margulies and Fred Massarik).

Christopher G. Worley is director, MSOD Program, Pepperdine University, Malibu, California. He is co-author of *Organization Development and Change* (7th ed.), with Tom Cummings, and of *Integrated Strategic Change,* with David Hitchin and Walter Ross.

Shaolin Zhang is senior manager of organization development for Motorola (China) Electronics Ltd. He received his master's degree in American Studies from Beijing Foreign Studies University, Beijing, China, and holds a Ph.D. in sociology from York University, Toronto, Ontario.

Afterword
to the Series

ON **1967,** Warren Bennis, Ed Schein, and I were faculty members of the Sloan School of Management at MIT. We decided to produce a series of paperback books that collectively would describe the state of the field of organization development (OD). Organization development as a field had been named by me and several others from our pioneer change effort at General Mills in Minneapolis, Minnesota, some ten years earlier.

Today I define OD as "a systemic and systematic change effort, using behavioral science knowledge and skill, to transform the organization to a new state."

In any case, several books and many articles had been written, but there was no consensus on whether OD was a field of practice, an area of study, or a profession. We had not established OD as a theory or even as a practice.

We decided that there was a need for something that would describe the state of OD. Our intention was to each write a book and also to recruit three other authors. After some searching, we found a young editor who had just joined the small publishing house of Addison-Wesley. We made contact, and the series was born. Our audience was to be human resource professionals who spent their time consulting with managers in their development through various small-group activities, such as team building. More than thirty books have been published in that series, and the series has had a life of its own. We just celebrated its thirtieth anniversary.

At last year's National OD Network Conference, I said that it was time for the OD profession to change and transform itself. Is that not what we change agents tell our clients to do? This new Jossey-Bass/Pfeiffer series will do just that. It can be seen as:

- A documentation of the re-invention of OD;

- An effort that will take us to the next level; and

- A practical effort to transfer to the world the theory and practice of leading-edge practitioners and theorists.

The books in this new series will thus prove to be valuable resources for change agents to keep current with the new and leading-edge ideas and practices.

May this very exciting change agent series be most creative and innovative. May it give our field a renewed burst of energy and awareness.

Richard Beckhard
Written on Labor Day weekend 1999 from my summer cabin near Bethel, Maine

About the
Series Editors

William J. Rothwell, Ph.D., is president of Rothwell and Associates, a private consulting firm, as well as professor of human resources development on the University Park Campus of The Pennsylvania State University. Before arriving at Penn State in 1993, he was an assistant vice president and management development director for a major insurance company and a training director in a state government agency. He has worked full-time in human resources management and employee training and development from 1979 to the present. He thus combines real-world experience with academic and consulting experience. As a consultant, Dr. Rothwell's client list includes over thirty-five companies from the Fortune 500.

Dr. Rothwell received his Ph.D. with a specialization in employee training from the University of Illinois at Urbana-Champaign, his M.B.A. with a specialization in human resources management from Sangamon State University (now called the

University of Illinois at Springfield), his M.A. from the University of Illinois at Urbana-Champaign, and his B.A. from Illinois State University. He holds lifetime accreditation as a Senior Professional in Human Resources (SPHR), has been accredited as a Registered Organization Development Consultant (RODC), and holds the industry designation as Fellow of the Life Management Institute (FLMI).

Dr. Rothwell's latest publications include *The Manager and Change Leader* (ASTD, 2001); *The Role of Intervention Selector, Designer and Developer, and Implementor* (ASTD, 2000); *ASTD Models for Human Performance* (2nd ed.) (ASTD, 2000); *The Analyst* (ASTD, 2000); *The Evaluator* (ASTD, 2000); *The ASTD Reference Guide to Workplace Learning and Performance* (3rd ed.), with H. Sredl (HRD Press, 2000); *The Complete Guide to Training Delivery: A Competency-Based Approach*, with S. King and M. King (AMACOM, 2000); *Human Performance Improvement: Building Practitioner Competence*, with C. Hohne and S. King (Butterworth-Heinemann, 2000); *Effective Succession Planning: Ensuring Leadership Continuity and Building Talent from Within* (2nd ed.) (AMACOM, 2000); and *The Competency Toolkit*, with D. Dubois (HRD Press, 2000).

Roland **Sullivan, RODC,** has worked as an OD pioneer with nearly eight hundred systems in eleven countries and virtually every major industry. Richard Beckhard has recognized him as one of the world's first one hundred change agents.

Mr. Sullivan specializes in the science and art of systematic and systemic change, executive team building, and facilitating Whole System Transformation Conferences—large interactive meetings with 300 to 1,500 people. Over 25,000 people have participated in his conferences worldwide; one co-facilitated with Kristine Quade held for the Amalgamated Bank of South Africa was named runner-up for the title of outstanding change project of the world by the OD Institute.

With William Rothwell and Gary McLean, he is revising one of the field's seminal books, *Practicing OD: A Consultant's Guide* (Jossey-Bass/Pfeiffer, 1995). The first edition is now translated into Chinese.

He did his graduate work in organization development at Pepperdine University and Loyola University.

Mr. Sullivan's current interests include the following: whole-system transformation, balancing economic and human realities; discovering and collaborating with cutting-edge change-focused authors who are documenting the perpetual renewal of the OD profession; and applied phenomenology: developing higher states of consciousness and self-awareness in the consulting of interdependent organizations.

Mr. Sullivan's current professional learning is available at www.rolandsullivan.com.

 **K**ristine Quade is an independent consultant who combines her background as an attorney with a master's degree in organization development from Pepperdine University and years of experience as both an internal and external OD consultant.

Ms. Quade draws from experiences in guiding teams from divergent areas within corporations and across many levels of executives and employees. She has facilitated leadership alignment, culture change, support system alignment, quality process improvements, organizational redesign, and the creation of clear strategic intent that results in significant bottom-line results. A believer in whole-system change, she has developed the expertise to facilitate groups ranging in size from eight to two thousand in the same room for a three-day change process.

Recognized as the 1996 Minnesota Organization Development Practitioner of the Year, Ms. Quade teaches in the master's programs at Pepperdine University and the University of Minnesota at Mankato and the master's and doctoral programs at the University of St. Thomas in Minneapolis. She is a frequent presenter at the Organization Development National Conference and also at the International OD Congress and the International Association of Facilitators.

About the Authors

Life is what happens to us while we're making other plans.

Thomas la Mance

Stephen G. Haines is the founder and president of the Centre for Strategic Management, based in San Diego, California. He has thirty years' experience as both a CEO and senior executive as an internal and external practitioner in change consulting. Haines was formerly president of University Associates (UA) Consulting and Training, a pioneer firm in the OD field that featured Applied Strategic Planning and OD among its public seminar courses in the 1980s and 1990s. Haines has worked intensely with over two hundred CEOs around the world in support of their strategic and complex change efforts.

A U.S. Naval Academy graduate, he received his master's in OD in 1975 at George Washington University. This included an advanced-level course and research paper on General Systems Theory. He then completed his doctoral work in psycho-educational processes at Temple University in Philadelphia. Coupled with in-depth exposure to Russell Ackoff in the 1970s and 1980s at Sunoco, Systems Thinking has been his "orientation to life" ever since.

Haines is a prolific author, with more than twelve books in print, including *The Systems Thinking Approach to Reinventing Strategic Planning and Management*. Contact Haines at stephen@csmintl.com.

Gail **Aller-Stead** is an experienced practicing OD consultant who has worked on both sides of organizational boundaries. From within organizations, she has worked as a senior internal consultant in the oil and gas, telecommunications, transportation, pharmaceutical, and consumer-packaged goods industries. As an external OD practitioner, her clients include executives in the consumer-packaged goods, financial services, health care, municipal government, not-for-profit, oil and gas, pharmaceutical, professional services, telecommunications, and transportation sectors.

Aller-Stead works with organizations to help them focus on both strategic and operational excellence and build upon key opportunities that lead to a sustainable competitive advantage. Based in Toronto, Aller-Stead is the change management practice leader and a Partner in the Centre for Strategic Management, a global strategic alliance of consultants and trainers. She holds a M.S.O.D. from the George L. Grazadio School of Business and Management, Pepperdine University, an undergraduate degree from Athabasca University, and two specialized college diplomas in human resources management. She can be reached at gailaller-stead@csmintl.com or www.csmintl.com.

James **McKinlay** is a co-founder of the Centre for Strategic Management and has made significant contributions to the development of the principles, practices, and tools of Systems Thinking. McKinlay holds a master's in human resource management and an undergraduate degree in honours recreation, as part of the Kinesiology and Leisure Studies Department from the University of Waterloo in Ontario.

Over a thirty-year career, McKinlay has been an internal consultant in the fields of community and leadership development in the Ontario and Saskatchewan governments. He was also an internal HR consultant for the largest investor-owned power utility in Canada. He established a government-wide, internal consulting services function.

In his present role, he is responsible for the growth and development of the Centre across Canada. He can be reached at jim.mckinlay@csmintl.com or through the Centre's website, www.csmintl.com.

Index

What will you find on pfeiffer.com?

- The best in workplace performance solutions for training and HR professionals

- Downloadable training tools, exercises, and content

- Web-exclusive offers

- Training tips, articles, and news

- Seamless online ordering

- Author guidelines, information on becoming a Pfeiffer Affiliate, and much more

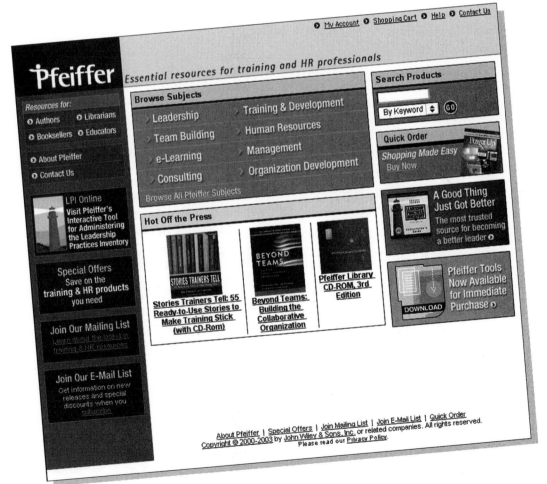

Discover more at www.pfeiffer.com

Customer Care

Have a question, comment, or suggestion? Contact us! We value your feedback and we want to hear from you.

For questions about this or other Pfeiffer products, you may contact us by:

E-mail: **customer@wiley.com**

Mail: **Customer Care Wiley/Pfeiffer**
       10475 Crosspoint Blvd.
       Indianapolis, IN 46256

Phone: **(US) 800-274-4434** (Outside the US: 317-572-3985)

Fax: **(US) 800-569-0443** (Outside the US: 317-572-4002)

To order additional copies of this title or to browse other Pfeiffer products, visit us online at **www.pfeiffer.com**.

For **Technical Support** questions, call **(800) 274-4434.**

For authors guidelines, log on to www.pfeiffer.com and click on "Resources for Authors."

If you are . . .

A **college bookstore, a professor, an instructor, or work in higher education** and you'd like to place an order or request an exam copy, please contact jbreview@wiley.com.

A **general retail bookseller** and you'd like to establish an account or speak to a local sales representative, contact Melissa Grecco at 201-748-6267 or mgrecco@wiley.com.

An **exclusively online bookseller**, contact Amy Blanchard at 530-756-9456 or ablanchard @wiley.com or Jennifer Johnson at 206-568-3883 or jjohnson@wiley.com, both of our Online Sales department.

A **librarian or library representative**, contact John Chambers in our Library Sales department at 201-748-6291 or jchamber@wiley.com.

A **reseller, training company/consultant, or corporate trainer**, contact Charles Regan in our Special Sales department at 201-748-6553 or cregan@wiley.com.

A **specialty retail distributor** (includes specialty gift stores, museum shops, and corporate bulk sales), contact Kim Hendrickson in our Special Sales department at 201-748-6037 or khendric@wiley.com.

Purchasing for the **Federal government**, contact Ron Cunningham in our Special Sales department at 317-572-3053 or rcunning@wiley.com.

Purchasing for a **State or Local government**, contact Charles Regan in our Special Sales department at 201-748-6553 or cregan@wiley.com.